HIGH ON GOD

THERE'S NO HIGH
LIKE THE MOST HIGH

by Matt Spinks

The Fire House Projects Ministries & Publications
Fort Wayne, Indiana USA

Cover and illustrations by: A. Deckler at StateBuilt
statebuilt.com

Published by:
The Fire House Projects Ministries & Publications
12222 US 30 E New Haven, IN USA 47664
www.thefirehouseprojects.com
Email: info@thefirehouseprojects.com

Publisher's Cataloging-in-Publication Data

Spinks, Matt, author.
High on God : there's no high like the most high / Matt Spinks.
New Haven, IN : The Fire House Projects Ministries, 2019.
LCCN 2019902084 | ISBN 978-0-578-45770-3 (paperback) | ISBN 978-1-68454-153-9 (ebook)
LCSH: Spiritual life. | Ecstasy. | Mysticism. | Supernatural (Theology) | Holy Spirit. | Laughter--Religious aspects. | BISAC: RELIGION / Spirituality. | RELIGION / Mysticism. | RELIGION / Christian Theology / Pneumatology. | BODY, MIND & SPIRIT / Mindfulness & Meditation.
LCC BV5090 .S65 2019 (print) | LCC BV5090 (ebook) | DDC 204/.22--dc23.

International Standard Book Number: 978-057845770-3
Library of Congress Control Number: 2019902084

CONTENTS

DEDICATION

To my amazing, wonderful, incredible, dedicated, gracious, beautiful, LOVE-DRUNK wife, Katie Rose! Without you I would not have stayed as incredibly encouraged and inebriated as I have! There is not a day that goes by that I would ever regret marrying you! Thank you.

ACKNOWLEDGMENTS

This book has been a holy experiment and a labor of love spanning some years, and drawing from experiences together with so many dear friends and partners in ministry.

Firstly, I want to thank all those who helped edit this book over the many multiple versions! Some of you I was able to ingrate your advice, and others not so much. But, each of you gave me your precious time and wisdom, and for that I am SO grateful! To Rob Hadziki, Tony Seigh, Pierre Morin, Eric Wilding, and everyone else who gave of themselves to help in the editing, cheers and may many blissful returns be upon you!

Secondly, to all those who gave me the rights to their amazing devotional meditations that make up the final chapter, thank you! Uncle Bert, Crystal, Dru, Shane, Luke, Britney, Nate, A.J., and Travis, there's such profound beauty flowing in your jacked up writings! You've helped me to complete my dream!

Also, to Aaron Deckler and the whole team at State Built in Austin, Texas, I want to say a profound, "THANK YOU!" You dealt with my impossible desires for the design of this book, and made it look incredible. I feel hammered drunk just looking at it! Your time and skill investment into this and your always encouraging support of my life means more than I can say. We are truly shaping history together, with Glory on our lives, bros!

I want to thank Georgian & Winnie Banov, John & Lily Crowder, John & Jean Scotland, Heidi & Rolland Baker, Jim Samuelson, Rich & Linda Brink, Benjamin Dunn, Dave Vaughan, Bill Vanderbush, Pete Greig, Francois & Lydia Du Toit, Eric Wilding, and all the voices who have spoken bliss and ecstasy into my life in Jesus! Some of you ministered to me personally, and others only from afar, but the impact was eternal! This book would not be here without you.

Brian & Emily Shilts you both have been my longest time friends in the joy of Jesus! Brian, your love and support, simply as a friend, over the last two decades has made so many things possible! You both have offered not only friendship, but audacious partnership in building dreams together. Living in Glory community with you, team Shilts, in the God-high, has empowered an actual tangible experience of heaven on earth! I'm so grateful, you dirty dawgs!!

Zach Pratt, thanks for always being such a real encouragement, a genuine friend and drinking buddy over the years. I know that, no matter what, I can always drink God with you. You are my true brother, and you get me... We're just getting started!

Nate Dickerson, I'm so grateful for that fateful Day that brought us together. We're also just getting started, haha! What wild adventures we've already had, but wow, where are we going, Lord?! I hope these lines provide you many eff-ed up moments as the winds of the Holy Ghost blow! And, may we ever drop ease across America and the entire cosmos!!

Chad Davis, thanks so much for the years of friendship in our Good Lord. I doubt you'll even read these lines, since you never give a rip about ministry stuff, LOL! But, that's exactly what I need on a regular basis, a friend who keeps me grounded and honest with a stiff drink. Here's to many good times to come! We will eventually go to the Philippines together!

To Luke Pratt, Crystal Niver, Chris Groleau, Dru D'Arnelle, Jennifer Perkins, Rainee & Ryan Perdue, Brandon Hartzler, Robin Grimm, Samuel & Angelynne TrueBeDOOR, Eli & Gia Winehart, Renee Jehl, Kristin Adams, A.J. Nichols, Mark & Sarah Howell, THANK YOU FOR BEING FAMILY in an era where long term Glory relationships seem like an impossible thing to find. Each and every one of you have showed up for me, in the whack, time and time again, bringing me your love and fresh perspective. You all matter to me, no matter what!

To Jared Gustafson, bro, your friendship and partnership has meant more to me than I could possibly describe! To begin to see communities of this Drink, in new fresh wineskins, springing up all across the world, it has been a dream come true! And, to have your ever loving and hyper encouraging voice right alongside me, I am beyond grateful. You sir, are the real deal!

To Kelsey Aper, thank you for your voice of encouragement and Glory in my life. I'm super excited about the adventures to come, higher than kites, transforming regions! FIRE! Your faith in the content of this book makes me brave!

To all our ministry partners in love and bliss, you have made so much of this possible! For those who prayed, and those who gave, THANK YOU! This book has been a long time coming, and I so hope it rocks your world as it has mine! Both Katie & I are forever grateful for your love!

To my Mom, Fran, thank you so much for all the tireless things you've done to support and empower me, and our family over the years. God gave us to each other, for sure! You are one of my heroines!

To my Dad, Lynn, what a wild ride we've been on! Thank you for your love and support of all the things I've ever done, including this book. You've been the most encouraging father that a son could ever ask for. How amazing is it to be able to get high on God with family!?!

ENDORSEMENTS

I can honestly say that I relate to feeling a sense of being high on God's love, as Matt Spinks shares in his new book *High on God*. In fact, Christians from all over the world use a wide variety of different verbiage to describe what Matt is conveying in *High on God*. But at the end of the day, it all means the same thing: being touched by the presence of God's divine love in a dramatic way.

To be honest, I have gotten a lot of backlash and judgments from Christians just for being seen in a photo with Matt or other Christians in the charismatic realm. But what people don't understand is that I have a child-like heart and I love to learn more about the body of Christ's different expressions of faith—from conservative to charismatic Christians. I am even planning to write a book about it. I will admit that I do understand why there is a bit of controversy though; some of the ways that Matt Spinks and other spirit filled/charismatics manifest can be strange. I would suggest that we all ask ourselves this question: What do you think Paul's body looked like when his spirit was being caught up into Heaven as he shares in 2 Corinthians 12? Or what did Ezekiel's body look like? We should think twice before we judge. A person may be having a very holy and pure Heavenly encounter while we may decide to judge them calling them a "weirdo." When the Divine touches our weak human vessels, there can be strange reactions as the intensity of pure bliss, loving kindness, and heavy divine peace overwhelms us to the point that we forget to care about how we look while experiencing the divine pleasures we are feeling.

Whoever you are, and whatever you believe, my advice to you would be to keep your child-like heart open as you read Matt Spinks' book *High on God*. You may not agree with every single word in the book, but I promise if you ask God daily to awaken you in similar ways, you will not be disappointed.

Brian Welch
Musician, Author, Speaker, Founding member of KORN

This book is such a key to tangible Holy Spirit encounter! The words and pages come alive with the heartbeat of Matt who lives what he communicates in an abandonment that is contagious and irresistible! I believe it will help many discover for themselves the intriguing adventure and bliss of our redeemed innocence and oneness! Oh how my heart longs for people across the planet to enjoy the matchless beauty of the God-adventure! Well done Matt!

Francois Du Toit
Teacher, Safari Guide, Author & Translator of the Mirror Bible
www.mirrorword.net

Some people seeking greater spiritual experiences ask, "How…?" Yet the letters and ideas in this question are better reordered as, "Who…?" As we know and experience Who our God is—Abba, Jesus and Holy Spirit—we know and experience who we and everyone is—one new creation in Christ. Spiritual experiences are the supernatural outcome of sharing in the supernatural Triune relationship. Matt Spinks' life and book demonstrate this gloriously. Each chapter is an agape feast that will take you from the ecstatic soaring "weeees" in Christ to the katastatic resting "aaaahs" of Christ in you. Enjoy the sober-inebriation!

Dr. Eric Wilding, The Gloryists
www.ericwilding.org

High on God is a beautiful union of scripture, history, research, experience, teaching, and practical application. Matt lifts the veil on the reality we were created to live in...glorious heavenly bliss from the constant presence of God IN us. This book makes joy seem easy, because it is! Find yourself overcome by the truth of all that life is meant to be through the words you read in these enriching pages.

Melissa Joy Wood
Speaker and Author of "Eliminating Fear"

Matt Spinks is faithful to Joy. One of the most mysterious aspects of the kingdom of God is the challenge toward bliss, mirth, merriment, or whatever buzz word for uber happy is culturally hot. In the years I've known Matt, he maintains a consistent electricity of authentic joy, and it's contagious. This book unveils what I believe are some key secrets to living in the unbroken and unbridled bliss of the Gospel.

Bill Vanderbush
Author, Pastor, Speaker

Matt Spinks is a crazy, creative character who loves the Gospel of Grace and whose life is marked by compassion, joy and humility. His door has always been open to the stranger, and he truly lives out what he believes. This is a fun book to encourage the ecstatic, experiential life of bliss we are created for in union with God, achieved effortlessly and single-handedly for us in Jesus. Thanks to the finished work of the cross, we have a nonstop cosmic ride of wonder and divine delight that is nothing less than what we were adopted for: to be recipients of the transcendent, intoxicating cup of the wine of His love. The love of God in Jesus is the tangible drink our souls thirst for. And just as the Creator created us for creativity, I appreciate Matt's unique style of expressing and living out the Gospel (and also his unique style of writing ... English majors beware: I have never seen anyone spell out their glossolalia before). For anyone who knows Matt, you will quickly recognize his heart in these pages. For those unfamiliar with him, Matt wears many hats: a teacher, a revivalist and of course a family man. But most truly he carries the gentleness of a pastor who authentically longs to see people realizing the unconditional love of Father, Son and Holy Spirit. ... Matt serves up an inebriating message of the eternal love of God in Jesus not tainted by religious formulas. Pure Grace is meant to be drunk straight.

John Crowder
Author, Missionary, Reformer, Speaker
www.thenewmystics.com

Every once in a while we have the privilege of bumping into someone who truly is a game changer. One who boldly goes where few have gone in history. I guess you could say a reformer of sorts. Matt Spinks is one of those people. He and his amazing wife Katie set out to experience over a decade ago a true heaven on earth reality. In this pursuit, living a sustained joy filled existence became the norm. Never once looking back, they proved the theory to be a reality. The book you have in your hands is not only an explanation of a "High on God" lifestyle, but also a living testimony years in the making. I trust you'll be offended, challenged, encouraged and built up by the goodness of the fullness of God that awaits you.

Steve Freeman
Local Indiana Pastor, Musician, Mentor

Satisfaction? You CAN get some! And, Matt Spinks' book, High On God, can show you the Way. Whether you're a religious striver, a schmoozing conniver or a Jesus deep-diver; whether you're afflicted, addicted or conflicted; whether you've had the real deal or a raw deal; whether atheist, creationist or CEASE AND DESIST! In a writing style that is approachable, funny and conversational, Matt has made a great attempt to describe what Paul, the Apostle, said was absolutely IMPOSSIBLE to describe: the EXPERIENCE of the ecstasies of being loved by God! NOT in some far off, isolated place of spiritual harmonic convergence, not after years of fasting and deprivation, or religious self-flagellation, level-climbing and humiliation, not after experimentation with mind-altering pharmaceuticals and esoteric education, but in the context of real, normal, everyday family and community life, the way life was always intended to be lived and enjoyed, set in motion by a God who is even MORE schnockered in love with us than most folks even dare to consider!

Matt and Katie are treasures, and Matt's book High on God is just an extension of the sparkling intoxicant that God has imaged in and through them.

If you need to get drunk, read this book. If you're confused, read this book. If you're depressed, angry, hungry, lonely or tired, read this book. If you're on top of the world, read this book. Read this book out loud to your friends and family. Your dog will love it, too. Read it to him. Then follow Matt as he follows Christ.

Mimi 'Blissed' Ross
Author, Musician, Speaker, Life Coach/Mentor

Matthew Raymond Spinks and I have grown up together. His friendship has been no small part of my life, rather it has been a great thread of palpable joy woven into my story by the Father of all. I have walked with him through much of what is detailed in this book, and I am here to say... it's all true! This message is not a fleeting trend nor is it a simple western evangelical theology to placate itching ears. I have seen it transform countless lives, Matt's especially. In these pages you can hear his authentic voice sharing a real message that he lives fully every day. So if you are looking for another modern book about emerging Christian concepts, this may not be for you (yet). But if you are searching for something ancient and tangible and expansive and utterly genuine, that can awaken hope and patience and pleasures in every part of your life.... then I think you're really gonna enjoy this!

Brian Shilts
Counselor, Musician, Friend
www.brianshiltslovesyou.com

INTRODUCTION

Shwwwooogah booogah! Life is so amazing and beautiful! I'm just so glad to be alive! There is a world-wide awakening happening. People are beginning to wake up to heaven, even here on earth. Right now is an absolutely incredible time! Even if no one else was living in the experience of this, I AM. You are included in it too, dear reader! I'm absolutely ecstatic at the realization that we can ALL live in the experience of pure bliss together! We can all be high and explore God's wonderland together!

My heart in writing this book is to be a clear encouraging voice. I believe that I am one of many that are emerging speaking of an awakening to true sustainable bliss, true heaven on earth. Jesus Christ is real! (And, if you don't believe in Jesus yet, please hang with me. It's all gonna be ok, I promise. I'm not proposing the right wing, moralist, control freak, kill joy Jesus that is so often misrepresented by the religious church.) The true Lord Jesus Christ has such a strong, pure, child-like reality that He's revealing to the world. Jesus' Gospel is simply this, "You are included in heaven on earth today in Me!" It's a simple, child-like message. The word Gospel means good news!

I have had the privilege for the last ten years, along with my beautiful wife and two amazing children, to be a part of a community that values being in a continuous altered state, based on Jesus' Gospel. (This may seem weird at first, but how else can you describe being overcome by the joys of heaven on earth in the here and now?) We are still young, and continuing to grow in many ways, yet we're beginning to come to some really amazing discoveries about life! There is absolutely no reason to ever be bored, depressed, discouraged, or anything other than purely blissed out on living in Jesus!! It is possible to live absolutely high ALL THE TIME! This is no shallow high either; it includes loving the needy, and serving one another in love. This is a full package of bliss!

Our local Gospel imbibing community has so wanted to share this experience with the world! Yet, so many people have a hard time comprehending what we're even saying. I mean, are we really saying that heaven is already on earth?!? It's a wild message to communicate! It sounds too good to be true. It sounds ridiculous to so many. But, out of this passionate desire to communicate, an unusual book is born.

We want to answer the questions and help people understand, if at all possible. We want to create a resource for the wave riders of bliss to refer to for years to come. We want to assist in global bliss inebriation. Simply put, I, as a friend, just want to share my joy with you! Yet, the questions, they emerge. Why have my wife and I named our child "Rainbow Glory Spinks?" Why do we just start laughing out of nowhere? Why are we not discouraged at times when so many people are? Why are our eyes often squinty? LOL! Why is it so difficult to upset us? Why are we so happy? I want to answer these questions and more. I'm so inspired to share a real love and lasting bliss with the world!

If you have ever dared to dream that you might be able to get absolutely high without drugs, if you are looking for authentic meaning in life, if you are a partier and just want the highest longest lasting high, this book is for you! If you want to see sustainable happy communities, if you want to see heaven impact impoverished countries, if you simply want to see yourself have patience with your spouse, this book is for you!

Really, no matter who you are, oh my GOD, we want to share this message with you! It's ridiculous, it's incredible. It doesn't wear off! GOD is f***ing awesome!! I am so high now as I write, so have mercy, and Holy Ghost, please help!! Heeheeheehee!!! Yay!!! You are real, Jesus!!!

- *Matt Spinks*

CHAPTER 1
BUT, THEN WE GOT HIGH...

Welcome to being high on God! It's the most amazing, incredible, jacked up experience of life! I am so excited to share it with you! Puff, puff, pass! (No drugs are needed here, just lightening the mood, and encouraging you to breathe in our precious Holy Spirit!) Oh, Jesus, thank ya, Lord! Bammm!! There you go!

I'd like to begin by sharing a bit of my personal story... why would I write a book like this???

I was born a poor black child....oh wait, no different story. Ummm, yeah! Oh wait, no, yes, it's testimony time. So, ummmm, I used to be really bad, and then Jesus changed my life at summer camp. I'm joking. Oh, ahlm, uhhhhhh, shakkkahzzzah... let me start over...

MY STORY

So, I grew up in a semi-typical American home and family, Christian, kind of. Parents separated, Dad went to jail, moved around a few times. I ended up attending Lutheran schools for the most part, all the way through high school. I always kind of had an awareness of God. Looking back, I've always had somewhat of a strange inclination towards God. I did my homework as a youngster, because somehow I knew that "God" wanted me to do it. I used to talk to God, but never felt that much response. I was raised learning about Jesus and grace. It wasn't much of actually communing with God, but general Christian teachings were present. (Does this feel like a cheesy summer camp testimony yet? LOL!)

In high school, I had two youth leaders. They were both very passionate, encouraging men. They always attempted to inspire me to live my life fully for Jesus Christ. They shaped me to have godly vision and plans for my life, to be a youth pastor or missionary or the like. They never pressured me, but encouraged me toward a spiritual life vision. I had always known that I wanted to love and serve God in some way. The problem was that high school, and life in general made me pretty disillusioned with the world. I saw a lot of hypocrisy in my religious schooling, and a major lack of passion in the church. I also had this pervading sense that as long as I was still in high school I would never be able to do anything that really mattered. Still, I didn't want to drop out. I figured that I at least needed to finish school. But, I stopped trying to get A's in my classes, began to just have fun as much as I could, and go to parties, etc. The last year of high school especially was experiments with LSD, DXM, marijuana, alcohol, and other drugs. I also spent a lot of time listening to and playing music. To be honest, though, I was all over the place in my head.

I would lead our high school youth group's worship gatherings on my guitar, while at the same time being high on LSD. It was a strange time. I did not feel great about using drugs and being a youth leader at the same time. I wanted to live for God in purity. I did wonder if drugs could fit in there somewhere. A lot of my Christian high school friends were pretty confused in many of the same areas. We believed in grace and God's love, so why couldn't drugs, sex, and questionable living be included in there somewhere too? We didn't know, and no one around us offered much clarity. We weren't exactly talking to the adults around us about it, but amongst our friend group we were pretty confused.

Around the same time, through our youth group's mission trip to Mexico, I encountered some radical charismatic type believers and missionaries. I met young people who were living together doing mission work and spending all day worshiping, praying, and telling people about Jesus. It made so much sense to me. I saw a glimpse of a new world. I so wanted to be a part of a group like this. They had more joy and passion than I had, for sure. They also seemed to be living honest and open lives with no double standards. Their way of life absolutely appealed to me! So, I made plans to join this mission organization and immerse myself in a new life-style. These missionaries lived as if they were hearing God, communicating with God in supernatural ways, and had a whole different culture of dedication. As soon as I was finished with high school I signed up to join this group of missionaries. I started off right away for a distant country.

A RADICAL MISSIONARY

As soon as I arrived, my training started in a whole new paradigm and culture of following Jesus. It was way more focused, intense, and dedicated. I joined a group of new students from around the world who were also being trained in missions school together. This year, 2001, was a very powerful time for me.

I remember, as I arrived in the foreign land, and was just getting to know my new school mates, going out to the beach with a friend who had also just recently quit doing drugs. We sat by the ocean and discussed if we thought that we could remain drug free, and how this new life was going to be for us. We both asked ourselves, "Is there not a way to be at least as high on God as we were on drugs?" We both were not even 20 years old. And, we both were sincerely asking one another that question. We promised that if we ever found out answers we would let each other know. It was such a genuine question, but we literally had no idea how to get high on God. We imagined it must have been possible. But, we honestly had no clue. I remember thinking how far away that reality felt. It was as if really living high on God would be only for the super spiritual person, or maybe for just a few special people that had figured out some weird secret. It took me until seven years later to encounter my first glimpses of someone who was experiencing these realities. I met a lot of spiritual people, but this experience did not seem to be happening with anyone. If anyone was experiencing this, they were keeping it quiet. I pretty much forgot about the whole thing for a long time. My first encounters with those who were high on God weren't until the year 2008.

Anyhow, I continued on with this missionary group, completing six months of their missionary training. At the end of the training I returned home to Fort Wayne, Indiana to pray about where to go on assignment. The night after I arrived home, I did have a truly profound life changing experience. I experienced something I now believe to be the baptism of the Holy Spirit. All of a sudden, I began speaking in tongues, reading some of the thoughts of the people around me, seeing a bit of the future, and hearing God speaking clearly. It was amazing! It truly changed everything! I immediately went to my parents and told them everything I had ever done. I told them all the old secrets that I had kept from them, the drugs and other stuff that's not really worth mentioning here. I began to really be focused and passionate for God. I have never abused drugs again since 2001, never again having a problem with alcohol abuse either. For the next seven years I helped lead youth revivals, lived in foreign countries, ran missionary schools, preached Jesus, built homes for homeless families, and was involved in all kinds of ministry work. Yet, as seemingly great as those years were, I was never overwhelmingly happy. My life is significantly different now, in some pretty incredible ways. I'll get into that here soon! Holy Spirit!!!

FROM DEDICATION TO OVERFLOWING JOY

During those seven years, I was absolutely dedicated to Jesus Christ. I still am to this day. However, what I am about to describe has often been hard to explain. It often confuses people. How I could have been so dedicated to God and yet lived day to day with such a feeling of lack? It can be especially hard to explain because depression has become so normal in today's culture. No one would have even classified me as depressed, but compared to now...I truly was!

What do you mean depressed? What are you actually experiencing now? Isn't it just a little warmth or a bit of future hope? I may try to use many different words, pictures, or ways of explaining, not because anyone reading this is stupid, but because I get asked these questions so many times, everywhere I go. In fact, the majority of this book will be to attempt to clearly explain what is different about my life now! As one of our friends once said, "The only problem left with this Good News is how to put it into words!"

One way to describe my experience is this...

During those seven years I was mostly driven by what some call the "fire of God." I was mostly doing things responding to need and lack. I was motivated by a consuming passion to fix the world. I was trying really hard to get everyone "saved." Needless to say, it was like carrying a ton of weight around with me all the time! I had a genuine ache inside me to see everyone whole and free. Now it's not a bad thing to care deeply about the world, but it always felt like something was missing. As I went to bed most nights, I would lie awake thinking over and over again about what more I could be doing. I would think about how much the world needed to change. I had so much "fire." That same fire of passion remains to this day, but I see now that there's something profoundly different about it. There's another side of the God-life besides working for God. There has come much more clarity now. That's what this book is about. I really want to communicate a realm that has been revealed to me, to us, to the planet!

For those seven years, I was driven to help people, yet I myself was not happy. I was trying to serve and bless everywhere I went, but I did not feel full and overflowing. I knew all the Bible verses about, "my cup overflows," and "the fullness of joy," but I could not really describe how that felt. My message to others was always about getting more of God, opening the heavens, changing the world, or how to release the supernatural. My life and message had a certain underlying theme of how we were all off track and needed to get things right in order to save the world. I had so much passion! I loved God and others genuinely! Yet, my view of reality was not leaving me fulfilled! It definitely wasn't producing happy healthy lives around me. My life was definitely not "joy unspeakable and full of Glory," as the Bible says in first Peter chapter one verse eight!

I would lead church meetings, and often we would have amazing music, amazing messages, and yet I felt dissatisfied at the end of every one. I would go to bed frustrated at night. And, trust me, I tried everything I knew to shake this feeling. I kept thinking that maybe I just needed to serve God more or do more to change the world! I tried multiple long periods of fasting, intense weeks of study and seeking God, serving in far-away countries, organizing city church leaders in unity, repenting for everything I had ever done, etc. Nothing felt like it was working. I was just never seeing enough change in myself or the world. I felt like almost everyone was missing out on God. If I wasn't doing enough in all my efforts, then surely very few of my fellow humans could be experiencing the real kingdom of God on earth. Like I said, no one would have considered me depressed. I seemed like the model of a good person. My frustration made me all the more motivated. I just became more and more disciplined. I just kept believing that eventually I would "break through." I was so intense, and was forcing my intensity on my friends and all those around me. I would always be looking for an opportunity to challenge them to more prayer, more Bible study, more service to God and to humanity. I look back now and see that my intensity was hurting as many people as I helped in those days. However, I was doing everything that good spiritual leaders around me would have recommended.

It was during these seven years, that I played a significant role in starting up a small home based spiritual community in Indiana. I gathered as many friends and like-minded folks as I could to attempt to live as Jesus followers in a radical way. We started to meet in homes in 2005 forming our own dedicated group of believers. And, as you may have guessed, it didn't take long before I was challenging them at every turn to do more and more and more! We met seven nights a week! I had them scheduling every hour of their day out on paper, showing it to others in the group for accountability. We all became convinced that we needed to make sure that each of us were growing more intense and disciplined each day. We wanted to see more supernatural activity. We wanted to hear God more clearly. We wanted to see our city and world changed! The intensity continued. I was a part of several local and international ministries. I was putting every ounce of energy into it.

I was married during this time, and my wonderful wife, Katie, joined right in with me in our intensity. We criticized and even dis-associated ourselves with "hypocritical" family members. We wondered how long it would take until the world would change, if ever. We were not going to be a part of that old system. We would call out and challenge anyone who we thought was a part of that system. We were speaking the truth in love, so we thought. We weren't even always rude. We still probably looked quite spiritual to many people. Many folks commended us for our dedication. They said that we were great examples and very humble Christians. We didn't really care about that stuff though. We honestly just wanted God to be glorified and we were going to do whatever it took to get the most people to glorify God. (My wife was much sweeter about all this than I was, just for the record, hehehe!)

WHACKED BY JESUS!

BUT THEN WE GOT HIGH!! AHHHHHHH!!!! YAY! LOL!!!!!!!!!!
In the year 2008, everything changed! The burden was lifted! We began to have a completely different experience of God, life, and everything! And, here's how. Here's how the hammer of the Most High fell upon us, LOL...

On the very first day of 2008, we were at a large spiritual gathering for prayer. During one of the meetings, a whole group of us began to speak in tongues. As we did, I felt literal spiritual winds blow through my belly, my body, my soul. The whole rest of the day I was in some sort of trance, and could really discern the spirits of people around me, literally I felt them. I also heard God in an amazing way that day, more clearly than ever before. Something opened up for me there. It felt amazing, and I was very aware of having a tangible relationship with God in some kind of new way. However, that wasn't the biggest thing to happen to me that year. Really, I didn't even feel high there. That experience of love was still just scratching the surface of what was about to happen in the next few months.

Something else worth noting happened at that same gathering as well. It was there that I met my first group of "God stoners!" (That's just a random term I am using, not an actual title they had. LOL!) Now, at first I didn't really know what was going on with them. It was a group of 12-15 young people that I kept running into, in the midst of countless thousands at this huge spiritual gathering. Yet, these guys were easy to spot because they were always laughing and falling over. You could always pick them out of the crowd. They also kept using their finger to poke the people around them. Whoever the person was that they poked seemed to get high and would start laughing and fall over as well. These guys would stand in one spot together for a long, long time laughing and just falling down and just kind of praising God in the spot where they were.

I decided to observe this group of whackos. To be honest, they made me pretty upset and irritated. But, I couldn't figure out why they bothered me at all. They were just laughing and falling. Why was this making me upset? I did know that I had never seen or experienced this myself, so maybe I just thought that they were faking it, or maybe I just didn't like what I couldn't understand, or something like that. I remember watching them for like an hour. I was obviously struck by what was going on. I kept wondering if this kind of behavior was beneficial in any way. I wondered if their lives were fruitful. I saw something later that day that really spoke to me in that regard. This same group of people prayed for a man in a wheelchair. They prayed with him, and hugged him for like an hour. He got up out of the chair! He was healed! They seemed to be the only group at this entire massive spiritual gathering with the kind of power flowing through them to heal someone so afflicted. Still, I just thought to myself that these people were pretty weird. At the end of the few days gathering, I couldn't quite figure out what truly bothered me about them. I decided not to give it much more thought.

My wife and I had gone to the gathering together. We left feeling encouraged, but mostly, life was the same as ever for us. We were becoming more disciplined, we thought. We kept becoming more and more intense, spiritually.

Then, something started changing. Within a couple months of that gathering my wife began to seem a bit intoxicated when we would pray together. It wasn't every time, but sometimes. We had been watching some videos from a particular female missionary in Africa who would often behave drunk when in prayer or while preaching. So, at first, I thought that my wife was just copying this woman. Maybe she was trying to act more spiritual or something I thought. At first, I would take my wife aside and try to tell her to stop. My wife was getting high on God, and I would rebuke her for it! I remember rebuking her so harshly one evening that I made her cry. She was just genuinely being touched and influenced by God, but I didn't understand it. So, I tried to shut her down. Thankfully, that only lasted a couple of months. We were both about to get blasted in a wonderful intense way!

On with our story! At that time, we would often lead city-wide prayer gatherings around our region. We would help with leading music and singing. This was all still during early 2008. However, one of these gatherings was about to have an interesting turn of events for us! We had been asked to lead the music and prayer for a gathering on a local college campus, to pray for the campus and "contending for revival." As it went along, about half-way through the gathering, I felt to sing a particular song with lyrics about opening up the flood gates of heaven. I was really feeling determined to keep singing this song until we saw something powerful happen. We literally sang that same song for like 30 minutes, but nothing noticeable happened. I broke several guitar strings from the intensity with which I was playing. Eventually, the meeting ended, and we all went home.

The next day a married couple who we had just recently met called Katie and I over to their house to share some food and prophetic experiences with us. We had seen some cool things in the lives of these guys. They were humble and yet powerful in the things of God. So, we excitedly drove over to their house to hang out. They shared several experiences and words with us that day. They prayed for us, and even laid hands on us to release some spiritual impartation. The most powerful thing for me, though, was a comment from the man of the house, a comment made almost in passing. It was a statement that has forever changed my life.

He began to describe, kindly and with much appreciation in his voice, the city-wide prayer gathering from the night before. The couple had been present there and seemed to have enjoyed it, at least somewhat. The man began to talk about the song that I had sung about opening the floodgates of heaven. And, here's the statement he made that changed my life forever. He said, "It's really great to sing a song about opening the floodgates of heaven, you know, as long as you know that the heavens are already open." I laughed, and said, "Yeah, totally, of course!"

Truthfully, I was struck to the heart at that moment. The words he said there resounded within my heart and mind for days afterward. This was the first time that I had ever truly realized the truth of what he had just said. We finished our beautiful time of fellowship with the couple and went back to our home. Yet, that phrase stuck with me. To this day, I can still feel it! I am so grateful to GOD!!!!

While I pretended to understand what "the heavens are already open" meant, it was obvious that I didn't understand it at all. Surprisingly, this was finally the beginning of my journey down the rabbit hole of the genuine message of Jesus Christ. A spirit of revelation was coming over me in a powerful way! I was hearing the Gospel for the first time! This message was somehow standing out as strikingly different from what

I had previously believed! Let me say that, even as you read, this may seem like no big deal at first. I have come to see, however, that many people are just like me. I had previously thought that God wanted me to get the conditions just right before He would heal and restore the planet. I had come to know that God wanted healing, joy, life, and passion in people's lives. Yet, I thought that these things would only be made real if we could, "rend the heavens", and get God to come down, or if we could make something really happen through our prayers or fasting strategies. Maybe then this heavenly life could be ours and our cities and world would be transformed!

All of a sudden this new message was rocking the understanding built previously in my life. I had valued God and His Presence coming to us supernaturally. I knew that God was the solution to all life. The issue was that I thought that something was stopping God. I was totally convinced that there were massive spiritual barriers and hindrances of many different names and sources. I had been taught, or somehow come to believe, that God's presence and blessings were at best only partially accessible. Now my heart and mind were being opened to a new possibility. What if heaven and earth were totally unified and open to one another? What if the Glory of God was all around, already flowing to all His creation like a waterfall, like a river?!?

This was early 2008, a time I now look back to as the greatest turning point of my life. It was a big set up! Not only did I see new things demonstrated by a new message that was changing my life, but at the very same time I was being introduced to a whole new community of folks who were experiencing this reality.

I would be remiss if I didn't mention by name some of the people I was introduced to at that time. Through two different friends, my wife and I began to plug into the conferences and work of Georgian & Winnie Banov, John Crowder, Benjamin Dunn, and Heidi Baker. You may be familiar with these Glory folks, or you may not. But, they had all either loosely or directly been associated with the Toronto Blessing movement of the 1990s. It was a controversial revival that has proved out to have borne amazing fruit over the years that have followed. It was marked by great joy, laughter, and tangible experiences of the Glory of God.

During this time, one friend gave me a book by John Crowder, and another friend recommended Mr. Crowder's videos. Through John Crowder, I began to listen to the music of Benjamin Dunn. Through both of these guys we began to attend conferences with the Banovs, and Heidi Baker.

While we were hearing from these ministers, my wife and I began to experience heaven! They spoke of a heaven that was nearer than we had ever dared to believe. Over the early months of 2008, believe it or not, we would be laid out on the floor just laughing and being overwhelmed, not by any change in circumstances really, but by a tangible felt Presence of God. Simply put, we would get overwhelmingly HIGH! Both my wife Katie and I had done drugs in the past. This was far greater! We began to feel a whole body buzz, a euphoria, a deep joy, a love for all, and so many more things which will be described later in this book! The only way to sum it up is to say, "We were high!" When we would gather with like-minded believers we would get so wasted, so jacked up as we would celebrate! It would then remain when we were alone, and on even into all kinds of circumstances. We began to feel God's heart so powerfully. We felt a love that was so far beyond what we had been able to muster before! Oh my GOD!

At that time, Katie and I would have a daily prayer time where we would spend an hour or two together each afternoon. Normally, it had been filled with pleading and crying out for so many things in prayer. All of a sudden, it was as if we were struck mute. (We actually were completely mute sometimes!) We would come to our prayer time already so overwhelmingly happy. All we could do was just sit and smile. There was just an absolute sense that Jesus had already finished it all. At that time we thought, "What more is there to pray for?" Heaven had come down! Was heaven already on earth? We laughed, smiled, and sat there in the tangible warmth of God.

This truly was the most transformative time of our lives. It was as if we had finally heard the best news in the cosmos! It changed everything. We became such satisfied people. We became such happy people. We felt so whole. And, the feeling of being high was constant! We would wake up stoned, and go to bed high, on God alone. It was amazing. It was exhilarating. It has never stopped!

FRUIT AND TRANSFORMATION

After that time, we continued to learn and experience so much more depth in this God-high. We began to see regular healings and wild supernatural miracles. Our local home fellowship community was rocked, and many began to get high with us. People moved from around the country to join our community, to live high 24/7 with us. It has been a wild journey! It has not been without persecution and challenges. Yet, the Glory has remained! The Presence is still so thick, it's incredible. Heaven is here to stay!

This book marks the time when we are finally ready to write about this to the world. We have lived and tested this material for more than eight years, through family life, community experience, and challenging circumstances. The bliss is real. The high remains! We now want to share this amazing experience with all humanity! It can be as simple as even now just looking around you and realizing the tangible Glory that is everywhere. It's not a complicated message! It can often seem too simple, or too good to be true. Sometimes it could sound too strange or unbelievable. I remember how crazy it seemed at first, trust me I do! But, please, read on!

There is more to this than just some weirdos looking for a cheap high. That was not my desire at all. In fact, I've lost so much of my personal reputation for believing this kind of stuff. I was on track to be a good little successful traditional evangelical missionary. But, I got hijacked by something. Something gripped my life. Something mind blowing, something healing, something precious invaded my little box of a world. I couldn't care less about making money off of this book. I don't give a rip about looking impressive in any way. I've already gone way too far out for that. Yet, maybe someone would dare to believe that this kind of stuff could happen in their life. Maybe that's you. Or, maybe you're skeptical and you just want to see what this crackpot has to say! Maybe you're the person who has already experienced some of this but you want to explore the depths together with us! Maybe you're just checking this out for the entertainment value alone! No matter why you find yourself reading these words, my friend, my desire is for you to read on! Why? Beautiful soul, my desire is to share this joy with you! Read on and be exhilarated by the glorious God-life you were created for! Enjoy the bliss of existence!! And, I say in conclusion, like the poet of old, "*Friends, drink, be intoxicated with love!*" - Song of Songs 5:1(HCSB)

CHAPTER 2
WHAT DO YOU MEAN BY 'HIGH ON GOD?'

The first thing you may be wondering is, "What exactly is going on here?" "What the heck do you mean by getting 'high on God?'" These are the first questions we are often asked! They are great questions! And, they have beautiful, pure, life-changing answers. However, I request your patience and calm consideration at first. Before any skepticism or prior experiences make conclusions on your behalf, give it a couple of chapters at least! Your questions may take a while to be able to answer for those who are new to the experience. And, yes, they really do need to actually be experienced to be fully understood. You may already realize that this is true about most spiritual experiences. Many times they are really only understood until years later! Think again upon the supernatural events and prophecies of the Bible. Rarely were they understood at the time. Even generations later they are wondered about and interpreted in vastly different ways!

This book is definitely not meant just to be read about! It is meant to be experienced! In fact, the best idea may be to just put the book down and simply realize the high right now! Christ is in you, and the whole earth is filled with the Glory of God! Bam! Feel the buzz of God washing over you even as you read! Mmmmmm, yeah! It can be just that easy. Take a moment and just sit in contemplation. See what God might do!

As long as we're looking into things with a context of something greater than mere surface language, there is often great value in discussing and understanding the things of the Spirit. So, please proceed ahead in reading while being open to a true present move of Holy Spirit in your life. God is eager to make this stuff real way beyond the words on the page! For many of you, though, the words you're about to read will really help to give clarity regarding the high of God. I honor and bless you, whatever place you may feel that you are at. Plunge ahead and be supremely blissed beyond words!

GOD IS THE HIGH!

First things first, then, what is the primary premise of this whole book? What is this high? The high is God! God is the high! Namely, Jesus Christ is the high! This is the foundation of it all!

What the heck are we talking about? We are talking about the tangible experience of God. Throughout history people have often become absolutely overwhelmed by the Glory of God. We will explore this in much greater detail later. Yet, for now, let's make just a very short list of some of the most potent examples. I want to bring to our attention, right at the beginning, some specifics of exactly what we are talking about. Let's get into the juice!

Did you know that there are many scriptural accounts where people would literally fall over because the Presence of God was so intense? In the book of second Chronicles chapter five, it says that all of the priests present at the day of the temple dedication were unable to stand because of the thick cloud of God's Glory! The prophet Daniel was also recorded to have involuntarily fallen on his face before God in the book of Daniel chapter eight. Another great example is John, the beloved apostle of Jesus Christ, who already knew God intimately. When John saw Jesus in the beginning of the book of Revelation he was forced to hit the deck as well.

What humankind often fails to realize is that God is not just an idea! God is not just a far off ethereal concept! God is personal. God has substance. Sometimes that substance is referred to in scripture as a literal cloud! And, what if that cloud was permanently living inside you, oh my, wow?!? This is the same cloud that knocked all the priests over in the temple!

Let's dive a bit deeper on this thought for a minute, just to help give an initial understanding of where we're going. Scientists are only beginning to scratch the surface of the connection between the spiritual realm and the natural realm. Discussions about consciousness and where "the spirit" or "awareness" of life comes from are happening more and more all over the media and scholarly world.

I am often asked the question, "Are you talking about the spiritual realm, or the natural realm?" The answer is, "Yes!" Could God be a natural, physical cloud? Yes! Of course, just being a natural cloud does not contain or fully describe God at all, in the fullest sense. Yet, the point is that God has a true, real, and living substance, ultimately revealed in the literal man, Jesus Christ.

Jesus Christ is God in a body, a tangible living physical body. Yet, Jesus in his physical body was not the first or only time where God appears in a tangible sense, in a way that can be experienced. The Gospel of John chapter four reminds us that God is Spirit. This Spirit can also be tangibly experienced. The spiritual realm is not a realm without literal effect! Even God, the Father, and God, the Holy Spirit, have tangible substance! Spirit is just as real as natural realities. In fact, it is quite likely that soon the spiritual realm will be scientifically discovered to be merely invisible realities that historically had not previously been perceived well by human observation. Scientific breakthroughs will continue to happen! Our best technology and scientific instruments will continue to grow and new discoveries will be made.

Not to get too far off topic, as I am not a physicist, nor am I a professional scientist by any means. I have however become quite experienced with being high on God. And, all that to say, it is quite a literal, tangible, real experience! Something is happening to every part of me, from my "spirit" to my big toe! The Gospel of Jesus Christ has become way more than just pie in the sky ethereal concepts for someday far away. I literally feel like heaven! It's affecting every part of me. Something is happening!

I've become convinced that there is a tangible substance being released in and around me. It's causing me to be high. Now, God includes so much more than being high, don't get me wrong. I am in no way wanting to limit God to just one facet or description. God's substance causes all of God's life and virtue to flow through me. God is an unlimited creative perfect and holy One! However, as we will continue to explore throughout this book, the satisfaction and fullness of a person feeling the God high is no small thing either.

There is something profoundly real and even scientifically tangible to this. Again, what is happening? Let me give another quick picture that I often use to help people understand.

If a whole room was completely filled with marijuana smoke, anyone who came into that room and took a breath, even just a little bit, they would get high. No one who inhaled in that room would be able to remain unaffected. A substance was released in that room! That substance affects everyone, no exceptions. It doesn't depend on their personality or mood. It doesn't really depend on anything. All that is needed is the substance in the air, and the ability to breathe. This is very simple science. We don't have to make spiritual things so complicated to understand! God is the substance, and hearing the Good News of Jesus Christ awakens our ability to breathe. And, so much healthier, fuller, and richer than marijuana smoke is the Glory Presence of God. That's some good Shekinah!

I honestly believe that we were created out of the substance of God. God's Spirit is our home. All things originated in God. So, experiencing God is like being fully home. God, the life source of all things, is so full and rich, filled with goodness, exploding with creativity. God's Spirit is invisible, just like the deepest parts of humans. These two were created to be one. We were meant to be! The goodness of this infinite source called God, uniting with our deepest parts, creates a euphoria beyond anything else that ever could be. This was the great goal of human history. The whole point of it all is for the two to experience oneness, the truest, most intimate relationship! Just like in a marriage, there is intense bliss around true oneness. Scientifically speaking, there is something real and observable going on here! Most likely, with the right tools we will someday be able to scientifically observe and measure this phenomenon. Until that time comes, I say we keep experiencing it for ourselves! Be a mystical cosmonaut, exploring God deeply and richly, like the mystics of old, like the disciples of Biblical times, like our Lord Jesus Christ laid out before us! His Presence has been freely given for us to partake!

As you recognize heaven all around and within you, namely the very fullness of the Person of God in Christ, you will experience this reality! This is what is happening to us! Somehow it starts with hearing the truth. This allows our hearts to open up to the substance that has always already been there. Like I mentioned before, the message of Christ enables us to breathe the Substance of Christ.

It is wholly true that God and heaven have always been right here, inside our bodies, and all over the cosmos! Yet, most people are living closed off to this reality mostly due to hurts and disappointments. This is why most people think we are crazy for being high on God. It has not been the experience of most people so far in human history. It seems too good to be true. It feels unsustainable, unrealistic, or strange.

Something does, however, seem to open up within us and around us, even physically, when we become convinced of the Good News of Jesus Christ! It's as if a whole new world lies revealed before us! This could easily sound like we are just going crazy. But, maybe it's just that we were crazy before. What if it is just now that we are coming to see the world rightly? This is why I brought up physics earlier in the chapter. Scientists are beginning to discover some things that confirm what I am saying here. There have been some studies done that reveal certain matter behaving differently when being observed. We are discovering that perception can literally change physical reality! What if realizing the truth, as revealed by Jesus Christ, that heaven is here, even when we don't see it with our physical eyes, is the very thing that shapes a new reality to be experienced all around us (Matt. 4:17, Mark 1:15)?

Humanity is also just learning about other dimensions. What if heaven has always been all around us, but we hadn't picked up on how to live in its' dimension? I believe that science will grow closer and closer to confirming something similar to this exact conclusion. What if there was a whole reality that we could be experiencing, but because our perception was not right, we were missing it?

Whether I have it right scientifically or not, I am pointing to a reality that I believe confirms scripturally, theologically, historically, and experientially. There is a whole new world that is all around us and within us. The whole earth is filled with the Glory of God (Is. 6:3)! This Glory has been so intense that it physically knocked people down throughout the ages. This Glory surely can affect us so powerfully. This is what is happening when we are getting high. It is the Glory of God tangibly affecting our beings! Wooohoooo! Just stop again for a second, and take another breath of THAT!

As soon as I began to realize that heaven was open and present to be experienced now in Jesus, I began feel literal, tangible effects, as I mentioned earlier. To give further help in letting you know what I mean, let me attempt to describe more specifically what some of these effects have been. Some of these may read as a bit childish or shallow at first. Yet, don't underestimate the value of simply being ravished and filled with pleasure! There is a powerful value to being overwhelmed with pleasure. We were made for it! We will discuss that more in chapter five. For now, I want you to know more specifically what exactly is available to you in the God high! Is this for real? What exactly happens when you are high on God? Oh, thank you, Jesus! Let's attempt to put together a list of literal descriptions of what being high on God is like. This list is in no way comprehensive, but it should be enough to whet your appetite. We were made to live in His ecstasy!

SYMPTOMS OF BEING HIGH ON GOD

THE BODY BUZZ – Literally, the physical body just begins to feel really good. Pain decreases, and your whole body can feel very light, or just generally comfortably numb. Sometimes there is literally no pain, even up to the point where you may feel like you have a brand new body. The body buzz is extremely common in varying degrees.

THE EUPHORIA – The sense that everything is just so great! You can feel extreme happiness, like everything is right with the world. You begin to believe in people again. An almost ridiculous positive outlook takes over. This is very common as well.

THE EXCITEMENT – Often a renewed passion for life will arise. It becomes easy to believe in your dreams and callings. You get energy for living with zeal again! This is also a common effect. This one can cross over and become a full on supernatural ability to do tasks, even impossible tasks.

CHILDLIKENESS – You can act silly, and easily have fun. You're relaxed. You have an innocence about you. You don't take yourself too seriously. This is extremely common.

LOSS OF MOTOR FUNCTIONS – Often, a person will slur speech, and walk/drive poorly. People will fall, or just be rendered immobile on the floor. This can also be called "ligature." When experiencing this, it is recommended that you be careful about engaging in activities that require motor functions. God has a way of protecting those in this state too, but proceed with caution!

PASSING OUT – This one is not quite as common, in my experience. However, sometimes in the weighty presence of God, you can get so absolutely high, you really can pass out. It can come on slowly, or very quickly.

RUNNING, MOVING, AND/OR SHAKING – The Glory of God is the purest most powerful energy! Many people who are experiencing the God high get the desire, sometimes an almost uncontrollable urge, to move, dance, shake, or even run. There have been many forms of this throughout history; holy shakers, quakers, and runners!

MUTENESS – In rapturous joy, I have honestly been struck mute on a couple of occasions. I've heard of this happening to others as well. The reality of heaven is so amazing, you are literally left speechless.

VISIONS – The holy counterpart to psychedelic drugs, being high on

God often causes visions of different sorts. From seeing simple pictures in your mind's eye, to full on "open visions", it all could happen. These are not quite as common. They seem to happen more to some people than to others. This includes all sorts of seeing into unseen realities, or distant events, supernaturally by the Spirit.

THE SATISFACTION – A deep sense that all is well almost always occurs. This could also be called the bliss. The real experience of Christ's perfect work in creation and redemption produces a profound stable sense of being satisfied.

THE REST OF MIND AND SOUL – As a result of the satisfaction, the whole being is put to rest. Worries fade away. The mind can become quiet and still. It becomes easy to trust in this place. You no longer are ruled by the tyranny of the urgent. You lose a sense of lack.

EFFORTLESS FRUIT OF THE SPIRIT – This is the greatest experience of all! It becomes so easy to fall in love with God and people. You lose temptations, because you are no longer filling a void. You feel full! You learn that joy is far more than a word! Peace rushes like a river. You feel stable, because of the satisfaction and rest. The virtue of God flows through you in long term relationships, and causes expressions of the fruits of the Spirit mentioned in the book of Galatians chapter five.

The greatest symptom of all, truly, is that you are LOVE – DRUNK! You literally feel full of God, who is Love! You are experiencing authentic union intimacy with the Trinity! You become empowered to be no longer simply a taker, but a giver as well. You are set free to overflow with generosity toward others. You begin to care about the world, with no hidden agenda. You find that you like people. You feel good, and are ready to help others feel the same. You are high on God/Love, so what would you expect?!!?

Now remember how I said earlier that God is the substance, and hearing the Good News of Jesus Christ awakens our ability to breathe? Let's discuss that in further depth. This is the good stuff!!! I feel like a Glory dealer about to deal you the best stuff ever!!! Hahaha!

As we close out this chapter, I just want to be totally clear. We get high on the person of God, Who is Love, which is the Glory, which is the substance of God!

Many people believe that God is good. We can know intellectually that God is Love. We can know that God is a consuming fire, as a fact, in our heads. However, it's obviously a whole other thing entirely to actually be consumed by a fire. You get high when you begin to experience the substance that is Goodness Itself/Himself/(Herself even, but most of you would need another book to be comfortable with me saying that one, so for most of this book I will use masculine pronouns when referring to God, LOL). The substance is Love itself. The substance is the consuming fire itself. The substance is God Himself!

The drug is God! God is what we are on! God is what we are high on, nothing else!

Here's some more really important stuff regarding all of this, as this chapter concludes.

Like I said before, God is the substance. And, it's hearing and understanding the Good News of Jesus Christ that allows us to breathe God's substance continuously.

Unfortunately, some folks throughout history have been intoxicated by the Glory of God, yet it only lasted for a short time, seeming to wear off later. Sometimes the Glory comes so strong, even when we haven't really understood the how to breathe it regularly. It can just overtake an individual. That experience is amazing and precious just as it is! However, hearing the Good News of Jesus, and truly understanding it, is THE big deal. Having a revelation of Jesus' Gospel enables the deepest places within us to remain open to His substance. Understanding Jesus' Message allows our hearts to trust God, even in times when life appears as a contradiction. Through the clear revelation of Christ we can REMAIN continually high!

For this reason, I want to continue to share what this Good News of Jesus truly is! It may seem like a broken record, but most of us need to hear it almost daily! Once we thoroughly lay a foundation of Jesus' Good News, we will also discuss what is the nature, history, and purpose of this high, this intoxication. (Some of you may have a problem with the word 'intoxication,' as though you are receiving something negative, something toxic. God's Glory is the exact opposite of toxic! However, we are using street lingo and slang that has been incorporated in the English language to have a meaning beyond the exact literal break down of the word. There may be other words like that, and may I encourage you to look to the overall deeper function of the word, not so much the form.) Read on for further depth of exploration to increase your understanding and to sustain your experience. I pray that the spirit of revelation be upon you as you read! This foundation of understanding will greatly help you to remain high on Him! Cheers! Deep drinks!

CHAPTER 3
HIGH ON THE BIBLE

To truly get into an understanding of the Good News that makes us high, we really must start with the Bible! The Bible describes in depth what the Gospel of Jesus Christ is! The Bible, despite what religious weirdos have done to it over the centuries, is packing a lot of bliss! The Bible is the highest book ever written! (Yes, I do know that the Bible is not one book, but rather, a collection of books.) The Bible contains the clear Good News message that enables our constant high!

Before we go any further with this book, I want to lay a foundation from the original book of ecstasy! There is a full and rich display of the God high throughout the scriptures! This will be extremely important for many of us to explore, especially if we grew up around the Christian church. Many people hear us talking about being high on God, especially

Christians, and they think that it must be some new strange phenomenon! They certainly don't think it could be Biblical! Yet, once you see it, you will notice that it's all over the scriptures! The Bible is the ultimate book on the God high!

BIBLICAL ORIGINS IN THE BLISS

In the beginning God was high. The Trinity, basking in their full and complete love of one another, have always been overwhelmed with the love and ecstatic joy of being! All bliss began in God! This only makes total sense when you have a full picture of God and the Glory of reality. From the very beginning the Bible points to the bliss! We see a major pointer to God being high from all eternity past displayed here in the book of Proverbs.

Proverbs 8:25-31 Before the mountains had been shaped, before the hills, I was brought forth, (26) before he had made the earth with its fields, or the first of the dust of the world. (27) When he established the heavens, I was there; when he drew a circle on the face of the deep, (28) when he made firm the skies above, when he established the fountains of the deep, (29) when he assigned to the sea its limit, so that the waters might not transgress his command, when he marked out the foundations of the earth, (30) *then I was beside him, like a master workman, and I was daily his delight, rejoicing before him always,* (31) *rejoicing in his inhabited world and delighting in the children of man.* (ESV)

This passage from the book of Proverbs describes Wisdom in the Trinity, rejoicing in delight, from the very beginning of the world! And, while the word 'high' is not literally used here, the childlike euphoria is definitely present. In context with the rest of scripture, I believe it points to God being high, in the relational life of the Trinity, from the very beginning.

Then, following along in the Biblical timeline, we have the creation of humankind as recorded in Genesis. Adam and Eve were placed in the Garden of Eden. The word 'Eden' is based on the Hebrew word for pleasure. God placed them in the Garden of Pleasure! And, as if that wasn't enough, do you know what the first thing that God did was when He made humankind?

Gen 1:27-28 - So God created man in his own image, in the image of God he created him; male and female he created them. (28) And God *blessed* them..." (ESV)

This passage says that God blessed them. Now, that may seem like just a simple religious statement. However, a blessing is a powerful thing. When God blesses you, it is way more than what you may have realized!

Webster's 1828 Dictionary reads as follows:

> **Blessed**
> BLESS'ED, pp. Made happy or prosperous; extolled; pronounced happy.
> BLESS'ED, a. Happy; prosperous in worldly affairs; enjoying spiritual happiness and the favor of God; enjoying heavenly felicity.

So, God placed them in the Garden of pleasure, gave them happiness, favor, and heavenly felicity!??! Sounds like the high life to me! It's definitely not some boring, just-getting-by existence. Adam and Eve were enjoying heavenly felicity in pleasure-land! This is the Bible folks. Who knew that it was filled with such ecstasy, such delight? It's not some boring kill-joy book! It's full of the goodness of God as the original motivation for creation. God created us to be high in pleasure-land!

Continuing on, the Bible says that in that Garden there was a tree that we were meant to eat from. Remember that story? What was the tree called? That's right! It was called the 'tree of life.'

Genesis 2:9, 16-17 - And out of the ground the LORD God made to spring up every tree that is pleasant to the sight and good for food. The *tree of life* was in the midst of the garden, and the tree of the knowledge of good and evil…And the LORD God commanded the man, saying, "You may surely eat of every tree of the garden, but of the tree of the knowledge of good and evil you shall not eat, for in the day that you eat of it you shall surely die." (ESV)

Sometimes the word 'life' can simply mean 'existence.' Yet, it can also mean 'quality of existence'. Jesus says in John 17:3 that, "knowing God is eternal life." This refers not to simply existing forever, but having the highest possible quality of existence. The word life could mean simply to exist, like when someone says, "The car accident didn't kill me. I still have life in my body." But, it could also mean, "I just did a high dive off of a 30 foot cliff, and I feel so much life."

When speaking of the tree of life, I think it means both. This tree sustains existence, and also gives the highest quality of existence. The tree keeps you alive, and also makes you feel SO alive! The Bible also says that Jesus is the way, the truth, and the life (John 14:6). Jesus sustains every living thing, and is the very life of all things. Jesus ALSO makes everything SO alive!

By this 'Tree of Life' in the garden we can see that from the very beginning humankind was meant to live forever, and LIVE forever! We were created to eat of *THE* Tree of Life and live the absolute highest form of life forevermore!

It's also very interesting to me that the other tree noted in the Garden of Eden in the book of Genesis was the one that we were not meant to eat from. This was the tree of the knowledge of good and evil. I believe that most people alive today are not truly 'living'. They are merely existing on a steady diet from this inferior tree. The tree of the knowledge of good and evil represents the very thing that caused the problems that the world is still experiencing on earth to this day. It's what killed the high life! Literally, there is more to this subject than you may realize.

The tree of knowledge of good and evil represents a state of consciousness. The tree of life, or living high on God, may seem to us like an altered state of consciousness. But, what if it was the original intended state of consciousness? What if we were created to be high, exhilarated with life, simply walking with God in the faith of Jesus Christ (THE Tree of Life Himself), rather than weighing out our own decisions of what is good and what is evil, living in a sober state of worry and independence? The state that most people find themselves living in today is usually a state of thinking that they have to take care of themselves. It seems to all be deeply rooted back to that tree. This is the mindset that says that we must be in charge of deciding in independence what is good and what is evil in order to make our lives and the world better. The Tree of Life gives us something completely different. The Tree of Life offers us God, from the inside out, as the infinite abundant source of the highest quality of everlasting existence. The Tree of Life represents an abundant unstoppable loving Person as our Source and Provider. This means that we don't have to be our own source. We don't have to be our own providers. We don't need to control and manipulate our world. Instead we can relax and live in an enjoyable trust!

The Tree of Life enables you to live dependent on God, and therefore high and at peace, while being an effortless success. Sounds too good to be true!?? I know, right! God created us to be happy and high in pleasure-land with His life flowing through us! Many times when I read the word 'life' in the Bible, I remember this. I remember that often it is not referring to mere existence, but the high of the God ordained quality of existence. Those two trees, oh what a difference! This is a huge deal! Let the reader be encouraged to meditate on this at length.

So, we've seen how the Bible points to our origin and purpose as having been created to live in God's bliss. What else can we find scripturally regarding the high of God? Let's explore some Old Testament prophets!

JACKED UP OT PROPHETS

We already mentioned the priests of the book of Chronicles, and the prophet Daniel falling out in the Glory. The Presence was so strong it literally made them fall over (2 Chron. 5, Dan. 8)! But, this didn't just happen to those guys alone. The prophet Ezekiel got blasted by the Glory and fell multiple times (Ez. 1, Ez. 3). Daniel's wasn't a one off either, by the way! Abraham also fell down (Gen. 17). The entire nation of Israel fell down on several occasions because of the Glory (Lev. 9, Num. 16, 1 Kings 18)!

Beyond falling out or falling down, there are numerous references in the

Old Testament of people getting an altered state of consciousness as a direct result of the Glory of God. Consider the following list of scriptures:

Zechariah 9:15 - The LORD of hosts will defend them. And they will devour and trample on the sling stones; And, they will drink and be boisterous as with wine; And they will be filled like a sacrificial basin, Drenched like the corners of the altar. (NASB)

Psalms 36:8 - They shall be inebriated with the plenty of thy house; and thou shalt make them drink of the torrent of thy pleasure. (DRB)

Song of Songs 5:1 - He: I came to my garden, my sister, my bride, I gathered my myrrh with my spice, I ate my honeycomb with my honey, I drank my wine with my milk. Others: Eat, friends, drink, and be drunk with love! (ESV)

Isaiah 25:6 - And in this mountain shall the LORD of hosts make unto all people a feast of fat things, a feast of wines on the lees, of fat things full of marrow, of wines on the lees well refined. (KJV)

Isaiah 55:1 - "All you people who are thirsty, come! Here is water for you to drink. Don't worry if you have no money. Come, eat and drink until you are full! You don't need money. The milk and wine are free. (ERV)
Psalm 4:7 - You have put gladness in my heart, More than when their grain and new wine abound. (NASB)

1Kings 8:11 - so that the priests could not stand to minister because of the cloud, for the glory of the LORD filled the house of the LORD. (ESV)

Isaiah 35:10 - The LORD will make his people free, and they will come back to him. They will come into Zion rejoicing. They will be happy forever. Their happiness will be like a crown on their heads. Gladness and joy will fill them completely. Sorrow and sadness will be far, far away. (ERV)

Isaiah 35:10 (35:9B) - and shall return, and come to Sion with joy, and everlasting joy shall be over their head; for on their head shall be praise and exultation, and joy shall take possession of them: sorrow and pain, and groaning have fled away. (Brenton)

Joel 3:18 - And in that day the mountains shall drip sweet wine, and the hills shall flow with milk, and all the streambeds of Judah shall flow with water; and a fountain shall come forth from the house of the LORD and water the Valley of Shittim. (ESV)

Psalms 32:1-2 - Oh the bliss of him whose guilt is pardoned, and his sin forgiven! Oh the bliss of him whom the Eternal has absolved, whose spirit has made full confession! (Moffatt)

Psalms 45:6-7 - Your throne shall stand for evermore; for, since your scepter is a scepter just, since right you love and evil you abhor, so God, your God, crowns you with bliss above your fellow kings. (Moffatt)

Psalms 65:4 - Happy is he whom thus thou choosest to dwell in thy courts, close to thee. Fain would we have our fill of this, thy house, thy sacred shrine- it's bliss! (Moffatt)

Psalms 73:28 - But to be near God is my bliss, to shelter with the Lord; (that I may tell of all your good works). (Moffatt)

Psalms 84:11 - For God the Eternal is a sun and shield, favour and honour he bestows; he never denies bliss to the upright.' (Moffatt)

Isaiah 55:12 - For you shall leave with joy, and be lead off in blissful bands. (Moffatt)

Psalms 65:4-5 - The emotions of passion were stronger than I,- But You can erase our sins. Happy he whom You choose and approach, He can dwell in Your courts full of bliss; In the house of Your holy retreat. (Fenton)

Those are some whacked out scriptures! Honestly, each one of those references points to something that these writers and prophets were tangibly experiencing. This is way more than a "joy deep down"! It is compared to drinking wine, to being drunk. It is described as bliss! It reads as if joy was taking complete possession of people!

Psalm 16:11 has always been one of my favorites! It is widely believed to have been written by the prophet-king David. "You make known to me the path of life; in your presence there is fullness of joy; at your right hand are pleasures forevermore." David was said to be a man after God's own heart. David was obviously experiencing something! He called it fullness of joy! He was tasting pleasures, plural, multiple eternal pleasures of God. David was getting high on God!

There are many stories in the Old Testament that seem to have prophets and other people getting high on God. You may have to read the rest of this book to be able to see what I see in those accounts. So, I'll leave that to your further exploration. Have fun noticing throughout history how many times spiritual revelation came to humanity through people who were high on God!

Now, something else you may have noticed is that the majority of people who lived in Old Testament times were not high on God at all. This is absolutely true. Even the most powerful of prophets seemed to only go into ecstasy on rare occasions. There is a key reason for this. It's what we discussed earlier. It's not that the Glory substance of God was not filling the earth. No! Isaiah chapter six reveals that the whole earth was filled with the Glory, even way back then (Is. 6:3)!

The issue was that the Good News of Jesus Christ had not been revealed to them! The Glory was there, but they were not aware of it. They did not know how to breathe it! They did not know the Gospel. They were in an era of lesser revelation. Jesus Christ had not yet appeared on the scene. Therefore, at best, the few who were tasting the Glory, only knew temporary tastes. They didn't stay high very often in the O.T. Enoch, and a few others, may have glimpsed the Good News and gone pretty far in the Glory. However, for the most part, the whack was scarce! There wasn't much Good News going on in those days! But, all that was about to change! God was about to become a man to show the world the ultimate High Life!

ALL JACKED UP ON THE NEW TESTAMENT

Jesus Christ was obviously embodying the Glory of heaven in every way. Jesus is amazing! How many men and women of all walks of life, all cultures, all eras of history have testified to the beauty of the life of this man, Jesus Christ? Jesus stands alone in the pure Light of His glorious Person! Jesus is the name above all names. And, as one who walked in the fullness of divinity and humanity, Jesus was definitely high!

Saying that Jesus is high is definitely offensive to some. So, once again, let me unpack this further. The whack of God is not a shallow, a merely acting drunk, or just a falling down phenomenon (though it can sometimes include that, as we discussed earlier). Being high on God is about having the fully exhilarated consciousness of the life of God flowing through one's being. Jesus Christ revealed what God was like, and what man is truly like. We were created to be in a different state of consciousness than what most people have grown up with. We were created for a rich, deep, and powerful state of consciousness, a fullness of joy and a rich bliss!

Jesus lived in this normal state of consciousness 24/7, embodying heaven on earth! Have you ever wondered what it felt like in the mind of Jesus, in the consciousness of Jesus? What did it feel like in the day to day? What state was he in when he would read people's minds, or confound the critical Pharisees? What was his mind state when he raised someone from the dead? How does it feel within to have pure unconditional love for the entire cosmos? This is the high we are talking about!

Jesus lived in a state that was absolutely childlike. Jesus lived in a state that was just "crazy" enough to move in those types of manifestations. Jesus lived high on the Presence of His Father, by the power of the Holy Spirit.

The book of Hebrews chapter one says that Jesus was anointed with the oil of gladness above all of His companions (Heb. 1:9). This means he was happier than anyone who had ever lived! The gladdest person to ever live! Now that's definitely going to be one whacked out individual! Jesus was also a man of sorrows too, as you might remember. Yes, it's true that Jesus experienced all the pain and suffering of this world as well. This is so beautiful and amazing to have a God like this, so deep and rich with His vastness! Wow! He knows what highs can feel like, and He knows what lows can feel like too! He knows what each one of us has been through for He has always been with us all. However, in the midst of taking on and healing all the wounds of this world, he remained more glad than anyone who has ever lived. This is a true God high! Jesus shows us what it's like to be totally whole, with the full range of emotional capacity open and activated, yet still extremely stable, AND also absolutely wasted on His Father, Holy Spirit and His love for all creation!

In the Gospel of Luke chapter ten it says, "He thrilled with joy at that hour in the holy Spirit, saying, "I praise thee, Father, Lord of heaven and earth, for concealing this from the wise and learned and revealing it to the simple-minded; yes, Father, I praise thee that such was thy chosen purpose (Luke 10:21)." The word for 'thrilled' there in the original Greek indicates a jumping, a spinning, and a leaping for joy! Jesus was not a boring, somber person. He thrilled in the Holy Ghost! I believe that Jesus lived a higher life than we've ever dared to imagine!

Jesus' apostles and followers also went into ecstatic states. Actually the entire early church was birthed in the God-high. In Acts chapter two, at the great outpouring of Pentecost, people thought Jesus' followers were drunk (Acts 2:13)! The apostle Peter spoke up and said, "We are not drunk as you suppose." But, in looking at the whole situation in context, it was obvious that something ecstatic was going on. They were not drunk on alcohol, as the onlookers "supposed." They were high on God! And all of a sudden, Peter, who just days before had denied Jesus, became bold as a lion. He became bold enough to preach before the entire Jewish nation! Thousands of people began to believe in Jesus through

Peter's preaching that day! He had been emboldened and empowered by the high of God! It's a well-known fact that drunk people are more bold!

Peter, the apostle Paul, and many others in the community of Christ followers were recorded as often going into high, trance-like states throughout the rest of the book of Acts and the New Testament. The word for trance in the Greek is 'ekstasis,' from which we get our English word 'ecstasy.' This root word for ecstasy is all over the Bible! Biblical ecstasy refers to an altered state of consciousness in which visions and revelation can occur. There is not an exact definition of this word in the Bible, as with so many Biblical concepts and words. You have to gather it's meaning by reading the context, and by having your own trances! Feel free to go into an ecstatic trance as you read the following scripture verses on the subject:

Acts 10:10 - And he became hungry and wanted something to eat, but while they were preparing it, he fell into a trance. (ESV)

Acts 11:5 - I was in the city of Joppa praying, and in a trance I saw a vision, something like a great sheet descending, being let down from heaven by its four corners, and it came down to me. (ESV)

Acts 22:17 - When I had returned to Jerusalem and was praying in the temple, I fell into a trance. (ESV)

2 Corinthians 12:2 - For instance, I know a man who, fourteen years ago, was seized by Christ and swept in ecstasy to the heights of heaven. I really don't know if this took place in the body or out of it; only God knows. (MSG)

It can also be interesting to note some other occurrences in the New Testament where the word 'ekstasis' is used in the Greek. These were when whole groups were struck by something amazing. It could be that they just wondered, or stood in awe. But, what if they were getting high on God? The Strong's dictionary on the word notes that this word could be used for going out of one's mind, or going insane! Check these out:

Luke 5:26 - And, astonishment, seized one and all, and they began glorifying God, and were filled with fear, saying—We have seen unaccountable things, to-day! (Rotherham)

Mark 16:8 - And going out quickly, they fled from the tomb. And trembling and ecstasy took hold of them. And they told no one, not a thing, for they were afraid. (LITV)

Acts 3:10 - And they recognized him, that it was the one who was sitting for alms at the Beautiful Gate of the temple. And they were filled with amazement and ecstasy at the thing that happened to him. (LITV)

The listing of scriptures in this book is meant to send you on your own Biblical journey. Explore the intoxication all throughout the Bible, and the little 'rabbit trails' it sends you on. Enjoy! This is by no means meant to be comprehensive chapter, merely an introduction. Crack open your Bible!

In the final portion of this chapter, I'd like to introduce you to the most intoxicating portion of scripture. We've saved the best for last! After these, we will transition into the next chapter to fully explore and develop the themes found herein. We're going to fully press the beautiful wine out of these scriptural grapes, so to speak. What grapes are we talking about, you may ask? The juiciest grapes I've found in all of writings of the world! These are found growing plump in the rich theology of the New Testament Epistles! These books are the most supremely intoxicating, especially the writings of the apostle Paul!

Paul and the other apostles developed the understanding of the Good News of Jesus Christ in ways that can honestly keep you jacked up forever! I pray that you might see what I see in these epistles, for it will produce a real joy unspeakable and full of Glory (1 Pt. 1:8)!

I'd like to absolutely eradicate the lie that says that theology could ever be boring. Theology is only boring when it is separated from experience (which makes it no theology at all)! The apostles wrote, in the New Testament epistles, of revelation which no eye had seen, and no ear had heard before! They wrote of incredulous scandalous things! It got most of them killed, because it was as shocking and irreligious then as it is now. Read on, if you dare!

May I suggest that you read these many multiple times, slowly, and with great openness! Some of the greatest inebriation of spirit is found in the following New Testament Epistle passages:

2 Corinthians 5:13-14 - For whether we *be beside ourselves, it is* to God: or whether we be sober, it is for your cause. (14) For *the love of Christ constraineth us*; because we thus judge, that if one died for all, then were all dead: (KJV)

1 Corinthians 1:4-7 - I give thanks to my God always for you because of the grace of God that was given you in Christ Jesus, (5) that *in every way* *you were enriched* in him in all speech and all knowledge— (6) even as the testimony about Christ was confirmed among you— (7) so that *you are not lacking in any gift*, as you wait for the revealing of our Lord Jesus Christ, (ESV)

Ephesians 1:3 - Blessed be the God and Father of our Lord Jesus Christ, who has *blessed us in Christ with every spiritual blessing in the heavenly places,* (ESV)

1 Peter 1:7-9 - so that the tested genuineness of your faith—more precious than gold that perishes though it is tested by fire—may be found to result in praise and glory and honor at the revelation of Jesus Christ. (8) Though you have not seen him, you love him. Though you do not now see him, you believe in him and rejoice with joy that is inexpressible and filled with glory, (9) obtaining the outcome of your faith, the salvation of your souls. (ESV)

Hebrews 12:22-24 - But *you have come to Mount Zion and to the city of the living God, the heavenly Jerusalem, and to innumerable angels in festal gathering,* (23) and to the assembly of the firstborn who are enrolled in heaven, and to God, the judge of all, and to the spirits of the righteous made perfect, (24) and to Jesus, the mediator of a new covenant, and to the sprinkled blood that speaks a better word than the blood of Abel. (ESV)

Ephesians 5:18 - And do not get drunk with wine, for that is debauchery; but *ever be filled and stimulated with the [Holy] Spirit.* (AMP)

As you become intimately familiar with the heart of the epistles you will notice certain themes. One these powerful themes is the astounding truth that we have been given the highest life ever in Jesus Christ, as a free gift! You may also begin to notice that the New Testament is not at all about behavior modification or attempting to live moral lives! Of course, loving lives will flow out as a natural result. However, it becomes clear that God's life for us is all about being ravished by the Presence of God which lives within us. The New Testament speaks from an absolutely unique perspective regarding theology. It records a message where God came in Christ to move from the inside out, satisfying the way we were built, enabling us to love and live out our co-created dreams with God and others!

The Bible was always leading up to this culminating revelation of Jesus Christ, as unpacked by the New Testament epistles. There is a mind blowing revelation in these books! It is the essential foundation for the bliss. This foundation is being seen more and more, even today, for God's nature is to always reveal more and more each day, week, month, year, and century. It's a never ending journey as Holy Spirit shows each generation ever more of the goodness of God, life, and reality.

I'd like to explore even more of unique Gospel foundation of the high in the next chapter. It will be a mostly theological chapter, but NOT boring by any means, trust me. In fact, those that comprehend this stuff will stay the drunkest, the longest, guaranteed! I've come to see that without this kind of foundation in truth your bliss will be temporary at best! But, with this foundation of happy New Testament theology, you will be empowered to be perma-high! Are you ready!?! Let's have fun with some theology!

CHAPTER 4
A HIGH VIEW OF THEOLOGY

Let me just start this chapter by saying that this stuff came to me while I was high. I mean high on the Glory of God, of course! That may sound funny, but it's true, and worth mentioning here. I think some people get the revelation and understanding first, and then the experience. Others seem to have the experience first and then the revelation. Maybe they both really come at the same time. I'll be honest with you, I am still learning! I do want to be as transparent as possible about this stuff, so as to be as helpful for others who are on a similar journey of awakening! I certainly haven't got it all figured out yet.

However, I do recognize that there are way too many "theologians" out there teaching by merely quoting information regarding God and spiritual life, and it's only material that they have read or heard from others. There are many voices out there spouting knowledge without experience. Also, it's unfortunate that many are speaking in the name of God, yet their "revelation" is not coming with love and humility. This definitely doesn't make their cause very appealing. It's made multitudes of folks around the world closed to even hearing about God at all. This is a big problem! Knowledge can puff up, but love builds up (1 Cor. 8:1).

In the same way, there are far too many "spiritual" people having "experiences" that are just based on psychoses or empty imaginations. I hate to have to say that as I am a part of a community of mystics and those pushing the envelope of experiential spirituality, I've seen this also happen many times. I find myself hanging out with intellectuals and mystics alike. I enjoy them both. Ideally, I'd like to see everyone embrace both the mystical and the intellectual. Yet, both sides of that same coin can have individuals or even groups that fall into those common pitfalls.

I so desire that this next generation would avoid the pitfalls of both exaggerated or shallow "spirituality", as well as the mere gathering of intellectual information and knowledge. True Christ life includes the joy of deep study AND the ecstasy of deep experience! Plus, there truly is no pressure on us to sustain our own progress on either side of that coin. So, if it doesn't depend on our own efforts, then there is no room for pride about how much we have learned or discovered. True theology is all revealed and sustained by the living person of Jesus Christ. True theology is also intoxicating! Those few disclaimers now having been said, may you read on with clarity! Hopefully you can now hear my heart to be absolutely as honest as possible with what I believe Christ has been revealing to me in my journey. I hope you can come with both an open mind and an expectant spirit to chew on what could be my most favorite chapter in this book. Why might it be my most favorite?

This is the chapter about the centerpiece of all joy and life! It's the great mystery of the ages revealed: Heaven here on earth, Christ in us!

Now before we really get into the meat of things here, let me give one last short aside. I did mention that I want to be absolutely open about how this stuff came to me in my own personal journey. So, like I was mentioning previously, I started getting drunk and high on God a short time before a full Gospel revelation came. Really it was right around that same time that I was hearing my first inklings of the Good News, just not in the clarity of what I know it to be now. All that to say, most of my revelations have sprung forth while in the experience of the whack itself, they dawned on me while I was in the gift of the altered state, high out of my mind.

I feel that this must have been what it was like for many of the prophets and apostles of old (not that you need to be some big shot "Apostle" to get high revelation, of course). I do now believe that these ecstasies must be similar to how the Biblical figures had their revelatory experiences. That being said, I don't want to give the impression that I wasn't influenced by other teachers and my own personal study either, by any means. I was profoundly impacted by a number of perfectly timed voices into my life and study at the time. A simple reading of the Gospels and the book of Ephesians helped quite a bit too! Yet, I needed to hear it resound deep in my own spirit, while intoxicated on the love of God, before it really settled in. In this state, the truth would ring so clear and powerfully to the depths of me that it ceased being mere information. Revelation would come springing forth out of the tangible Glory Presence, confirming with my study and learning. And so, I began to get the whack, and God quickly made sure I was given enough understanding to sustain it. It has been a wonderful journey of discovery in the Gospel and the inebriation in both personal experience and intellectual study ever since.

THE GOOD NEWS – SOURCE AND ENABLER OF THE WHACK

So, let's get on with it! Let's explore this incredible message that is the Gospel of Jesus Christ! Did you know that Jesus himself really only had one main message? Jesus Christ had ONE message that he spoke everywhere he went during his earthly ministry 2000 years ago. ONE simple message that will make us all high forever! The most jacked up message in the universe! Unfortunately, I grew up my entire life around Bible believing people, and never heard this message, not in a way that I could understand anyways, not even once! Yet, this was the main thing that Jesus said to people everywhere!

The main dude of the whole Bible is Jesus. And, this dude really only had one thing to say most of the time. He really only preached a few sermons that we have recorded in the Gospels, maybe only three sermons in total! However, according to scripture, he had one message that he preached everywhere he went (Lk. 8:1, Mt. 4:17, Mk. 1:15). This message must be pretty important then, am I right? That's my point. Yet, like I said, I personally never heard this message as I grew up in the church. How could that have been? How could we have missed it?

Well, regardless of whatever reason I missed it my whole life, I pray that no one else would have to do the same. So what is this message!!??

It is here in this next verse, pure, beautiful, and simple.

Matthew 4:17 - From that time Jesus began to preach, and to say, Repent: for the kingdom of heaven is at hand. (ESV)

There it is! It's one simple phrase. Now, you might be thinking, "What? What's so intoxicating about that!?!" Well, let me explain. It's way drunker than you might think!

I'll sum up the conclusion right here then I'll explain to you the background. What this verse is essentially saying is, "Heaven is here!" Wait! Think about that for a second! Could this mean that the things that most of us thought were reserved for some day, far off in heaven, those very things are here NOW! Oh my God! The enormous implications of this one statement! THIS is why we are high! When this simple message of Jesus becomes real for you, there is no way to come down! You will be high forever too! You will begin to live in heaven, even here on earth!

The biggest problem people have with this revelation is that it seems too good to be true. It's seems crazy. Learned theologians might even call it "over-realized eschatology!" So let me explain. I AM saying that heaven is here on earth now. I know that many of you thought that the Bible was all about believing in God so that we could go to heaven someday after we die. Yet, actually, there is very little in the Bible to support that claim. Just try to name one scripture that talks about going to heaven later, or after you die. It's hard to find that in the scriptures.

What IS clearly in the scripture is this simple message of Jesus. It's what he preached everywhere he went! Here it is again in the book of Mark:

Mark 1:14-15 - Now after John was arrested, Jesus came into Galilee, proclaiming the gospel of God, (15) and saying, "The time is fulfilled, and the kingdom of God is at hand; repent and believe in the gospel." (ESV)

In that particular verse in Mark, it says, "kingdom of God." In Matthew it says, "kingdom of heaven." I love the slight difference in wording there because God IS heaven, and heaven IS God! When we say that we are high on heaven, we are also saying we are high on God. It's the same thing! Jesus was telling people that God's original perfect world is now on earth, filled with His Glory substance, restoring all things to better than the garden of Eden! The kingdom of God is where God rules, a place where everything is beautiful, perfect, holy, joyful, loving, high, and whole!

When people heard this in Jesus' day, they knew it was good news. The Jews had been looking forward to the day of the kingdom of God for hundreds of years. Their prophets had been prophesying it for generations. They knew it was going to be the high life. They just didn't understand exactly how high it was going to be!

The Jewish people had become so focused on an outward physical and political kingdom. They missed out on the fact that it was meant to start from within their own hearts. They didn't understand the nature of Jesus' ministry. This is no knock against the Jews, people of every culture and generation have done the same thing. Every tribe, nation, culture, and subculture have longed for something like the kingdom of heaven on earth! Where humanity has so often missed out is in understanding HOW this heaven was going to be brought to earth. Jesus Christ, God Himself, came to earth to clear up our confusion, to open our eyes to a heaven that is always near, springing from within.

Obviously, I am not going to attempt to give a full theological dissertation on the nature of the kingdom of heaven and its' coming in this book. I do, however, want to give an overview. It's just so intoxicating! I want to give enough understanding to lay a strong foundation for the bliss. I'm trusting that you will go on your own rich juicy theological exploration of the rabbit hole that is the Gospel of the kingdom of heaven on earth. It is so deep and so wide! It's the very meaning of life! It's what the whole cosmic drama has been leading up to!

The foundation of this all is that Jesus would go from town to town preaching one simple message, announcing that the earth is heaven's home in the now. Now God is ruling His planet in bliss. God's eternal purpose was that it would always be on earth as it is in heaven. Jesus made this clear by His life, death, and resurrection. As we see this Good News, a river springs up from within us! This Gospel of Jesus reveals that everything that we thought was reserved for heaven some day is here with us!

The nature of heaven on earth often does require some great description. Like we mentioned, the Jews together with almost all of the people of Jesus' day totally misunderstood it! Most people today are still misunderstanding it. We want to be as clear as possible about what we are saying. We want to clearly reveal this scandalous message to a world that God so loves! It seems that Paul the apostle spent most of his ministry announcing and meticulously describing this mystery more than maybe anyone in history so far, for these very reasons. It says in several places in scripture that Paul was given a revelation of this Gospel that had never been revealed to mankind before! So, I'll give a simple explanation, and then why don't we dive into a bit of Paul's revelation on the subject!

The simple explanation is that Jesus Christ, in His person, preserved the original design of God, for a united heaven and earth, for a united God and man. Jesus Christ preserved in Himself the union of heaven and earth. Meditate on that phrase for a while!

At the fall of Adam and Eve, mankind forgot what life was about. We forgot that God always wanted to be with us in paradise. God always wanted heaven and earth to be together! The planet fell into disarray when the consciousness of humanity fell from reality. This caused all kinds of nasty things to happen to this world. Since we weren't satisfied in God, we destroyed each other and the world in many horrible, painful ways. These ways could also be called the kingdoms of this world. When Jesus appeared on the scene, however, through His incarnation, life, death, and resurrection, He revealed that God had never given up on the original reality of his design. He was still committed to being God with us in paradise! Though we had messed up the world in so many ways, building our own dark kingdoms, Jesus had preserved the original world inside Himself. He came to re-present that to us, and to invite us to re-join it!

The Jews kind of understood this. Unfortunately, they were looking for an outward forceful revolution to take over the planet for God. That type of revolution was just another fallen idea. Jesus came for something way deeper. God's kingdom is so much more than just an outward circumstantial rightness that would need to be kept by force. God's heaven starts from within!! Jesus came to win back our hearts. Jesus came to awaken us to the kingdom that starts inside. Only from there could the kingdom manifest to the outward world, through intimacy and spiritual union with God, moving through love to restore the world to reality.

Many people have misunderstood Jesus and what He was about. He came to ravish us with heaven from within, which would then, in turn, move outwardly and reveal heaven to the world. This is why He spoke in the following scripture:

Luke 17:20-21 - And when he was demanded of the Pharisees, when the kingdom of God should come, he answered them and said, *The kingdom of God cometh not with observation:* (21) Neither shall they say, Lo here! or, lo there! for, behold, *the kingdom of God is within you.*

This has major implications for us! The kingdom is within us! God's throne is in us! Heaven is in us! This is the foundation that keeps you high! I mean just think about that for a minute! The priests of the Old Testament couldn't even remain standing on their feet while in the Glory of God in 2 Chronicles 5. Now all of that Glory now lives inside of you!! Can you feel that?! Can you taste the sounds?!?! Are you even aware of a fraction of what that means right now!?! THAT is intoxicating, for real!

Heaven is here! God is here! His address is you! Wow! Could any street drug compare with that? I mean could LSD or DMT ever touch that? Talk about ecstasy!

That's my simple theological explanation! Jesus came to announce that heaven starts now, not someday far away. We can live in it, even here, as a free gift. There is no secret to unlock heaven. It already here, preserved in the person of Jesus Christ, inside of us.

PAUL'S REVELATION OF HEAVEN ON EARTH

Paul the apostle had the clearest revelation of this heavenly reality. Many people in Jesus' day didn't understand what He was going on about. Yet, Paul's eyes were opened. The man could sing in prison, while in shackles, for goodness sake, I mean, he HAD to be high (Acts 16:25)! Paul was so inspired by God that some say he took the Gospel to the entire known world of his day! He wrote more of the New Testament than anyone else! I'd say his revelation must be pretty powerful! Let's taste and see a little bit of the Glory that Paul was packing.

Paul's message can be summarized very shortly, just like Jesus' message, in a few simple words. The summary of Paul's joy can be found in both of the following passages:

Ephesians 1:9-10 - making known to us the mystery of his will, according to his purpose, which he set forth in Christ (10) as a plan for the fullness of time, to *unite all things in him, things in heaven and things on earth.* (ESV)

Colossians 1:27 - God's plan is to make known his secret to his people, this rich and glorious secret which he has for all peoples. And *the secret is that Christ is in you, which means that you will share in the glory of God.* (GNB)

Paul wrote those words 2000 years ago! What a powerful summary of the same message that Jesus preached! This is what Paul was expounding upon throughout all of his epistles. What's the big secret? It's that heaven and earth are One in Christ, and that same Jesus Christ lives inside you! To describe this a little bit more, Paul goes on in the next chapter of the book of Colossians.

Colossians 2:9-10 - For in Him the whole fullness of Deity (the Godhead) continues to dwell in bodily form [giving complete expression of the divine nature]. (10) And you are in Him, made full and having come to fullness of life [in Christ you too are filled with the Godhead—Father, Son and Holy Spirit—and reach full spiritual stature]. And He is the Head of all rule and authority [of every angelic principality and power]. (AMP)

Paul's message will get you jacked up! You are filled with God in Christ! Remember, God's entire original high world was preserved in Christ. And, Paul says that Christ lives inside of you! In essence, everything good that ever was is living inside your body! Not only inside your body, but even the whole earth is filled with the Glory of God! Isn't it crazy that we have been unaware of this for so long?!!? The fall of mankind was a fall in our consciousness. It was at that point that we began to believe lies about reality. Both Jesus and Paul ministered in order to re-awaken us to this amazing intoxicating truth. Heaven is here, in Christ, in you, and filling the whole cosmos. This is the foundational awareness that keeps us high!

Paul goes on to declare in several more places just exactly what this means. Paul's letter to the Ephesians has some amazing insight into heaven on earth. Check out these verses:

Ephesians 1:3 - Blessed be the God and Father of our Lord Jesus Christ, who has blessed us in Christ with every spiritual blessing in the heavenly places, (ESV)

Ephesians 2:6-8 and raised us up with him and seated us with him in the heavenly places in Christ Jesus, (7) so that in the coming ages he might show the immeasurable riches of his grace in kindness toward us in Christ Jesus. (8) For by grace you have been saved through faith. And this is not your own doing; it is the gift of God. (ESV)

Ephesians 3:18-19 - so that you, together with all God's people, may have the power to understand how broad and long, how high and deep, is Christ's love. (19) Yes, may you come to know his love---although it can never be fully known---and so be completely filled with the very nature of God. (GNB)

Paul had a unique understanding of the intoxicating Gospel. While Jesus, and even John the Baptist, had preached that the kingdom of heaven was here, Paul described in detail what that meant, and how it was manifesting in Christ. The other apostles revealed this as well, in some profound ways. However, it is most obvious to me through the writings of Paul how the heavenly life has come to us.

Jesus preached that heaven was here. Then he demonstrated it through His life. He lived as though the normal rules of earthly life could not contain Him. He healed the sick and raised the dead. Yet, there is even more to Jesus than that. Jesus Christ, simply by being alive, by being both fully God and fully man, revealed an unbreakable union of heaven and earth. Paul expounded on this, to help us grasp how this could be so.

Paul described how the point of this union was spiritual first, all about intimacy with God in the spirit. Heaven on earth starts from the inside first, deep within.

Ephesians 5:31-32 - As the scripture says, "For this reason a man will leave his father and mother and unite with his wife, and the two will become one." (32) There is a deep secret truth revealed in this scripture, which I understand as applying to Christ and the church. (GNB)
Paul reveals that it's all about our union with God in Christ. Exploring our spiritual oneness with God will bring so much bliss, the truest depth of the heaven on earth Gospel. The love drunkenness of union with Love Himself is the supreme high of all! Oh, the glories of intimacy with the Divine!

Paul also reveals that this isn't just some positive thinking, an ignoring of reality. In fact, we see that being "in Christ" is an alternate reality, or the original reality, that trumps the fallen lesser reality that we have created through our fallen consciousness. Paul writes about this clearly in his letter to the Colossians:

Colossians 3:1-4, 11 - Therefore if you have been raised up with Christ, keep seeking the things above, where Christ is, seated at the right hand of God. (2) Set your mind on the things above, not on the things that are on earth. (3) For you have died and your life is hidden with Christ in God. (4) When Christ, who is our life, is revealed, then you also will be revealed with Him in glory. (11) a renewal in which there is no distinction between Greek and Jew, circumcised and uncircumcised, barbarian, Scythian, slave and freeman, but Christ is all, and in all. (NASB)

Here Paul encourages us to keep our minds on the true original reality, aka "things above, where Christ is all." This is HOW TO STAY HIGH!! Meditate on the meaning of that Colossians 3 passage. You will come to see that Paul is not talking about denying the physical realm, no that would be what theologians have called a "gnostic heresy." That would be simply foolish. What Paul is talking about is remaining aware of the greater reality or truest dimension of Christ. You see, life in Christ is another dimension that is presently co-existing with what we have thought was the true dimension. The "in Christ" dimension is coexisting with our fallen reality until we all wake up. At that time all there will be is what always truly has been, and that is Christ, Christ as all and in all. Hang with me here, I know this can sound a bit strange or crazy at first!

The word 'above' in that Colossians chapter three scripture does not mean "in the sky," or in some far off place called "heaven." It means "greater" or "first in priority." Paul is giving us the key here. There are obviously people who are not experiencing the high of heaven on a regular basis. This is because their minds are set on the things of the earth. This is not referring to the natural earth, but to what the Bible calls, "the world (1 John 2:15)." This is the fallen subjective reality that has been created by our fallen consciousness. It is when we learned to prioritizing things from the outside in, in so-called "independence from God". This is the non-intoxicating, non-love-drunk consciousness and the reality that it creates. This is the fallen man. Most people live in this sober, unhealthy world. But, Jesus and Paul have good news! You don't have to live there! This is not the greater reality! The higher reality that is "above" all of this is in Christ!

Christ is the ultimate reality, the original reality, the only reality that will last! Truth is, we are already in Him, and He in us. Yet, when we are not aware of that, we do not see the kingdom of God. Only those like a little child can see the kingdom, those willing to embrace an entirely different view of reality. The good news is that it is already here. The whole cosmos and everyone in it has already been included in Him. As the consciousness of the planet is made aware of this Good News of Jesus Christ, we will all be high! We will all experience complete wholeness and liberty from the bondages of this world! The world will be gloriously revealed to have already been heaven on earth in Christ from all eternity past! It is finished!

Have you been able to follow the pattern of thought here? This theology can be quite shocking! To say it again, Jesus came to reveal, as described through the revelation of Paul and the apostles, a heaven on earth reality that flows from the inside out, yet is already completely here, existing in the alternate dimension called "in Christ." He is the original dimension, the greater dimension. You will seem as if you are in an altered state when you live aware of His dimension. You will live in the Lord's joy, the joy of the Lord! You will be overjoyed and overwhelmed by the Glory substance of God flowing together with all of heaven's virtues!

The final conclusion then, of this Gospel revelation, is this: because He is in you, and you are in Him, now, everything that Jesus is and has, you are and have! All that we thought was reserved for heaven is ours here and now. This means perfect intimacy with God and others. This means the ability to flow continuously in perfect healthy relationships. This means healthy emotions. This means a healthy mind. This means love, joy, peace, patience, and all the fruit of the Spirit. This means a perfectly sanctified heart and soul. This means physical healing. This means financial prosperity. This means the power of God flowing. This means endless love for all people! The list of benefits goes on and on! Study and meditate into the depths of it for yourself! What all is included in heaven on earth in Christ?!!? Dig deeper! Especially if this sounds non-Biblical or heretical, or crazy, or too good to be true, read the scriptures I mentioned for yourself. Go on an exploration with God. Could the good news of Jesus be better than we ever thought? One thing is for sure, His truth will set you free! His truth will make you higher than a rocket shot to outer space!! Don't be afraid to look deeply into the teachings of Jesus. Study the writings of Paul and the New Testament writers. Their books have gotten me higher than anything rolled up into papers ever could!!!

CHAPTER 5

A PSYCHOLOGY OF THE BLISS

Alright, now it's time to approach the issue of hedonism! I again need to be totally honest with you. If you haven't figured it out by now, I want to get it all out in the open. I am an unashamed hedonist! Surprise, surprise, right!? In order to have even a chance of hanging with much more of this book, you're going to have to make some key conclusions in your heart regarding that. One of the chief tenets of this book is to admit that if we are honest, every one of us is hedonist at heart. And, there's nothing wrong with that!

Wait, what!? Isn't that a sin? Isn't that a shallow way to live? Well…let's check it out.

What is hedonism?

Hedonism = A guiding belief that pleasure is a proper aim of human life.

Hedonism has gotten a bad rap amongst responsible people of the world, in many cases for good reason. However, I want to provoke you through this chapter to consider a new conclusion about hedonism. This conclusion is important to embrace so that you might give yourself and others a long term permission to stay high, a.k.a. a long term permission to enjoy life.

Firstly, I want to ask the question, "Is happiness good or bad?" That might sound very silly to you depending on how you have been brought up. To push it even further, let's ask, "Is happiness a chief goal of existence?" Let's explore further.

I once was having a conversation with a middle aged man about life. As we were chatting, I was telling him how excited I was just to be alive every day. I told him how my every day felt like a party! He immediately interjected, "Well, my party days are over. I got all that out of my system, and now I'm doing the things that a man should." As we continued to chat, though, it was obvious that he was very unhappy and dissatisfied with his life. He worked all day, came home, fixed things around his house, coached his kid's sports team, enjoyed an occasional movie, and went to bed. He did the same thing each day. He had been active in serving his community for years, volunteering at his local church and community groups and being a model citizen. As we continued to talk it became more and more obvious that he had little value on fun or joy. He did seem to have a high value on doing what was right. He confided in me that he was depressed and had few friends. I really felt a deep compassion for this man.

How many of us know multitudes of people all around us who are living exactly like this man? These are people who are involved in so many good activities, and would be a respectable citizen, yet they've lost the spark of life. They have adopted the idea of "service and doing the right thing," but they are mostly depressed, lonely, bored, or emotionally stoic in daily life.

Now, I am by no means encouraging pleasure as opposed to being a generous and responsible citizen. That's where some misinterpret this and make it sound like some drug induced hippie hallucination. To them it initially sounds like a life of irresponsible, destructive consequence. What I really want to communicate here is to challenge some deep misconceptions about joy, fun, and pleasure. I want to present that life in God is meant to be a life of extreme happiness! Radical joy, extreme pleasure, and ecstatic happiness are major values in God's kingdom! And, these don't have to be at odds with excellence, servanthood and selfless love. God wants you to be happy AND holy! Yet, many folks have lost sight of what a happy holiness could be like. This is tragic! You were created by God to function best when absolutely and overwhelmingly happy!

CREATED TO BE HAPPY

One of the biggest misconceptions that spiritual people struggle with is the thinking that we were created for service over joy. To put it another way, we have often thought that we couldn't truly love, serve, AND be happy. It's as if we thought that living for God was the right thing to do, but not necessarily the most satisfying thing.

Why do these have to be at odds with one another? Why do we think we were put on the planet to toil, rather than to celebrate? It's like the idea we often have in regards to eating food, "Well, if it tastes good, it must be bad for me. And, if it tastes bad, it must be good for me." But, the Bible says, "Taste and see that the Lord is good!" (Ps. 34:8)

We've also often forgotten what Jesus came to reveal about God being our Father. What good father isn't concerned for their child's happiness? I mean what father has children just so that they can work for him? Pretty sick idea, huh? There have been so many ideas we have pinned on God that just aren't true. What if God created us on this earth giving us the whole world just to enjoy?

We already explored earlier in the book about God creating us and put us in Eden, the garden of pleasure. But, what are the whys behind this? Would God have really just made the whole world as a playground? Could this simply be a place for us to explore, enjoy and experience pleasure together? Wasn't there some hidden motive that God had? Didn't God need us to work for Him or worship Him or something like that? I no longer think so. I'd like to present to you a God that is a healthy father, a father that just wanted His kids to be happy!

DOES GOD NEED YOU TO WORK FOR HIM?

But, doesn't God need me to help fix the world? Don't I need to be worshiping or praising God in some way in order for Him to "get Glory?" Isn't that why I am here? Well let's address those misconceptions too.

I love the finished work of Jesus Christ! You may or may not be familiar with that term, "the finished work of Jesus Christ." It is the teaching that Jesus' death on the cross already fully completed all of the restoration that was needed in the world. It's the greatest revelation of the goodness of God expressed in the fact that He took upon Himself to save the world, fully and completely, and that this work is done. Most of the world has not realized this yet, but when we understand the finished work of Christ, we see that in reality heaven is on earth now. As we covered in the last chapter, it all exists in the original, authentic reality, in Christ! Truly, nothing is lacking!

God is big enough to handle the planet. God didn't need us to fix it for Him. Infinite Love has the passion and power to take care of us all. We do get to participate in the manifestation of this good news, but ultimately it doesn't depend on us. This is a huge realization, a massive revelation. Indeed, it is THE message of the ages! It's the absolute key that keeps us high!

I want to propose to you that while the revelation of this "finished work of Christ" is still currently dawning on humanity, yet even this dawning is not by our efforts. We were created to be along for the ride, to watch and enjoy as what God has done unfolds before the eyes of the world. We were created in Christ Jesus for good works that God had prepared in advance for us that we may walk in them (Eph. 2:10). This means that even the service, even the heaven on earth service that we do to share this Gospel is just effortlessly walking out what was already done beforehand, as we are carried along by the Holy Spirit.

I want to propose that we were not created to work for God! We were made to enjoy life! God didn't need our help. God wanted our company! God wanted children with whom to share the ecstasy and joy of living!

You can think of it this way. Many times a father and a young child will work on a project together. However, the father doesn't need the child in order to finish the task! Let's say that they were in a wood shop together making a wooden chair. My guess is that the child would mostly just get in the way, and even hinder the work. The father could easily just get it done faster and better without the child. But, for the joy of relationship they work together! The child always wants to join in what the father is doing, it's only natural. In a healthy relationship both father and child just enjoy being around each other, and doing things together. So it is in the Spirit! Our heavenly Father has given us tasks, and brought us to work with Him. Are we necessary to complete the work? I don't think so. I think that even as we grow in the knowledge of who we are and begin to function as mature sons and daughters, we are still along for the ride, primarily for the joy and pleasure of it all primarily. It's still all about the relationship! It's still all about the joy, the intimacy, not the work.

THE SCRIPTURES ENCOURAGE HEDONISM

The Bible confirms that we are here simply for the joy of living! We exist for pleasure! There is no shame in that. Check out the following scriptures:

Psalm 16:11 - You make known to me the path of life; in your presence there is fullness of joy; at your right hand are pleasures forevermore. (ESV)

John 15:11 - I have told you these things, that My joy and delight may be in you, and that your joy and gladness may be of full measure and complete and overflowing. (AMP)

1 John 1:4 - And we write this to you to make your happiness complete. (GSNT)

Hebrews 12:2 - our eyes fixed upon Jesus as the pioneer and the perfection of faith — upon Jesus who, in order to reach his own appointed joy, steadily endured the cross, thinking nothing of its shame, and is now seated at the right hand of the throne of God. (Moffatt)

Even Jesus Christ went to the cross for the joy of what He was going to receive! He didn't have some martyr complex. He knew that the cross would awaken US! This gave Him incredible joy looking forward to reciprocated relationship with us. He did it all for the joy of experiencing intimacy with us. Even the cross was all about pleasure!

DENYING OUR SELF?

Seeing that even Jesus Christ ultimately wasn't denying Himself pleasure can give us another big shift in thinking. Again, I am hoping to share with you, as the reader, the joy I have found in being a true healthy hedonist! In order to allow ourselves the freedom to fully enjoy life, we must clarify some common misunderstandings about what it means to "deny ourselves." This is another area where we humans can get all bound up and confused. Doesn't the Bible teach us to deny our self? Yes, it absolutely does. Jesus, himself said this in the book of Mark chapter eight. It is truly important too!

There are two sides to the coin of self denial. In our old fallen mindset we believed in and built up a false sense of self. This was a self of independence from God, of darkened understanding, of selfishness. This false self thinks of humanity, God, creation etc. as separate, not interdependent. The true self sees us all as One, in reliance upon the Father, in Jesus, through the Holy Spirit. The false self pursues pleasure at the expense of others. The true self knows that there are pure pleasures that benefit the whole. Jesus came to destroy the false sense of self so that the true original self could emerge!

So, did Jesus teach us to deny our self? Yes! Jesus taught us to deny the false self, the self that was never truly us to begin with. The Bible also teaches that we should take up our cross daily, and follow Jesus. Yet, just as Jesus showed us, even the cross was about joy! Though Christ's cross was obviously painful and horrible on one level, Jesus was experiencing a deep pleasure within that made it a delight for him to undergo. Looking even deeper, none of us will ever have to carry a cross like Jesus did. He died once, for all, to save the world. So, also, part of us carrying our cross is recognizing that his cross already completely finished the job of salvation for us all already.

In conclusion, to deny our true self would only create a world where no one is being who they were created to be, nor enjoying life at all. Jesus' teaching on denying self is all about denying our false self. This is a self that is already dead and removed at Christ's cross anyways. If the false self exists at all, it's only in our minds. Galatians chapter two says it this way, "I have been crucified with Christ. It is no longer I who live, but Christ who lives in me. And the life I now live in the flesh I live by faith in the Son of God, who loved me and gave himself for me." The reality of the matter is that carrying our cross means to recognize that our false, selfish self already died with Christ. We carry this cross daily by continually being conscious that the lesser version of our self already died with Christ, and now we are going to live as a new creation, our original design renewed and elevated to be seated with Jesus in the heavens (Eph. 2:6).

Think about it! If everyone was supposed to deny themselves pleasure we would end up with a world where no one was happy at all! This could result in us serving and helping a lot of people, but even then, they would not be a good person if they allowed themselves to enjoy it! What a "catch 22!" What a sad cycle! Yet, much of the church has become just like this. Many spiritual people live for others, which may have some profound benefit, but they never let themselves enjoy life. We have so many miserable servants in spirituality who feel bad about feeling good.

WE HAVE HOLY HEARTS, SO WE CAN TRUST OUR DESIRES

There is an even deeper matter at hand here. It has a whole lot to do with why many spiritual people feel so bad about feeling good. We need to have a clear grasp of who we are and how we were created.

Understanding the nature of our true self, created in Christ Jesus, can help so much to prevent a miserable double-minded existence! Many of us have thought that we had evil hearts. We might not outright say it, but we feel like we are flawed at the core in some way. In the old, fallen, selfish, false self that was very true. However, this is not our authentic identity, as we briefly discussed previously.

Many religions teach us that we are by nature wicked and evil. If that be true, then, of course, it only makes sense that what we would consider pleasurable would have to be evil too! Following that logic it would only make sense to make a life out of doing the things that we don't enjoy, denying our wicked self and denying our desires.

This was so much of why Jesus came, to remove the lie and end the religious bondage! Jesus came to show us our true identity. We are daughters and sons of God, created in God's very image and likeness! We forgot who we were, but Jesus reminded us, with authority. Jesus restored us. Jesus redeemed us. Jesus reveals our deepest, truest nature, a whole and holy self, created to walk in union with God!

This has profound implications regarding a happy life! Think about it. If God made us perfect to begin with, and Jesus has restored that, then can't we trust that our desires are perfect too? What if we are no longer stuck in darkness, with darkened hearts? What if we have been restored and it is a finished work? That would mean we have a holy heart! I believe that this is what it talks about in Hebrews chapter 8. "For this is the covenant that I will make with the house of Israel after those days, declares the Lord: I will put my laws into their minds, and write them on their hearts, and I will be their God, and they shall be my people (Heb. 8:10)." The ways of God are in our hearts!

When you remember who you are, your tastes change. You no longer desire selfish pleasures. Yet, you do have a desire for pleasure, just as Jesus did. It's amazing how deep the desire for pleasure goes. No matter how twisted your life got, you still wanted pleasure. In the same way, no matter how clear and healthy your life becomes, you still have that same drive within. You were made for pleasure! That will never change! Like we covered earlier, even Jesus endured the cross for the joy set before Him (Heb. 12:2).

Jesus Christ appealed to this holy drive for pleasure when he spoke many times. Remember when Jesus said blessed are the meek, blessed are the poor in spirit, blessed are the merciful, etc.? Many times Jesus would tell people about the blessed life throughout his teachings. This in itself is an appeal to pleasure. The word blessed, as we explored earlier in this book, means to be made happy! Jesus was inviting people to live a life that would truly make them happy. He was basically saying, the highest people in the world are the meek, the merciful, the peacemakers! Want to be high? Here's the pleasurable high life! Jesus shows us the way of true pleasure!

Jesus knew that he could naturally appeal to us because we were in built for pleasure. The Bible calls Jesus the desire of the nations (Hag. 2:7). Even those that have no clue about Jesus have a desire for Him! Why? One reason is because they desire pleasure. This is not by mistake! Our hearts were made for pleasure!

I'm especially longing to see a shift in understanding this in the body of Christ overall, in the churches. Can you imagine a church where they believed that their members had holy desires? Can you imagine a church that set their members free to live for whatever was the most fun? Oh yes, this is the Gospel, being truly free to enjoy life! We do not need to manipulate or control our church members! We only need to teach them who they are, give them the good news of heaven on earth, and encourage them to keep living the high life! I love church, but if it is a group that encourages us to distrust our redeemed holy hearts, I cannot support it. This kind of church will only produce bound up, fearful, shells of what could be. I am envisioning and participating in a new kind of church in my hometown. We get high, we serve, we encourage and we enjoy life. We trust the desires of our hearts and let ourselves experience them!

JESUS CAME FOR YOU FIRST

There are far too many people who think, "for God so loved the world that He came to put us to work!" I say that kind of as a joke, but it's true. What if God so loved the world that He gave His Son so that we may have everlasting life (Jn. 3:16)? What if He didn't come so that everyone in the world except you can have life. No, listen to that again. What if He came for you? What if He came that YOU might have life, first and foremost?! He has the capacity to feel that way about each one of us!

He didn't come to put you to work. He came that you might have life!! So many of us have thought that we were helping God out, all the while not allow Him the very reason that He came…for us…for each, individual one of us…to have LIFE! He did it for you. He would have done it just for you individually. The life starts with Him…and you, experiencing His life personally, first and foremost, before you can share it with others. Unless you are experiencing that everlasting life, there's no point in sharing it with anyone else.

In fact, the "everlasting life" of John 3:16 means enjoying God, the earth, your family, and all creation! So many evangelism programs would be a better benefit if they shut down until each worker firstly became an enjoyer of everlasting life! We can only spread the amount of joy that we first are experiencing! If you want to see the whole world experience everlasting life, it has to start with you.

How are you enjoying the life in your family? How are you enjoying God's Presence today? How high are you on life!?!? Be the change you want to see in the world! Let yourself be free to be high on God! I use the word HIGH here, and throughout the book, because I don't just want the world to experience a little bit of joy. I want the whole world to be absolutely wildly happy! I want everyone to have a life beyond their wildest dreams! Yet, you can't spread what you aren't familiar with. You can't share wild joy with someone if you don't know what it's like! Enjoy life, for yourself! Then, enjoy life, for the world's sake! Enjoy life for God's sake! Be high on Life for everyone's sake! It's more than ok! It's what you were created for!

PRAISE COMES BEST FROM BEING RAVISHED

This brings me to another topic that has so often been misunderstood in spiritual circles. It's the subject of praise and worship. I asked the question earlier, "Didn't God make us to praise and worship Him?" This is something that has been written about and talked about almost to death! They say, "It's all about praise. It's all about worship." Could this be making God out to seem like some kind of insecure, self-seeking monster? Let's explore that idea.

What is praise? We praise things all the time. We praise our friends for being good at things. We praise people's songs, sports achievements, or successes in an occupation. We praise the food we eat. We say, "Oh, wow, that was a great dinner." We praise what we appreciate. We praise what we enjoy! Worship is what we do when we deeply, deeply appreciate and enjoy that thing.

So what if even praise and worship were all about enjoyment and pleasure too? What if God calls us to praise Him because He knows that the most joy and pleasure come from His Presence? I see it as more of a call to taste God's goodness and then simply express ourselves when we do. Most of us feel an even greater pleasure when we express the pleasure that we are experiencing.

We are called to delight ourselves in the Lord (Ps. 37:4). Well, that's easy! God's Glory is the highest high in the universe! Praise and worship spring naturally from this. The expression of this delight makes the delight all the more full. So, God calls us to express our delight in the highest high. Now that sounds like a kind and extravagantly loving God to me!

There have been so many worship programs throughout the world formed as if praise was just a ritual or maybe just a way to get God or the gods to do something greater for us or the world. But, what good father needs to be buttered up before helping his kids? This is not the true God of love! There is a higher way. So much attention has been given to proper worship formats and structures. God is only looking for a genuine expression of real affection and enjoyment as the truest praise. And, He only likes praise because it means all of us are having a great time experiencing reality!

You can think of it like this. Which person wants their romantic lover participating only because they are commanded to? Who wants to be hugged out of obligation? Now, when it's a spontaneous response to a spark of passion and delight, oh how sweet it is!! Praise and worship are all about delight and pleasure!

GREATEST PLEASURE IN NOT BEING SELF-SEEKING

We already touched on how this authentic high is not a seeking of how to fulfill oneself independently from God. To be clearer, we are not advocating spending a life trying to find the most individual, or selfish, high only. It's not about drinking a lot of alcohol, staying up all night, avoiding responsibility, being lazy, irresponsibly traveling the world, and not caring for those around you. No! In fact, I am not advocating "seeking pleasure" at all. At first, yes, you will seek pleasure, for you were built this way. Everyone is seeking pleasure until they meet Jesus Christ. From that point on they are continuously filled with the pleasure of experiencing God, His Presence, and His leadership. Thus begins the experience of the exhilarating co-adventure of time, space, and all reality together, in satisfaction, in complete bliss.

This can seem kind of strange to understand at first, but it becomes clearer over time. The highest high is God. Once you taste God, you will never be satisfied with anything else. Then, in Jesus Christ we find that this God is permanently united with us. We are one with God in Christ. So, the pleasure seeking ends. We have found the Pleasure! Or, rather, we have been found by Pleasure.

From this point on, we get to remain in the endless dance with our Lover, God, as we explore life, high together. The whole world becomes our oyster! We begin to dance through existence continually ravished from the inside out.

The ultimate pleasure is found in union with God. We begin to enjoy what God enjoys. We begin to enjoy God in everything, as we're led by the Spirit, in everything. We may forget this reality, this bliss, for a moment due to the illusions projected upon us from wherever, at first. Yet, eventually, we will no longer get distracted. Eventually, all the other voices cease. Our pleasure seeking here ends, and rather, we flow completely, always in bliss, to do the highest will of God and our true self in all things.

In our true self, we can enjoy God as well as His pleasure in other things. Yet, we are not seeking anything else to fulfill us, nor allowing any other thing to master us. We may enjoy the finest of food and drink, and find joy there, but not to the point of distraction or harm. We can enjoy everything in the healthiest way, not going to excess in anything other than God, of which there is no possible excess. Yes, and because we are in a co-dance with God, we only move in ways that honor the oneness of Christ, our beloved, in all things. We are no longer looking to any pleasures of the world for satisfaction, because we are in no way in need of satisfaction.

Having become one with God in Christ our highest and greatest pleasure comes in giving and caring for others. This is not in some guilt driven sense of obligation. We will actually become a most healthy and responsible citizen. Not as we once were, though, doing things out of duty, or repressing ourselves. We now move in a very free flowing way, like the wind. It's a passionate, joyful, even whimsical servanthood.

It may look like one expression at one time, and like something else at another. They key mark of this joyous life is that it will always leave people feeling loved, at least as long as they are open to being loved. It will always be a blessing. "The greatest among you is the servant," Jesus said (Matt. 23:11). He also said that it is more blessed to give then to receive (Acts 20:35).

There comes a point when we are confident in who we are that we will find the most exhilarating high in blessing and caring for others. This will NOT be at the expense of our own joy, but enhancing it, expressing it! This is when we see us all as One, as Christ, and we literally begin to feel the pleasure that our neighbor feels when we bless them, for we are one. This may all seem like just semantics. However, I believe it is a journey that God invites us to go on in our consciousness to enjoy life as He does. We were built for it. We were built for love, true love.

This is the love that exhilarates us in loving, not at the expense of our own high, but only enhancing it. We were built for a wild high adventure, enjoying the pleasures of both heaven and earth, in God, as One with all creation, a loving adventure, an adventure of caring, serving, and blessing the world, BECAUSE we like people AND for the fun of it!!! Whew!

PHYSICAL BODY WORKS BEST WITH PLEASURE AND JOY

"Laughter is the best medicine," is an often repeated quote. Have you ever pondered the depth of it? Doctors are coming to prove this phrase even further. There is even a part of the brain that is now being called the joy center. This joy center has been shown to be able to protect and release greater health to the body in many ways, when functioning properly. Of course, that only makes sense. We truly are well made by God! Depressed people usually have many other health problems as well. The body was simply wired for joy.

COUNTRIES ARE SWITCHING TO HAPPINESS RATHER THAN MONEY AS SUCCESS SIGN

The world is beginning to wake up to this reality too! Have you noticed that the United Nations is now considering changing their measurement of a nation's success from gross domestic product to gross domestic happiness? This means they are measuring, through polling, the happiness of the average person in a nation, rather than how much they are producing monetarily or otherwise. This makes so much more sense to me! Like Jesus said, "What good is it for you to gain the whole world, but lose your soul (Matt. 16:26)?" The world is beginning to see that it's all about being high on life, not necessarily producing more stuff.

NO TEARS IN HEAVEN, WHEN CAN THAT START?

Now, for my last happy holy pleasure trick, let me riddle you this! Just kidding, kind of, but here we are at the last section of this chapter! Have you ever thought about the end of the whole story of life? Meaning, like I mentioned earlier in the book, what are we going to be doing forever in heaven? And, if Jesus' message was instead about heaven being now established on earth, rather than waiting for some far off day, what does that mean about pleasure? Did you think that we were going to be avoiding pleasure for all eternity? Heavens, no!! In fact, one of the specific verses in the book of Revelation says that there won't even be tears anymore!

"And I heard a loud voice from the throne saying, 'Behold, the dwelling place of God is with man. He will dwell with them, and they will be his people, and God himself will be with them as their God. He will wipe away every tear from their eyes, and death shall be no more, neither shall there be mourning, nor crying, nor pain anymore, for the former things have passed away.' And he who was seated on the throne said, 'Behold, I am making all things new.' Also he said, 'Write this down, for these words are trustworthy and true.'" – Rev. 21:3-5 (ESV)

That passage sounds to me a lot like second Corinthians chapter five, a chapter that speaks of something that is already finished! If God is having us live "on earth as it is in heaven", then it sounds like the plan must be for extreme joy! If that passage in Revelation chapter twenty-one is the end goal of the story, then it sounds like we can just start now!

I'm not suggesting that we shallowly ignore those who haven't entered into a tears-of-sorrow-free existence yet. Instead we get to demonstrate a new world to share with them. Just as Jesus, who was always experiencing the oil of joy above all His companions even while weeping with those who wept, we also get to live in heaven's joys, even while we take those joys to those who are hurting. We may even weep with them, but right in the midst of that our inner ecstasy never has to fade. We'll talk about that more later on in the book. Right now, let's revel in God's Glory, to the point where our heavenly existence explodes and expands to become the experience of all those around the world. Let's live it up, in heaven on earth, that the whole world might taste this Glory too!!

CHAPTER 6
THE GOD HIGH THROUGH HISTORY

At first glance, it may seem like this altered state of consciousness, what in this book we are calling, 'being high on God,' is a new or super unusual thing. However, while it is quite unusual to the average person at the time of this book's writing, it is by no means new! Obviously, it has not been the norm during any time of human history either, for sure. Does that therefore make it irrelevant or relegate it to the category of being strange or unimportant? Many things have been uncommon throughout history, only later to be realized as a key breakthrough or an important truth. Human slavery was considered normal for many, many years. Only in the modern era are we beginning to see a widespread rejection of this horrific practice. It was once commonly thought that the earth was both flat and at the center of the solar system! We see that many things have been the normal status quo belief, only to be changed by a few key pioneers or explorers.

I'll be honest, I do want to be one of the pioneers that introduces being high on God to the planet! I think it's too important to miss. It's just downright lovely. It's the bees knees! At the same time, I also want to be sure to take plenty of time in acknowledging the many who have gone before me! There have been many "ecstatics" throughout the generations. They may have been few and far between at times, but they're there. Scattered throughout history, there have been God junkies and heavy Jesus drinkers. Sometimes they made a big deal about their intoxication on the divine. Other times you have to dig deep into their life and writings to find the God high. Either way, we have had a whole lot of holy whack pioneers on this planet already!

For the sake of brevity and the fact that this is not a history book, I won't be exploring all the bliss pioneers from our past. We've already taken time to mention Jesus Christ Himself and many ecstatics from the Bible. I also don't have time to explore the many countless God drinkers that are alive today (though I will mention a few). What I do want to do in this chapter is mention just a handful of those who became intoxicated on God, mostly examples from the last 2000 years of church history, as it were. Also, there are a few books out there already that engage this material much more thoroughly than I can here. However, it would be remiss not to include at least some of these in a book that's all about the high of heaven! Would you go with me on a journey of looking at some of these who have been wasted on God? I bet that you'll learn some things and your own bliss will be encouraged by their testimony. It may help you to know that this is not just a modern feel-good concoction of nonsense! There is a rich history to the God high!

Brother Lawrence (1614-1691)

Let's start with one of my favorites, Brother Lawrence! Brother Lawrence, also known as Brother Lawrence of the Resurrection, was definitely a pioneer of the whack! This guy was high on God all the time…literally, all of the time! I, personally, really like Brother Lawrence because his bliss was not associated with just certain times of the day, week, or year. He was one of those few in history who began to live in an altered state continuously. He lived in a Carmelite monastery, not as a priest or pastor, but simply as a brother. He worked primarily on menial tasks, cleaning, washing dishes, making sandals, and the like. Lawrence experienced profound ecstasy in the midst of all of life!

Here are a few historic quotes from him or about him:

This King, full of mercy and goodness, very far from chastising me, embraces me with love, makes me eat at His table, serves me with His own hands, gives me the key of His treasures; He converses and delights Himself with me incessantly, in a thousand and a thousand ways, and treats me in all respects as His favorite. It is thus I consider myself from time to time in His holy presence. My most usual method is this simple attention, and such a general passionate regard to God, to whom I find myself often attached with greater sweetness and delight than that of an infant at the mother's breast; so that, if I dare use the expression, I should choose to call this state the bosom of God, for the inexpressible sweetness which I taste and experience there. (The Practice of the Presence of God – by Brother Lawrence 2011 edition pg. 32)

I have quitted all forms of devotion and set prayers but those to which my state obliges me. And I make it my business only to persevere in His holy presence, wherein I keep myself by a simple attention, and a general fond regard to God, which I may call an actual presence of God; or to speak better, an habitual, silent, and secret conversation of the soul with God, which often causes in me joys and raptures inwardly, and sometimes also outwardly, so great that I am forced to use means to moderate them, and prevent their appearance to others. (The Practice of the Presence of God – by Brother Lawrence 2011 edition pg. 31)

That his prayer was nothing else but a sense of the presence of God, his soul being at that time insensible to everything but Divine love: and that when the appointed times of prayer were past, he found no difference, because he still continued with God, praising and blessing Him with all his might, so that he passed his life in continual joy… (The Complete Works of Brother Lawrence with Notes and Scripture References – By Brother Lawrence, edited by Kevin H. Grenier, pg. 41 2009)

Often during his life people would gather just to watch Brother Lawrence experience God! There was such an obvious living Presence on Him. His life was an amazing demonstration, a true pioneer of the God-high!

St. John of the Cross (1542-1591)

St. John of the Cross is another beautiful example of a God bliss forerunner. John was a Spanish priest, reformer, and poet of significant achievement. And, while He was not necessarily one who was always writing happy-go-lucky, grace-based revelations; He did drink deep from the God high. He was a true mystic. His extensive experience with pain, even being tortured, did not stop him from writing the following:

In the inner cellar
Of my Beloved have I drunk; and when I went forth
Over all the plain
I knew nothing,
And lost the flock I followed before.

There He gave me His breasts,
There He taught me the science full of sweetness.
And there I gave to Him
Myself without reserve;
There I promised to be His bride.

My soul is occupied,
And all my substance in His service;
Now I guard no flock,
Nor have I any other employment:
My sole occupation is love.

If, then, on the common land
I am no longer seen or found,
You will say that I am lost;
That, being enamored,
I lost myself; and yet was found.

(A Spiritual Canticle of the Soul and the Bridegroom of Christ – By: St. John of the Cross, translated by David Lewis Section 26-29 1909)

That "canticle", or song, was written while he was imprisoned in a six by ten foot cell! His joy was definitely beyond physical circumstance. His high was based on something else. Here's another stunning writing from this St. John:

The spark touches and is gone, though its effect lasts for some time, and occasionally for a very long time, but the spiced wine and its effect are both accustomed to last long, and this, as I say, is love's sweetness in the soul. Sometimes it lasts for a day, or for two days; at other times, for many days, though not always at the same degree of intensity, since it weakens or increases without the soul's ability to control it. Sometimes, when the soul has done naught in the matter, it feels this sweet inebriation of its spirit and the enkindling of this Divine win within its inmost substance…(Spiritual Canticles and Poems – By: St. John of the Cross and R.H.J. Steuart pg.98)

St. John of the Cross was definitely a pioneer of the ecstatic experience! He even remained intoxicated through extremely trying times. Beyond that, St. John was living proof that you can be an amazing reformer, activist, poet, and world changer while at the same time being drunk on the Divine.

Joseph of Copertino (1603-1663)

Joseph of Copertino is the patron saint of air travelers, aviators, astronauts, and those with a mental handicap! He was another seemingly average guy, even below average in the areas of education and intelligence. Still, the dude was a Holy Ghost drunk who became known for his many cases of literally lifting right up off of the ground in ecstasy. He also earned the nickname "Boccaperta", meaning 'the open mouthed gaper!' As you would imagine, a guy who walks around mouth open looking high and levitating would definitely experience some misunderstandings. Joseph was for the most part of his life quarantined by the church and kept away from the public eye. He did gain respect, however, as leaders began to recognize that his love for God was producing some powerful results.

Here are a few quotes about Brother Joseph:

At the command of the Inquisition he had said Mass in their church, dedicated to St. Gregory of Armenia, and there was raised in ecstasy above the altar. This occurrence so increased the fame of his holiness that it penetrated to the royal palace. (St. Joseph of Copertino – by: Angelo Pastrovicchi pg. 17-18)

Uttering his usual cry, "Oh," he seized the nobleman by the hair and lifted him from the floor as he rose in ecstasy into the air. The saint held him thus for a time to the amazement of those present, who with the nobleman, now fully restored, praised and thanked God for working such miracles by His servant. (St. Joseph of Copertino – by: Angelo Pastrovicchi pg. 38)

During the remainder of his life he had not the least intercourse with anyone except with the Bishop, his Vicar-General, the religious of the monastery, and, in case of need, with the doctor and surgeon…He was nevertheless contented in his seclusion and was wont to say, "I live in a city, yet it seems to me that I live in a forest, or, rather, in a paradise." In very truth he could call his new abode a paradise; for his soul was almost continually enraptured. Heaven only knows of all the sweet ecstasies which here united him with God. Many however, became known… At times the religious found him in his chapel wrapped in ecstasy, and would carry him like a corpse to his room. Occasionally these raptures lasted for six or seven hours. (St. Joseph of Copertino – by: Angelo Pastrovicchi pg. 107-108)

There was no stopping this guy's ecstasy! And, in case you're wondering, there are many accounts of the wild exploits of his life. Do some research on him! History is full of things that may just blow your mind! History is full of those who have experienced the God high. Sometimes you just have to poke around a bit to find them!

Catherine of Sienna (1347-1380)

Poking around a little bit farther back into history, we can find St. Catherine of Sienna. She lived to the age of only 33 years, but wow did she pack a whole lot of Glory! St. Catherine is a well-respected mystic and even a doctor of the Catholic church. She is also considered to be a patron saint of Europe. She experienced what she called a "mystical marriage" to Jesus, and wrote extensively on the love of God. Through her writings it becomes obvious that she was quite familiar with the God high. Here are some heavily intoxicating quotes by and about St. Catherine:

This soul, yearning with very great desire, and rising as one intoxicated both by the union which she had had with God, and by what she had heard and tasted of the Supreme and Sweet Truth, yearned with grief over the ignorance of creatures, in that they did not know their Benefactor, or the affection of the love of God. (Dialogue of St. Catherine of Siena – by: St Catherine of Siena pg. 186 1907)

Without delay you come to the open side of God's Son. There you find the fiery abyss of divine charity. At this second (scalene), his open side, you find a storehouse filled with fragrant spices. There you find the God-Man. There your soul is so sated and drunk that you lose all self-consciousness, just like a drunkard intoxicated with wine; you see nothing but his blood, shed with such blazing love. (Catherine of Siena: Spiritual Development in Her Life and Teaching – By: Thomas McDermott pg. 92 2008)

Sometimes when she talked of God in this way, she was lifted up in ecstasy. Her body became rigid, her eyes tightly shut. She could not see or hear anything, and if anyone touched her she could not feel it. One observer said she looked more like a statue than a live human being. Her friends reported that at times they could see her body slowly rise toward the ceiling, remain there for a time, and then slowly descend again before she woke from her ecstatic state. (Catherine of Siena: A Biography – By: Anne B Baldwin pg. 40)

Then she: 'If Thy truth and Thy justice permitted it, I would that Hell were utterly destroyed, or at least that no soul ever more should descend thither, and if (so I were still united to Thy charity) I were put over the mouth of Hell to close it, in such wise that none should ever more enter it, much would I rejoice, so that all my neighbors might thus be saved.'" "And when she said these words, she was abstracted from her senses and rapt in ecstasy. But, when she returned to herself, she was white as snow, and began to laugh loudly and to say : 'Love, Love, I have conquered Thee with Thyself. For Thou dost wish to be besought for what Thou canst do of Thine own accord.'" (Saint Catherine of Siena – by Edmund Garratt Gardner pg. 15 1907)

Talk about high on God, some of those quotes could literally send you into an ecstasy just by glancing at them! Unfortunately, Catherine seems to have died from being too hard on her body. This happened to a number of mystics who didn't fully understand grace and Christ's finished work. Yet, she definitely pioneered some Glory whack! She was high on

Jesus Christ and his love in ways that we are still learning from to this today.

Theresa of Avila (1515-1582)

Theresa of Avila was a whacked out reformer nun. She was kind of a female counterpart to St. John of the Cross. She has too many stages and steps included in her "ascent" into the Glory for my liking, yet she was surely still a pioneer of the intoxication. She wrote a book called "Interior Castle" which has some of the most in depth descriptions of spiritual inebriation ever recorded. All this and she lived it out 500 years ago! We are still catching up to some of the mystic revelations that St. Theresa had. Read some of them for yourself:

The soul is itself no longer, it is always inebriated; it seems as if a living love of God, of the highest kind, made a new beginning within it...(The Life of Saint Teresa of Avila by Herself – By: Saint Teresa of Avila pg. 143 Translated by David Lewis 2009)

It doesn't seem the King wants to keep anything from her. He wants her to drink in conformity with her desire and become wholly inebriated, drinking of all the wines in God's storehouse. Let the soul rejoice in these joys. Let her admire God's grandeurs. Let her not fear to lose her life from drinking so much beyond what her natural weakness can endure. Let her die in this paradise of delights. Blessed be such a death that so makes one live! (Saint Teresa of Avila by Mirabai Starr pg. 66 2010)

May it please his Majesty to give us this prayer often since it is so safe and beneficial; to acquire it is impossible because it is something very supernatural. And it may last a whole day. The soul does about like a person who has drunk a great deal but not so much as to be drawn out of his senses; or like a person suffering melancholy who has not lost his reason completely but cannot free himself from what is in his imagination - nor can anyone else. These are inelegant comparisons for something so precious, but I can't think up any others. The joy makes a person so forgetful of self and of all things that he doesn't advert to, nor can he speak of anything other than, the praises of God that proceed from his joy. (The Interior Castle – By: Saint Teresa of Avila pg. 142-143 1979 edition)

Yes, St. Theresa was a true imbiber of the divine Presence! She was also recorded to have lifted off of the ground in levitation ecstasies a number of times, as well. Her life and resources provide an amazing stepping stone to where we are today. As with any mystic or teacher, we must eat the meat and spit out the bones so to speak. All that being said, Theresa paved a way in the whack for many to follow after.

John Wesley (1703-1791)

When speaking of John Wesley, let me say, right away, that he was not known to be an exceedingly happy fellow. In fact, the religious attitude, and absolutely sobering demeanor of his daily life almost made me want to not list him here. But, there were enough manifestations of the God high in his life, and especially in the lives of those present in his meetings, that it wouldn't be right not to mention them. Also, it must be said that the culture of the world has come a very long way in being able to talk about God in a happier manner overall. John Wesley, when studied in depth, could easily seem very critical and judgmental, and in fact he surely was in some respects. Still, he spoke of the love and grace of God in ways that were really quite radical and refreshing for those in his day and age.

John Wesley is also credited as the founder of multiple church movements, including Methodism. He was a very essential part in sparking the "first great awakening" both in Europe and the United States. He was an Anglican clergyman that was one of the first ministers to actually consider preaching in the streets, rather than just in church buildings. This was absolutely revolutionary at that time, and not without much opposition.

Wesley was on fire to preach to as many folks as he could. In the days before big sound systems and modern stadium gatherings, he would gather tens of thousands of folks at a time by preaching his passionate lungs out! It was during these gatherings that many would be struck with unusual ecstasies and wild outbursts of laughter and joy. There were all sorts of unusual manifestations in his public and outdoor meetings. Wesley was not really expecting these kinds of things to happen, still they continued. Sometimes he was convinced that they were of the devil! Other times he believed that they were of God. This is a typical tension among spiritual people, especially when they are new to the phenomena. If you embrace the God-high, be prepared for many, many questions, opposition, and persecution! Wesley himself sometimes openly criticized the ecstatic folks. He also had much harshness and judgment in his preaching overall. At the same time, He also was proclaiming the Glory and love of God in a way that most definitely intoxicated people. One account of Wesley embracing the inebriating effects of the Gospel is mentioned here:

There were also outbursts of laughter reported, though, unlike in Bristol in 1740, they were welcomed as expressions of the joy of salvation (except when they interrupted a sermon). Another oddity was that a high proportion of those affected were children and teenagers. Wesley investigated and was intrigued and impressed. He read an account of these meetings to the York society and was delighted that it provoked similar reactions. (John Wesley: A Biography – By: Stephen Tomkins pg. 157 2003)

Sarah Edwards, wife of Jonathan Edwards (1710-1758)

A great example of a true Glory drinker is the wife of famous Protestant theologian Jonathan Edwards, Sarah Edwards. Often Protestants are not familiar with the wild manifestations of God's Presence that happened in the history of some of their most favorite leaders. Ever hear of "the Quakers" or "the Shakers"? These are widely accepted groups from the history of Christianity. Heck, one of them is even featured on the front of your Quaker Oat Brand oatmeal cereal. People are usually not aware that the Quaker and Shakers would shake and bake in the Glory of God, quite literally!

Sarah Edwards was not a part of those movements particularly. She was however deeply experienced with the God high. Sarah and her husband Jonathan were instrumental in the Great Awakening in the United States. They pastored a Reformed church. Her father founded Yale and her husband founded Princeton! She was considered a model wife and female leader in her day. It is, however, not commonly known that she regularly got jacked up on the Glory of God! Check out the following reports:

On Wednesday morning, January 20, 1742, Sarah Edwards was enraptured by spiritual ecstasy that continued for more than two weeks. Repeatedly she was physically overwhelmed by her spiritual raptures, sometimes leaping involuntarily to praise God and more often so overcome by joys and transports that she collapsed physically. Jonathan was out of town on his scheduled preaching tour...On his return, Jonathan was elated to learn of his beloved's transfixing encounters with the divine. They far surpassed his own raptures, yet they fit the same patterns...He wrote down her account of the entire episode as she dictated it...She often retired by herself to meditate...and much of her ecstasy took place in solitude or at night. Sarah's experience, he argued, perfectly fit the highest spiritual standards to which the most mature Christian should aspire. (Jonathan Edwards: A Life – by: George M. Marsden pg. 240)

For hours on end, she felt sensations of God's love, as her "soul dwelt on high, and was lost in God." Her soul seemed almost to separate from her body, but Edwards, growing more moderate, noted that she was not in a trance and did not lose her bodily senses. Nevertheless, she sometimes lost her strength and became mute. The joy of Christ even caused her to leap involuntarily...Sarah became Jonathan's ideal test case for fruits of the revival, and she demonstrated love, goodness, and holiness in abundance. "If such things are enthusiasm," he concluded, "and the fruits of a distempered brain, let my brain be evermore possessed of that happy distemper!" (The Great Awakening – by: Thomas S. Kidd pg. 133)

Sarah and her husband Jonathan were both in favor of experiencing God's Glory in profoundly joyful ways. Their theology has been widely accepted. And, while it still comes off as too critical and angry sounding to me, I deeply respect that they experienced the drunken Glory, and took a stand for it in front of the whole world.

William Seymour (1870-1922)

William Seymour was a one-eyed African American holiness preacher around the turn of the 20th century in the United States. He is known as one of the pioneers of the Pentecostal movement in America. He was also a Holy Ghost drunk! His work in helping to pioneer what is now known as "the Asuza Street revival" brought tongues speaking and being drunk in the spirit back to the forefront of many places around the world. Asuza street had a massive impact on the spiritual climate of the planet, and still does. The meetings Seymour helped to lead in California were often very free flowing and open to whatever the Spirit would lead them to do. It's reported that fire fell from heaven when they gathered! The stories from those days on Asuza street are many. Here are a few accounts regarding the God inebriation released through Seymour's life:

What happened on April 9, 1906, in the Asberry's home changed the religious face of the 20th century. Seymour had just come from praying for a Mr. Owen Lee for healing. Mr. Lee began "speaking in tongues" as Seymour prayed for him, and evidently received the baptism of the Holy Spirit. Arriving at Asberry's home, "He related what had just happened with Edward Lee. This news caused the faith of the people to rise higher than ever before, when suddenly, 'Seymour and seven others fell to the floor in a religious ecstasy, speaking with other tongues.'" (Ice on Fire – by: Scott T. Kelso 2006 pg. 140)

The scenes at Azusa Street as described by Seymour and Bartleman were nothing new to many holiness people. The "Fire-Baptized Way" was already well known, especially in the South and also in the Middle West.

Many of the holiness people had felt that some physical evidence would often accompany sanctification to prove that a person had "prayed through." Some thought that the best proof of being baptized with the Holy Ghost was the ability to perform the "holy dance." Others taught that "hallelujah earthquakes" would be felt by the newly-baptized, while some thought the best evidence was a shouting in drunken ecstasy, like the disciples on the day of Pentecost. (The Holiness-Pentecostal Tradition: Charismatic Movements in the Twentieth Century 1997 pg. 109)

Mr. Seymour was definitely not the only whack pioneer during this era. Thankfully there were many who were experiencing the God high by this time. However, William deserves to be honored for helping to bring this ecstatic joy to the forefront in a powerful way. So many of those who are getting drunk in the Spirit today can trace their roots back to Asuza Street and the impact of William Seymour's ecstasies.

Kenneth Hagin (1917-2003)

One only needs to do a short search on the internet to find videos of the drunken escapades of Glory pioneer and teacher Kenneth Hagin. Brother Hagin helped to form an entire movement of Bible based churches referred to as "Word of Faith" churches. His teaching pamphlets and resources have circled the whole world wide. I honor him as a Holy Ghost drunk who sincerely and powerfully lived a long life of integrity both to the scriptures and in leadership.

Brother Hagin was a clear and consistent voice amidst many wild and controversial years of American Pentecostalism. The churches that were powerfully influenced by him, to this day, are, among many things, familiar with the Glory intoxication. He didn't do much writing on the subject, but it was very present, especially in his meetings. He rightly taught that it was about trusting God no matter what you were feeling. Then the whack would often manifest spontaneously from believing the truth of the Good News of God. Kenneth Hagin had an influence of spirituality around the world, and received a lot of opposition. And, while some of his teachings may have been abused, he himself was a pioneer of experiencing heaven on earth.

Ruth Ward Heflin (1940-2000)

Speaking of heaven on earth, there is a another woman who would often see wild heavenly manifestations, even within recent years, yet she still remains somewhat unknown. Her name is sister Ruth Ward Heflin. Her life has likely been brushed under the rug by many because she saw so many seemingly unbelievable things. Her gatherings would be filled with angelic visitations, jewels appearing from out of nowhere, and gold dust coming out of people's skin! More important than all of that to me is the extreme joy and holy laughter which she carried.

Sister Ruth ran a camp in the southern USA that would often gather crowds from around the world. People wanted this joy! People wanted to experience heaven on earth! Her movement definitely has had some very religious people involved with it up to this very day. However, she encouraged being high on God and living hammered on the bliss of heaven. Here are a couple of quotes from her own books:

The glory that I was witnessing began to come into my eyes and into my spirit, and I became drunk in my spirit from the glory I was witnessing. (Revival Glory by: Ruth Ward Heflin 2013 edition pg. 125)

He is waiting for you. Cry out in His presence, not from pain but from ecstasy. He wants us to know the ecstasies of this intimate relationship with Him. Worship and adore Him. (Glory by: Ruth Ward Heflin 1996 pg. 111)

Rodney Howard Browne (1961-present)

A man mightily blessed by God to restore laughter and holy intoxication to the world is one Rodney Howard Browne. It is quite interesting, and saddening to me, that he's no longer as enthusiastic about this fact as I am. Still, probably more than anyone walking the earth today, Rodney is responsible for introducing the holy inebriation to the modern world.

A South African by birth, Rodney was used mightily in the United States, being credited as a primary influence in both the "Brownsville Revival" and the "Toronto Blessing." There are numerous videos of Rodney and his gatherings online. You can watch the high of heaven come over them and take over thousands of people at once. (Although, as this book is being edited, I've noticed some of those videos being deleted.)

Some have accused Rodney of merely abusing the power of suggestion or human psychological dynamics, but the fruit of his life has brought much love and blessing to the nations. Rodney has been highly criticized, and experienced many challenges in his life and ministry, and today does not encourage the types of things that I am promoting in this book. Here are a few quotes from Rodney's older writings:

My whole body was on fire from the top of my head to the soles of my feet. Out of my belly began to flow a river of living water. I began to laugh uncontrollably and then I began to weep and then speak with other tongues. I was so intoxicated on the wine of the Holy Ghost that I was literally beside myself. The fire of God was coursing through my whole being and it didn't quit. I began to realize why we would need a glorified body. (The Touch of God by: Rodney Howard Browne pg. 89 1991)

We were in a meeting in Pittsburgh, Pennsylvania in January of 1990, and the glory of the Lord was in the place. Most of the people were not in their seats. They were lying on the floor under the power of God. The presence of God came in like a cloud and people were filled with joy. It was bubbling out of their bellies. People were totally drunk in the Holy Ghost. The anointing of God was on them and they were in a place of total Holy Ghost ecstasy, total joy. They were beside themselves. The Lord spoke to me and said, "You are tasting the powers of the world to come. This is a little bit of heaven, a glimpse of heaven, a glimpse of glory." (The Touch of God by: Rodney Howard Browne pg. 116 1991)

Toronto Blessing (1994-present)

The "Toronto Blessing" was definitely known as a laughing and intoxicating move of God. It has restored joy, laughter, and inebriation of the Spirit to the ends of the earth in our day. Many of the current Glory bliss teachers and ecstatics have come out of this Toronto experience. Many modern revelators of the whack have been directly influenced by the gatherings that have happened at the Toronto Airport Christian Fellowship. TACF (or what is now called "Catch the Fire") has been led by John and Carol Arnott throughout the entire movement. Another man by the name of Randy Clark was the one preaching at TACF when the movement began. There are too many names to mention of all of the gloriously intoxicated people who have come forth from this "Blessing." I myself, though I have never been to this Toronto based gathering, would not be writing this book if it weren't for what God did there.

The Toronto Blessing began in 1994 and was marked by people coming from all over the world to receive the news that God was a happy God filled with deep unconditional love for His children. The manifestations of the Spirit were powerful and unlike anything most had ever seen. There was laughing, falling, gold dust, angel feathers, strange sounds, shaking, jerking, running, rolling, and just a whole lot of people doing strange things! Along with the seemingly strange occurrences, many families were restored, bodies physically healed, lives filled with love and peace, and all around wonderful fruits of the Holy Spirit were awakened. The Blessing went under a whole lot of scrutiny worldwide. Still, the influence from Toronto has been vast and long lasting. Probably more than any one group today, the folks at TACF in Toronto have spread the high of heaven to the planet in this generation. I am so thankful for them. I honor the leaders and pioneers from this movement.

It's here, at the end of this chapter, that I want to propose something. Let's take it even further! I mean, let's get more drunk than this world has ever seen! Let's get so whacked up on Jesus that His bliss becomes famous. I want to propose that we take the revelation and manifestations revealed in Toronto and throughout our entire drunken history even farther!

I know that there is a temptation to back off because of the whole mess of persecutions and misunderstandings. It's true that this high of heaven, though existing in pockets and places throughout the ages, has almost always been opposed. However, I believe it is high time. What if getting high on God became a regular household practice!?!? It's just too amazing to hide away in a corner. It was never meant for just a few super spiritual few! Let's build on the foundations laid by our forefathers and foremothers! Let's get the whole planet drunk!

CHAPTER 7
HOW TO GET HIGH

By this point in the book we've covered a variety of foundational aspects to the high of God. I'm betting that a lot of you are ready to get right to the point! Let's get down to it! Let's get high already! Maybe you've not yet had much personal experience with the intoxication. Are you ready to get wasted!?!

The biggest question I get asked, both in person and through the internet is: "How do I get high on God?" So, while I have already pretty much answered this in one way or another already by this point of the book, it is for the folks that really demand a step by step that I write now. I do want to clearly and directly write a chapter specifically on the subject, so there would be no doubt in anyone's mind about how we get high. For some of you this chapter will be exactly what you are looking for, a no holds barred straight up prescription for the drink! For others of you, you are already familiar with the experience. Maybe the experienced drinkers will enjoy the other chapters more. Either way, for the record, here we go!

YOU ARE ALREADY HIGH

Let me frustrate your precious logical mind here right away! There is actually no way that you can get high on God! It's not by the wisdom or efforts of man, it's not a process that you must go through. This often frustrates people with the common western mindset of linear thinking and self-reliance. However, it's amazingly good news! Why? You are already high! It's not something you have to chase. It's not for the especially wise or intelligent. It's not for the lucky or elite. All of humanity is included inside of Jesus Christ, already included in His high!

"Well, I don't feel it!" you may be thinking. That's often the first thought right away. Fear not, we will walk you through that in this chapter too. However, if you step back and look at things objectively, you will probably agree with me that it's a good thing that all people are already included in the high. It's good news for the whole world! This bliss is already yours!

The truth is that all people are absolutely, wasted, whacked, jacked up, and thoroughly high on God. Experiencing the high of God is simply becoming aware of the experience that we have been included in on. Becoming aware that you have been included in Christ causes you to experience His reality now as yours. Yet, the objective truth is that it always was yours in Him.

This is why you can experience the growth in just a few minutes of what it would have before seemed to take years, whether emotionally, spiritually, or even physically. This is also why miraculous healings can happen. The recovery of a sick person in just a few short seconds can happen. This is called heaven's reality being made manifest. You are seated together with Christ in heavenly places (Ephesians 2:6). That's as high as it gets! It's already a reality. It's already true now. You are already high. Whether you like it or not, whether you believe it or not, whether you've ever even heard about it or not, it's still true.

Now, this can sound ethereal, too "Eastern," too intangible or frustrating. But, it actually works to the advantage of the whole world. It makes things so much easier. You don't have to follow a whole bunch of steps to get high. It's as easy as waking up! Your eyes simply open to the reality, and you begin to feel the reality. It's what I have often called our subjective reality becoming aware of the objective reality. Or, to put it in a crazy, hilarious way, you could say it's like your true self saying to the old false self, "Fool, you'd better recognize!"

So many things in the kingdom of God work exactly like this. It's what we talked about earlier in the book regarding Jesus' Gospel. Heaven is already here! It's all already here. We are just waking up to that. It is the same way with the high. When you become convinced that you are permanently high, regardless of your behavior that day, regardless of whether or not you prayed or meditated enough that day, regardless of any mental, spiritual, emotional, or physical thing you did or did not do that day, it is then that you will begin to experience or feel the high every day. You are high because Jesus Christ is high, and you are hidden in Him (Col. 3:3).

This is why I don't really like how to's. This chapter truly is a misnomer. There is no how to, there's only an already done! How to's will always leave it up to you to get yourself high. How to's promote a works mentality, aka working for something that God has already given to us freely. How to's are like spell casting, like illicit drug taking, like witchcraft. How to's will leave you feeling proud if you succeed, and feeling condemned if you fail. They lock you in to the fallen system of darkness. So, despite the title of this chapter, I cannot truly give you a how to. The how to already happened! You already are everything that you need to be now in Christ! You were created perfect and have been preserved perfect, lacking nothing, in Him.

Now, if you are struggling to wrap your head around this, do not be discouraged! It is truly good news! I promise. And, we will still help your experience to reflect this! I would not have written this book if I didn't want to help encourage your bliss! However, it truly has to come from a new and fresh perspective. It has to flow from a non-linear, non-western type of thinking, though it is still semi-logical and can make perfect sense in the renewed mind. It's got to start from a place of recognizing the perfection of all the cosmos in Christ! We must start from the finish line! Now, that will keep you whacked! Rest, you don't have to get yourself high, God's already taken care of that! Sit back, relax, and dare to believe that a high is overcoming you right now, because it always was part of you, completely independent of your efforts!

AWAKENING TO THE HIGH

So we discover that Jesus has already included us in His experience of life in every way (1 John 4:17). He has already made us high as kites, among so many other beautiful things! Now we are merely awakening to that reality. That awakening can happen quickly, as it does for some, or slowly, as it does for others. I'm convinced that this awakening will eventually happen for all, but that's a different topic for a different book. However, the topic of the speed of the awakening to this high is dynamically related to this chapter. I am sure that if you are reading this chapter you just want to get as high as possible, as quick as possible. Good news! That is God's desire too! God has already shown that He's willing to give his all to get you high.

Simply put, for those of you that just cannot move on without a how to, here's how to get high, even though I don't like that language! Just commune with the real Glory of God all around you and all within you! Be conscious of your union with the Glory-substance of God for even a second! However, really you won't be able to do that without the initiating gift of the Holy Spirit to enable you. Holy Spirit is the ultimate enabler, in a truly healthy way! To put it another way, no one can wake themselves up. You get high by realizing that you are living now in heaven on earth. Holy Ghost's primary job on the planet is to cause this awakening to Glory in us. It takes God to initiate this communion high! This kind of awakening was too scandalous for the people of the Old Testament days! Indeed, it confounds the religious and self-help oriented folks to this day as well! Jesus Christ appeared on the scene at just the perfect time, when humanity was just beginning to be ready, to awaken the world. The awakening is simply to realize with all your being that you are immersed in God! Become conscious of that, and you will be high! It's as simple as that!

For some of you, you will be able to get absolutely high just by reading the truth written in this book, or even these sections once or twice! You may want to read the inebriating truth multiple times, especially the scriptures! I'll say it one more time right here again too. You get high by becoming aware of the Glory of God all around and within you in Jesus Christ! No matter what other ways that God may use, or that we may discuss, it will always come back to that simple realization. In fact, all of the other "ways" we are about to discuss will simply be things that the Holy Spirit will use so that our being can hear this Truth.

Faith comes by hearing, and many folks do not truly hear the first several times. For whatever reason, it can take a shorter or longer amount of time for people to truly hear the good news that heaven is here on earth in Jesus Christ. It might be so that we won't turn it into a self-reliant formula that builds pride and independence in the heart of the preacher or communicator of this truth. For whatever reason, I've found that most people seem to need to hear it over and over and over in order to awaken to this glorious, scandalous reality!

It's also important to see that you get high by a holistic realizing of the Glory of God's heaven on earth reality, not merely by an intellectual realization. Our whole being, or consciousness must receive a true revelatory awareness of heaven on earth in Jesus. It's like the "aha moment", like when the lights come on for you that you are in heaven, in God, in the Glory! This will always, always, always be the way that makes you high! It's not complicated. Also, it doesn't have to take a big process. For most people, Holy Spirit leads them to some similar ways (notice I didn't say methods, processes, or programs) to receive this revelatory experience.

Again, I repeat, it is by true revelation! And, revelation is by nature something that must happen TO you, not BY you. Information can be discovered BY you. It's something that can be searched out. Revelation, however, must be revealed by another party. It cannot be searched out. It must be revealed. Revelation must be revealed. The high must come upon you, be revealed to you. You can't get yourself high. You are already high. The high must be revealed to you, by the Holy Spirit. As much as any man, or method, or ministry, or activity may seem like they can get you high, it can only come as a gift from the Holy Spirit. Now, if you think that Holy Spirit is stingy or ineffective, then that could sound like discouraging news. However, this is just not the case! Holy Spirit is more generous, loving, and powerful than we could ever imagine! Holy Spirit does a great job AND cannot be stopped!

Just as in Jesus Christ you are already preserved totally high all the time, so the Holy Ghost is utterly committed to making you aware of this truth. Just as salvation was ensured by Jesus Christ, so awakening to that is ensured by Holy Spirit. Hearing the truth of Jesus' Gospel, that heaven is inseparably united with earth will enable you to be high on God. And, Holy Spirit is committed to ensuring that you hear this Gospel to the depths of your being! This is how you get high! Holy Spirit gets you high, by revealing the Good News of Jesus to you! It doesn't depend on your efforts, how many sermons you hear, or how much prayer or Bible study you do. Only God can reveal the Glory to you and enable you to experience your high! And, that is what God does best, in just the perfect way, in just the perfect time!

NAVIGATING THE "WAYS WE GET HIGH"

Now, what I am about to write is also very important. Many people can get confused by misunderstanding the absolute dependence of this high on God. It can get as confusing as the age old debate over freewill vs. predestination! If it all depends on God, then is there any point to praying, reading my Bible, or going to fellowship gatherings? Or, to put it more clearly, "Can I just continue a life giving no attention to God and still just expect to randomly get high on God?" If it's all finished and dependent on God, do healthy choices even matter in awakening to the high of heaven on earth?

Obviously, once you awaken to the continual high of your true self in Christ, you will naturally begin to make healthy choices. Prayer, Bible study, fellowship, serving, loving, giving, and the like will become what you do, not to gain awakening, but because you are awakened! You will make healthy choices because you truly are healthy. Let it be said, as well, though, that even if you are not feeling awakened, healthy choices are still good and worth it! Not yet being awakened is not an excuse to hurt yourself and others! This chapter, however, is written especially for those who have not yet felt much awakening to Jesus' bliss. This is for those who have not yet become experientially high in their regular daily lives. Is there any benefit to the "spiritual disciplines" of prayer, meditation, study, listening to teachers, etc, to help me experience my high?

Again, for some of you, these questions are not as relevant, because you found it super easy to just engage and get high. Some folks just hear the truth, and get the revelation quicker. This does not make them better, or more attuned in any way. They have just been subjects of grace, to display that it is by grace. Each one of us will receive that grace, do not be discouraged. You are just as loved, just as important to God. Your life will not be wasted. You will get wasted on Life!

It is for these folks that continue to struggle to get high that I especially want to continue to write. There are some ways and situations that Holy Spirit often uses to awaken us. I do not want to prescribe these as spiritual disciplines. Prescribing spiritual disciplines has been a common thing to do throughout the world over the centuries. In certain ways maybe that could possibly be beneficial. However, it has to be understood in a very careful and delicate way. I look at "the disciplines" rather as ways the Holy Spirit has often used to bring awakening. In understanding this, you must have a disillusionment in trusting any of them as a "means of grace" in any formulaic, ritualistic, or rigid way.

In fact, the best way I can describe to grow in awakening would be to simply follow your heart, or respond to the grace that you are being given at the time. This comes back to the fact that in Christ you have been given a holy heart! You can trust what is going on inside you. To bring it back to the point at hand, specifically, if something is getting you a little high right now, and producing good fruit, GO WITH IT! If you are experiencing the genuine Glory of God in ways that have love, joy, peace, patience, etc. on them, then go with that.

Following your holy heart as the most important thing, the Glory has also historically been revealed to folks while engaged in certain activities. Sometimes the Glory just awakened someone in quick overwhelming ways, like knocking the apostle Paul to the ground on the road to Damascus. So, you just never know when awakening is going to strike. And, I believe that it is true that God's love is inescapable. Even if you choose to run and hide, like the prodigal Son, you will eventually be drawn back to the Glory of the Father. His love is just too good!

The point that I'm wanting to get to here, though, is that there remains great benefit and wisdom in living in the ways that have historically blissed people out. Holy Spirit is a person, and has a personality. Holy Spirit has ways that are consistent and reliable. These are ways that will become a normal and a spontaneous outflow of who you are once you are aware of the high. I also want to recommend that you begin to engage these ways even when you are not feeling it at first. This is not meant to be a 'fake it until you make it' idea, although it could look like that from an onlookers perspective. Hear me out! I'm not prescribing a fake spiritual life. I am prescribing to make healthy choices even before you feel it. Holy Spirit will absolutely meet you in these places and choices. These choices can also minimize the damage of unawakened activity. There is practical wisdom in the ways of God, even when you don't feel them. You might feel like killing someone while in an unawakened state, but don't do it! That might make you laugh that I would even have to write that, but you'd be surprised at the ways that some people misunderstand spiritual teaching!

Another thing I am not saying is that you should try really hard, to the point of exhaustion, fasting and praying for days or weeks on end for a breakthrough. No! In fact, I'm not even sure if fasting was ever a truly beneficial activity, but that's another one of my side topics. What I am saying here is much more basic. I'm just saying that even if you don't feel awakened, still please take care of your family! Please still feed your dog and cat. Please still fulfill your commitments at work, school, and at home! Please keep doing the things that you know are basic blessings and beneficial. This includes your spiritual life. Don't throw out your Bible and stop hanging out with friends and believers. You may be shocked that this common sense is even necessary to write, but many people have gotten frustrated and given up on everything. Folks have misunderstood the finished work of Jesus Christ to mean that they no longer need to take care of their family or themselves at all. Hey, if it's finished, then why go to work, or school, or read a Bible, or whatever?

No, there is a Trinitarian dance that is going on! Even once you are awakened, there will still be things that God empowers you to walk out with wisdom. It will be all God, but God moving through YOUR life! God included YOU! God did not finish the job so you can just get out of the way. No, God finished YOU as perfect so that you in union with Him could have real adventures, participating fully together in time and space! Yes, and even before you are awakened to your true self, the healthy activities and adventures of the new creation person will still have benefit in living them out.

So, even if it seems that you are not yet experiencing the God high in the way that you want to, I recommend that you continue to follow in the ways of those who have gotten high before you. There is still this mysterious happening wherein awakening can even be sped up or slowed down, many times, while engaging in certain activities. Again, do not strive in these ways, for that usually tends to make them completely ineffective, burning your heart out on God, as if God is a stingy miser not giving you what you thought you were working for. Do them while enjoying your life as much as you can! No, none of these ways will work in and of themselves.

To put it another way, let me just say that more people have seemed to get high while in meditation, or while serving their neighbor, than those gorging themselves on unhealthy behaviors or lifestyles. To be sure, God has met many people in the midst of outright rebellion, while they were shooting up heroin, or even murdering folks, like good ol' apostle Paul. While we were yet sinners, Christ expressed his love! But, to use that as an excuse to continue in unhealthy behaviors would be foolish. Not to belabor the point, but God will even use the very rebellious behaviors to bring us to the end of our independent confidence, to open us up to the Glory. So, all things will in the end work to our benefit! Oh, the complete victory of light over darkness! Oh, the power of God's grace!

There are, however, healthier and more beneficial activities to engage in that have seemed to speed up the intoxication of some. Just use these with caution. They are like rockets that could easily shoot you right into religious pride or disillusioned discouragement just as easily as they can blast you super high into the Glories of the Christ high! Truthfully only Holy Spirit working through the inspirations and winds that blow through your heart can rightly direct these rockets!

WAYS THE HOLY SPIRIT OFTEN USES

So, there ARE some activities that people are often doing when they get the revelation from Holy Spirit of the inseparable union of heaven and earth in the person of Jesus Christ. These are all just things that can and have often been more heavenly in nature, they tend to look like heaven, and therefore they lend to the Glory awareness. These are not truly how to get high, as we've already covered! The only way to get high is by realizing heaven's reality. You are already high, filled and flooded with God in every way! These ARE common ways that Holy Spirit has moved in and upon people to awaken hearts to the whack! I recommend filling your life with them, both before and after you experience the joy of being all jacked up in the Holy Ghost. I have also called these, "How to have a real party!" They are the activities of heaven's party. They are truly the most glorious things to engage in, both in heaven and on earth!

ANOINTING ON SPECIFIC INDIVIDUALS / GIFTS OF THE SPIRIT

One way that Holy Spirit loves to use to get people high is getting folks to simply be around those that are already carrying a tangible atmosphere of heaven. Previously in the book we explored the truth that everyone is heavenly and perfect. It's important to know, however, that you will still sense special Glory on specific people that are anointed to minister to you. You might know this when you encounter a person and a deep desire arises to want whatever they are walking in. You may see certain people that are high in a way that you want to be high. Be sure to be confident in your own individuality. At the same time, we were meant to receive from others too.

There is no shame in being around these empowering people as much as possible. I say get around them until you are confident that you are walking what they have to impart to you. Obviously, you will never look just like them. You are made to be you! But, God loves to release what is called "impartation" through other members of His body because there is a special joy in being able to experience God through others. We are the body of Christ, not created to be alone, but to be full together! We were created to release Glory back and forth to one another like blood flows through a body, or like currents of electricity flow through our body. It's ok to receive these invisible impartations from just being around others. Some of you may receive your biggest awakening to the high as you simply hang out with Glory people. It's a big deal!

This can seem like a pretty mysterious thing. I don't really have a desire to fully explain impartation, nor could I, really. Yet, Holy Spirit has so often used it in getting us jacked up on heaven! It can be a major blessing! Some individuals are especially gifted or anointed by God to get people high. They may seem to get way more of the people around them high than other people do. This is not wrong. We all have different gifts. You have it all in Christ, but many times God empowers certain people to release the whack in a special way. Don't over think it! Just go with the flow! Get around those who empower what you want to walk in.

ART

Another way that Holy Spirit can use to awaken you to the Most High is through the experience of creative art. Some people receive through art more than in any other way. There is a mysterious beautiful thing that can happen in someone's creativity where it's packed with Glory revelation! Creativity is absolutely everywhere throughout heaven. So, it only makes sense that we can get high on heaven when we experience creativity. Engage art and see what God does to awaken you to heaven on earth. You may just get wasted on God through art!

This kind of art could be in any form really, paint, music, drawing, sculpture, cooking, dance, etc. There is no limitation! The amount of folks who have gotten whacked through music is probably too many to number! There is so much to explore regarding God and Glory expression through art. It would take a whole other book to develop that!

COMMUNION

Receiving the bread and wine while remembering Jesus Christ in the Lord's Supper is surely a powerful way to whack people right up! There are countless stories of mystics throughout the ages becoming wildly intoxicated on God whilst easting the bread or drinking the cup. This was surely one of the main reasons that Jesus instituted the feast! Feasts are for partying!

The very simple physical elements of bread and wine are something we can tangibly taste, touch, smell, and see. Jesus starts with something that is so common and easy to experience in physical bread and wine, and says, "Hey, just like you have these common things that you partake of every day, now realize that my very Presence is like this. You can partake of Me and my Love just this easily. Eat, drink, and remember that!" I mean, meditate for a moment on the fact that Jesus used wine to symbolize the Presence of God! Remember the body broken at the cross, remember the blood spilled, and realize that God's Presence will never leave us, even when we completely rejected God. There is so much revelation on taking communion, it's ridiculous. Partake of the Table, and see how Holy Spirit may just sneak up and whack you out of your mind in ecstasy. He's done it before!

FAITH ACTIVATORS - TOKING/BREATHING THE GHOST, DRINKING WITH YOUR HANDS, ETC.

This one can seem pretty unusual to those who haven't heard of it. Indeed it is probably one of the newer phenomenon to appear on the spiritual scene, in a sense. In another sense, it could be quite similar to taking the Lord's Supper (don't stone me for saying this, I don't mean it irreverently). What I am talking about is something I like to call "faith activators"! One particular faith activator that has been used among many of my friends is known as the infamous "toking the ghost!" Toking the ghost is literally acting like you are smoking an invisible joint, but remembering that you are breathing in the Holy Ghost instead of smoking anything. Other common faith activators have been things like putting your hand to your mouth as if you are drinking a drink, or looking like you are grabbing a big barrel and lifting it all the way up to your mouth. Another common one in certain circles is putting your hand to your neighbors arm and looking like you are giving them an injection.

These are seemingly silly little actions these "faith activators," but they can be strangely powerful. There might even be some more appropriate term for them. I'm not sure. I have heard the term "faith activators" several times over the years from folks beside myself, so that's what I'm going with. There were many people especially in the United States and the United Kingdom during the late 1990s until the present writing of this book who would do these actions when getting high on God, often with great effect! I don't mind calling them faith activators because they kind of give a simple physical action that can engage the being of a person in believing the truth; the truth that they ARE getting high. Just putting your hand to your mouth like you are smoking an invisible joint can remind you that communing with the Glory is just that easy too! At that very moment God may combine that silly action with a gift of awareness. I've experienced it time and time again myself! I know many others have as well.

There was a point where so many people were doing these activators that they even became a bit religious or legalistic about them. As I said before, none of this will actually get you high by themselves. God just uses them sometimes to awaken you to the high that you already have in Jesus Christ. Isn't it true that God is more accessible to us than the air we breathe or the drinks we drink? An even greater scandal for many people is that it is easier to get high on God than marijuana, crack, alcohol, or any drug. I say smoke your invisible spliffs all you want!

Don't put your faith in them, put your faith in Jesus! But, don't ignore whatever might help you realize His nearness! It can make for a fun and powerful little time! You just might get reminded of heaven on earth and start getting stoned on the Glory!

FELLOWSHIP AND COMMUNITY

I already mentioned how Holy Spirit likes to use the gift of other people as a way to awaken us to the whack. I also want to specifically include fellowship and community here, in a sense of being a part of an intentional group of believers that do heaven on earth life together. God is a long term community, also known as The Trinity! The nature of heaven is that of intimacy and being known in a group!

Many people are in a place where their heart has been closed off due to past hurts. Usually these were inflicted upon them by those close to them. This can cause many to shy away, and even miss out on the grace of Glory family. However, Holy Spirit loves to move through spiritual community and spiritual family to open the hearts of the hurting up to the love of God, to the high of heaven! There is a whack that can often just begin to overwhelm you in the midst of a group of close friends, or fellow believers. It is good to be aware of this, and to include it as an important part of your regular life practice. We'll talk more about this in the later chapters. It's one of the primary focuses of our life and ministry!

GOING ON MISSION OR EVANGELISM

There is something about engaging in activities with intention to spread the Good News of Jesus Christ. Even if you are just beginning to experience the fruit of this Gospel, it can be of great benefit to you to share it!

Don't do this in some religious or guilt driven way. No need to share the Gospel if it isn't yet making you overflow with life! However, no matter how long you've been a believer there is a river that you can feel flowing through you as you give it away. Go pray for someone! Share Jesus with someone with just a little bit of expectation in your heart and watch the bliss begin to increase. Get some training and practice in flowing in the spiritual gifts! Holy Spirit absolutely loves to explode in these kinds of endeavors!

LAYING ON OF HANDS

Holy Spirit will often use the hands of another person to awaken you. Again, many times this has become religious or formulaic, with people putting their faith in this activity rather than in Holy Ghost. This can make folks disappointed when it doesn't work like a charm. Yet, throughout scripture and church history we have also seen the laying on of hands be mightily used of God, when there's Glory on it.

I personally have been in atmospheres where someone laid hands on me, and I got mega-intoxicated. It's not even just the hands. It could be having any kind of point of contact. I've seen the laying on of feet! Sometimes even handkerchiefs from an anointed person can release Glory! I've even, at times, worn a jacket or sweatshirt that was carrying an energy from God that helped me realize the Glory! It's worth listening to Holy Ghost and being open to any of these kinds of ways! They all can be powerful. Sometimes when it seems the strangest thing to you, it is that very thing that God has packed with your great awakening!

LOVING AND BEING LOVED

This one should be obvious to all of us, still sometimes it gets overlooked. Loving your spouse, or kids, or friends, strangers, or even enemies can bring the most incredible awareness of heaven on earth! Or, visa-versa, let them love on you! The love of God is THE whack. What a privilege it is to have love flow through us! Anywhere that love is there is a tangible power to awaken hearts. This is true both in the giver and the receiver. Just a hug, a conversation, or an expression of compassion can be the very catalyst for someone to get hammered drunk forever on the Glory! May we never underestimate Love!

MENTORSHIP

Mentorship can be big for many people. It's amazing how few people take advantage of it. If you find someone who inspires you in the Glory, consider embracing the humility of allowing them to mentor you. God loves to work through His people. You don't need them as some kind of go-between between you and God. They can, however, speak powerful reality into your consciousness.

Remember, being high is all about realizing the Glory of what is. It's all about consciousness change unto the truth of heaven on earth in Christ. Having a mentor who is living these realities intentionally reminding you of them can really help. Don't become reliant upon them solely, but let them help. Don't demand of them to fix you, or to get you whacked, but see them as a stable pointer to who you truly are. I know it can often be hard to find a mentor. True fathers and mothers are rare at this point of history. Still, do not be discouraged! You always have Christ living inside of you. God in you is always more than enough. However, if you find someone who you think could be a good mentor, it's worth going lengths to team up with them!

MUSIC, PRAISE, AND WORSHIP

We briefly discussed music in the previous art section, but it is so dynamically connected with praise and worship that I wanted to include it here. Yes, praise and worship can be such powerful means that God uses to whack us up! Of course, as with any of these ways, it also can be misused. Unfortunately, there are vast movements of the body of Christ that have almost come to "worship the worship." Music is so powerful in touching our emotions that it can often be misunderstood as the whack itself, when all it was, was a good song!!

Don't be distracted, it's about communing with God in the music! However, yes, extended times of music, especially with a praise and worship focus, can so often be times where Holy Spirit opens our eyes to the Glory! Short little times of praise can be great too! Some have prescribed praise as the way to get into the Glory, because praise is so often used of God. Well, as we have already discussed, we are always in the Glory. Praise just often works so well engaging many parts of our being in declaring truth about God.

Praise is more for us than it is for God. God doesn't need people stroking His ego all day! God has us praise Him because it can help us to be aware of the goodness of Reality! Praise and worship sessions can also become really dry and lifeless when approached religiously or as a formula! Be led by desire in worship! You will find that filling your life with praise, worship, and even just plain old 'secular' music can be such a tool for awakening in the hand of God! There is a lot more that could be said, but you get the point!

NATURE

There is a lot of Glory on nature! Trees, mountains, oceans, rivers, animals, planets, and all creation speak of the Glory of the God who made it all with just a word! God in nature can definitely make you drunk! In fact, there are a whole host of mystics throughout the ages classified as "nature mystics" because of their regular communion with God in forests, on mountains, or in pure natural environments. So take a walk! Go and sit somewhere in natural beauty. You may be one of those that receive heavy intoxication while looking to God in natural beauty. This is not unusual. It is beautiful and powerful to ponder and experience all that God has made. You might just watch it respond to the glorious liberty that you have as a child of God (Rom. 8)!

PRAYER, MEDITATION, SPEAKING IN TONGUES

This is another common and obvious one. It could use some good new creation clarity though too. True prayer is simply moving with God's Spirit, or vibrating with God energetically. It is not about finding the right words or sitting in the right way or place. It's not about finding a way to get God to do what we want. Prayer is a broad term for the many ways of experiencing and communicating with God.

One way to pray is to meditate. Meditation is a re-minding of reality. It is intentionally or unintentionally giving attention to what is real. Speaking in tongues, at least in the prayer form, is another type of communing with the Holy Spirit. While using the gift of tongues, vibrations are coming through our vocal cords, tongue, lips, etc. in order to express prayers beyond rational thought, at purely the vibrational level. All types of prayer are connected and meant to flow freely back and forth and all together. This is a natural activity of a divine human, just like breathing. None of these guarantee awakening. However, engage in them in a fun and refreshing way regularly, and you will likely find awakening occurring within them. Much could be written about this, as with any of the ways listed in this chapter. Prayer is a deep experience, which can be as simple as saying a few words to God in our mind, or it can be as mysterious as feeling frequencies and vibrations of love flow through our entire being causing all sorts of mystical experiences.

PREACHING/TEACHING

There is nothing like a good Gospel message in my ears, oh my! It truly never gets old! Hearing of how God created us all to experience the bliss of communion in the person of Jesus Christ, preserved one with heaven forever? Yes, Lord!! The Bible does say that faith comes by hearing, and hearing by the word of Christ (Rom. 10:17). Again, this is not a formula. Yet, I do recommend a steady diet of hearing the Gospel taught in all its depth and richness.

Unfortunately, at the writing of this book there is not a superabundance of pure new covenant Gospel preachers out there in the world. You will know them by how they confirm with what I wrote earlier in this book (not to be proud, but I believe my Gospel!). They may have many different ways of preaching and teaching the message, but there is only one Gospel. You may want to hear more than one preaching or teaching per week at first especially, whether in person or by recording. This can be so helpful when done in a restful, non-striving way. I highly recommend it.

RECREATION & HOBBIES

This one will definitely scandalize the formulaic mindsets of many spiritual people. God loves to awaken us when we are just hanging out, having fun, or even while doing nothing! Just relaxing and sitting around can be such a sign of trust in the Holy Ghost! It also could just be laziness, which isn't what we're recommending, LOL! Still, many times when you are just sitting around, or going to the beach, or engaging in your favorite hobby or sport, it can be used of God. We were created for fun and enjoyment!

When we are just having fun or doing something we enjoy, we can often easily just slip over into an awareness of the heavenly life! It's not complicated! I recommend including a healthy amount of fun and games and shooting the breeze into your life! It will help you, quite likely, to stay whacked! It allows you to engage in the slow enjoyable pace of heaven. You can stop taking yourself and your efforts so seriously and just enjoy life. This has been used in so many people's lives that I couldn't even tell you. It's a big deal. Chill! Hang out around the house. Go play a game. Go to a movie. You might just find yourself awakening to a world of heaven on earth!

SERVING/GIVING

Jesus Christ is alive and well in everyone you meet! Serving people can often cause you to see God everywhere! "What you did for the least of these, you did unto me," Jesus said (Matt. 25:40). The love that you feel when you are genuinely there to help or bless someone else is the heart of heaven, isn't it? Many people have been awakened by Holy Spirit while they were washing the dishes, mowing the lawn, or distributing food to the needy. Just giving a friend a bed for a night or giving money to a person in need can be such a bliss! This is the nature and character of heaven. Holy Spirit so often moves to awaken the giver's heart in these kinds of endeavors. Go on a service trip or a mission project to help someone in need! God loves to show up powerfully on these trips and adventures! You truly can't out give God. Generosity is the nature of God! It's your nature too! Establishing a regular lifestyle of cheerful service and giving will feel natural to you. It's the heavenly norm. Not to mention, it will bless a ton of folks! It's a win-win!

STUDY

Learning and exploring are a part of your new nature too! We will be exploring forever in heaven on earth! It's also an amazing way to commune with God. For sure, some folks have become too much "in their heads". That does not mean that study should be thrown out altogether! In study you get to receive from others, even others from generations past, by reading of their discoveries in God. This can be an amazing way to expand your awareness by the Spirit. There have got to be things that we can receive from every generation before us, right?

You may want to study spiritual or theological subjects. However, you also can often encounter Holy Spirit while studying all kinds of subjects, of course! Check out some biology or space exploration, or linguistics or film-making or whatever! God can definitely meet you powerfully in the ecstasy of learning and discovery. We are not created to be fools. Get in there and see what God has for you in books and research. God has made a whole wide world! Holy Spirit has often released massive revelation of the Glory to the students, the scientists, and the humble learners.

This Glory is not about promoting ignorance or putting a ceiling on learning!

GO WITH THE HOGO FLOW

There are so many ways to encounter the Drink! So many ways that Holy Spirit loves to creatively use! In conclusion, as you begin to learn of heaven on earth, and awaken to the whack, as we've emphasized here throughout, it's really all about doing what you enjoy from your new creation heart. There is absolutely no benefit in religiously creating a formula of "spiritual activities." Your true self is perfect in the image and likeness of God, preserved perfect in Christ Jesus. I will write more about flowing spontaneously, being led by desire, in the later chapter, "Staying High". For now, just know and remember that it is a big deal, even when you are first getting high, to begin to trust Christ inside your desires and go with the flow from deep within. This is following the Holy Ghost!

None of these ways of Holy Spirit mentioned in this chapter are meant to replace a simple going with the flow. They are intended to be used as pump primers and beginning points! They are simply healthy activities that you will often find yourself doing naturally anyways, as a healthy child of God. Establishing these ways as a regular part of your life, combined with a deferring to the bubbling up of the Holy Ghost from your belly, will give such glorious opportunity for an awareness of the Glory to appear! Remember, the Holy Ghost is always here, utterly committed to getting you high on God! You don't have to sustain your own awakening! No matter where you are, or how stuck you may have felt. It is going to be ok! God is extravagantly good! Jesus is going to get you high!

CHAPTER 8
A HIGH FUTURE

By this point in the book you may be asking, "Where is this whole thing going?" I mean, what would the world be like if everyone was just wasted out of their minds? Asking questions regarding the ultimate result of any teaching is surely a wise thing to do. It is these very questions I'd like to address in this chapter! I want to present an extremely hopeful and positive picture of not only what could happen, but what I believe will happen. Actually, I already see it happening. I am supremely encouraged to watch as God inebriates the whole of planet earth on His Glory-love! As you continue to read with me, just have a big drink of Glory right now! You may very well need it to dare to believe the radical goodness of what God is doing on the planet!

ON EARTH AS IT IS IN HEAVEN

This may not be new to you at all if you have hung out in charismatic or radical spiritual circles in recent years. I am a wide-eyed optimist regarding heavenly life becoming normal for planet earth! I honestly believe that the normal day to day life of every person on the planet is going to be "on earth as it is in heaven!" Wow! Yes! This sounds way too good to be true for most people to believe. Still, may you suspend any jaded thoughts for just a little while and read what I am about to write in this chapter. I may not be able to convince you, but just maybe you will read something that will give you a little bit more hope. Maybe you will read something here that will start to click, opening your heart towards the possibilities of a greater future than you've ever dared to dream. I'm not saying that I have it all figured out, but based on the goodness of God, I'm willing to dream as positive and hopeful as I possibly can! Can we exaggerate God's goodness?

"On earth as it is in heaven?" What does that mean? Does that mean God ordering us all around like He orders around angels or something? Does that mean that we will all be playing golden harps on lily white clouds? Does that mean we will all become like robots that are unable to sin? People have many questions and misunderstandings when it comes to what heavenly life could be like. I don't pretend to have all of the answers. However, I do believe that some things are made clear through scripture or direct conclusions springing from scripture.

Firstly, the Bible says that the earth is the Lord's (Ps. 24:1). This may seem obvious, ha, and it is! But, have you considered the implications? The Lord has not lost the earth to sin, sickness, devils, destruction, or even unruly humanity. This planet is still God's domain. He created it with a dream and a vision for it! I don't believe He's giving up on it, ever! In fact he made promises to certain people groups about possessing portions of it for all eternity. God also included in the scripture, in the book of the Revelation, some interesting things about this.

One passage that has often been misunderstood is Revelation 21:1. It says, "Then I saw a new heaven and a new earth, for the first heaven and the first earth had passed away..." Now, this can seem to imply many different things. I have mentioned many times in my writing and teachings that Revelation 21 is an interesting chapter. It has several eerie similarities to 2 Corinthians 5 and Hebrews 8, both foundational new covenant scriptures. Almost all scholars agree that the new covenant era of history began with the death and resurrection of Jesus Christ. I am implying that it could be very likely that Revelation 21 was already accessible to humanity to live in from that time on. What if the new heaven and the new earth were just the very new creation that is spoken of in 2 Corinthians five? "Behold, all things have become new!"

Many have misunderstood the book of Revelation to be saying that God was going to destroy the whole world physically, and either re-create a new one, or just take us all off somewhere to heaven. However, what if the book of Revelation was just visionary language describing what God already accomplished in Jesus Christ's first coming, with maybe only a few exceptions? The full name of the book of Revelation is actually, "The Revelation of Jesus Christ!" What if it was simply a picture of the Jesus Christ that already came, being revealed to the planet, in what he had already accomplished?

Regardless of what you believe about the book of Revelation, I believe that we can live as much of heaven here on earth as we want. I don't think that God has given up on planet earth! We are not destined to perish or to wait for the planet to be destroyed. God loved the world, and sent Jesus to save it! I believe Jesus succeeded! These simple truths cause me to believe that the world is going to keep getting better and better. In fact, I believe the world was always preserved in an alternate dimension called, "in Christ," which is a lot more simple and less creepy than it sounds, LOL! I believe that humanity is simply waking up to the Christ dimension. This is the very same altered state of consciousness we tap into when we are intoxicated on the Glory. I believe that more and more people are going to get high on God, causing that new Jerusalem to descend through our consciousness and be clearly seen here on planet earth. It's already here, but in the future, every eye will see it! "Beloved, we are God's children now, and what we will be has not yet appeared (1 John 3:2)."

Jesus taught us to pray that it would be, "on earth as it is in heaven." I don't believe that He would have had us pray that, if it wasn't meant to be. Jesus taught us to pray the heart and purposes of God! So, since God has not given up on the earth, and his purpose was for heavenly life to be lived on earth, I believe this is what is happening! This is what is going to continue to happen! In fact, in Christ it has always been happening!

WHAT COULD HEAVEN ON EARTH LOOK LIKE?

So, what does it look like when heaven on earth becomes the reality in our experience? What will it be like specifically? What is happening to the planet? What can we eagerly expect!?!?

Let me start by saying that God has hinted at it throughout all of history! From the beginning God put us in a Garden of pleasure, and gave us the ability to easily care for and enjoy the earth. Yet, the level of heavenly experience that we can begin to live in now is far greater even than the Garden of Eden! Throughout the scripture God made promises and indicated many pictures of this kingdom of heaven on earth.

God promised to the Jews many things regarding literal heaven on earth life. In fact, they were expecting the coming Messiah to usher in a kingdom much like the one we are receiving. They just misunderstood it, not realizing that it had to start in the invisible realm first. They misunderstood that God wanted to bring the kingdom starting from the inside of humanity, THEN permeating through to the outside. The kingdom wasn't about to come by conquering and violence, but by love and inner transformation. Still, the promises of the Old Testament were talking about something. I believe they were ultimately talking about what God wanted to give to all peoples through the Gospel of Jesus Christ. Isaiah chapter sixty and sixty-one, and Zechariah chapter eight give us a couple of beautiful pictures that apply to where this whole thing is going! The true messianic kingdom flowing from the heart, from the inside out, transforming the planet to truly see heaven on earth!

Carefully read the following verses, especially the emphasized portions:

Isaiah 60:1-22 Arise, shine, for your light has come, and *the glory of the LORD has risen upon you.* (2) For behold, darkness shall cover the earth, and thick darkness the peoples; but the LORD will arise upon you, and his glory will be seen upon you. (3) And nations shall come to your light, and kings to the brightness of your rising. (4) Lift up your eyes all around, and see; they all gather together, they come to you; your sons shall come from afar, and your daughters shall be carried on the hip. (5) *Then you shall see and be radiant; your heart shall thrill and exult, because the abundance of the sea shall be turned to you, the wealth of the nations shall come to you.* (6) A multitude of camels shall cover you, the young camels of Midian and Ephah; all those from Sheba shall come. They shall bring gold and frankincense, and shall bring good news, the praises of the LORD. (7) All the flocks of Kedar shall be gathered to you; the rams of Nebaioth shall minister to you; they shall come up with acceptance on my altar, and I will beautify my beautiful house. (8) *Who are these that fly like a cloud, and like doves to their windows? (9) For the coastlands shall hope for me, the ships of Tarshish first, to bring your children from afar, their silver and gold with them, for the name of the LORD your God, and for the Holy One of Israel, because he has made you beautiful.* (10) Foreigners shall build up your walls, and their kings shall minister to you; for in my wrath I struck you, but in my favor I have had mercy on you. (11) Your gates shall be open continually; day and night they shall not be shut, that people may bring to you the wealth of the nations, with their kings led in procession. (12) For the nation and kingdom that will not serve you shall perish; those nations shall be utterly laid waste. (13) The glory of Lebanon shall come to you, the cypress, the plane, and the pine, to beautify the place of my sanctuary, and I will make the place of my feet glorious. (14) The sons of those who afflicted you shall come bending low to you, and all who despised you shall bow down at your feet; they shall call you the City of the LORD, the Zion of the Holy One of Israel. (15) *Whereas you have been forsaken and hated, with no one passing through, I will make you majestic forever, a joy from age to age.* (16) You shall suck the milk of nations; you shall nurse at the breast of kings; and you shall know that I, the LORD, am your Savior and your Redeemer, the Mighty One of Jacob. (17) *Instead of bronze I will bring gold, and instead of iron I will bring silver; instead of wood, bronze, instead of stones, iron. I will make your overseers peace and your taskmasters righteousness. (18) Violence shall no more be heard in your land, devastation or destruction within your borders; you shall call your walls Salvation, and your gates Praise.* (19) The sun shall be no more your light by day, nor for brightness shall the moon give you light; but the LORD will be your everlasting light, and your God will be your glory. (20) Your sun shall no more go down, nor your moon withdraw itself; for the LORD will be your everlasting light, and your days of mourning shall be ended. (21) *Your people shall all be righteous; they shall possess the land forever, the branch of my planting, the work of my hands, that I might be glorified. (22) The least one shall become a clan, and the smallest one a mighty nation; I am the LORD; in its time I will hasten it.*(ESV)

Isaiah 61:1-11 The Spirit of the Lord GOD is upon me, because the LORD has anointed me to bring good news to the poor; he has sent me to bind up the brokenhearted, to proclaim liberty to the captives, and the opening of the prison to those who are bound; (2) to proclaim the year of the LORD's favor, and the day of vengeance of our God; to comfort all who mourn; (3) to grant to those who mourn in Zion— to give them a beautiful headdress instead of ashes, the oil of gladness instead of mourning, the garment of praise instead of a faint spirit; that they may be called oaks of righteousness, the planting of the LORD, that he may be glorified. (4) *They shall build up the ancient ruins; they shall raise up the former devastations; they shall repair the ruined cities, the devastations of many generations. (5) Strangers shall stand and tend your flocks; foreigners shall be your plowmen and vinedressers; (6) but you shall be called the priests of the LORD; they shall speak of you as the ministers of our God; you shall eat the wealth of the nations, and in their glory you shall boast. (7) Instead of your shame there shall be a double portion; instead of dishonor they shall rejoice in their lot; therefore in their land they shall possess a double portion; they shall have everlasting joy.* (8) For I the LORD love justice; I hate robbery and wrong; I will faithfully give them their recompense, and I will make an everlasting covenant with them. (9) Their offspring shall be known among the nations, and their descendants in the midst of the peoples; all who see them shall acknowledge them, that they are an offspring the LORD has blessed. (10) *I will greatly rejoice in the LORD; my soul shall exult in my God, for he has clothed me with the garments of salvation; he has covered me with the robe of righteousness, as a bridegroom decks himself like a priest with a beautiful headdress, and as a bride adorns herself with her jewels. (11) For as the earth brings forth its sprouts, and as a garden causes what is sown in it to sprout up, so the Lord GOD will cause righteousness and praise to sprout up before all the nations.*(ESV)

Zechariah 8:1-12 And the word of the LORD of hosts came, saying, (2) "Thus says the LORD of hosts: I am jealous for Zion with great jealousy, and I am jealous for her with great wrath. (3) Thus says the LORD: *I have returned to Zion and will dwell in the midst of Jerusalem, and Jerusalem shall be called the faithful city, and the mountain of the LORD of hosts, the holy mountain. (4) Thus says the LORD of hosts: Old men and old women shall again sit in the streets of Jerusalem, each with staff in hand because of great age. (5) And the streets of the city shall be full of boys and girls playing in its streets.* (6) Thus says the LORD of hosts: If it is marvelous in the sight of the remnant of this people in those days, should it also be marvelous in my sight, declares the LORD of hosts? (7) Thus says the LORD of hosts: *Behold, I will save my people from the east country and from the west country, (8) and I will bring them to dwell in the midst of Jerusalem. And they shall be my people, and I will be their God, in faithfulness and in righteousness."* (9) Thus says the LORD of hosts: "Let your hands be strong, you who in these days have been hearing these words from the mouth of the prophets who were present on the day that the foundation of the house of the LORD of hosts was laid, that the temple might be built. (10) For before those days there was no wage for man or any wage for beast, neither was there any safety from the foe for him who went out or came in, for I set every man against his neighbor. (11) But now I will not deal with the remnant of this people as in the former days, declares the LORD of hosts. (12) *For there shall be a sowing of peace. The vine shall give its fruit, and the ground shall give its produce, and the heavens shall give their dew. And I will cause the remnant of this people to possess all these things.*(ESV)

The book of Revelation also gives a beautiful picture of what I believe God wants us to expect for the immediate future! If you look closely you can see the high of God, the changing our consciousness, and the enabling of us to be the releasers of this kind of heaven on earth reality! Meditatively read these passages from the book of Revelation, especially the emphasized portions:

Revelation 21:1-6 Then I saw a new heaven and a new earth, for the first heaven and the first earth had passed away, and the sea was no more. (2) And I saw the holy city, new Jerusalem, coming down out of heaven from God, prepared as a bride adorned for her husband. (3) And I heard a loud voice from the throne saying, *"Behold, the dwelling place of God is with man. He will dwell with them, and they will be his people, and God himself will be with them as their God. (4) He will wipe away every tear from their eyes, and death shall be no more, neither shall there be mourning, nor crying, nor pain anymore, for the former things have passed away." (5) And he who was seated on the throne said, "Behold, I am making all things new."* Also he said, "Write this down, for these words are trustworthy and true." (6) And he said to me, *"It is done! I am the Alpha and the Omega, the beginning and the end. To the thirsty I will give from the spring of the water of life without payment.*(ESV)

Revelation 22:1-5 Then the angel showed me the river of the water of life, bright as crystal, flowing from the throne of God and of the Lamb (2) through the middle of the street of the city; *also, on either side of the river, the tree of life with its twelve kinds of fruit, yielding its fruit each month. The leaves of the tree were for the healing of the nations. (3) No longer will there be anything accursed, but the throne of God and of the Lamb will be in it, and his servants will worship him. (4) They will see his face, and his name will be on their foreheads. (5) And night will be no more. They will need no light of lamp or sun, for the Lord God will be their light, and they will reign forever and ever.*(ESV)

Now, those scriptures may be difficult to understand. So it goes with so many of the prophetic writings of the Bible. So much of it is spiritually applied, ultimately pointing to the life, death, and resurrection of Jesus Christ. However, it is all also describing literal promises of God, fulfilled in Christ, transforming the human experience on planet earth to something absolutely heavenly. In my study and communion with the Holy Ghost, I have seen specific manifestations already that are about to be revealed. Let me describe them as best I can, to give an even clearer more specific picture.

SOME DESCRIPTIONS OF THE GLORIOUS DESTINY OF HUMANITY

I do honestly believe that in time and space, God wants to completely reveal a humanity living in heaven on earth! This means we are going to all be able to commune easily with the invisible realm, angels, vibrations, creatures of other dimensions, and most of all God: Father, Son, and Holy Spirit! This means the world is about to see the best art and music, food, drink, and architecture, all of the arts will flourish in new and unforeseen ways! Heaven will literally manifest here!

We will have absolutely healthy functional families! Husbands and wives in glorious long term love and intimacy, children and parents loving and being loved, all this will be normal worldwide! Wars will cease. Violence will cease. Crime will cease. Authority figures will not use manipulation or control to motivate anyone to live their way. We will care for our bodies and land. Aging will cease. There will be worldwide unity, respect, harmony, honor, and peace.

The book of Romans chapter eight speaks of "the creation itself being set free from its bondage to corruption and obtaining the freedom of the glory of the children of God." (Rom. 8:21) I believe that this means that as we realize who we are, through the altered states of Holy Spirit perspective in our life, we will see all creation restored. This means crops growing much bigger and healthier, businesses prospering in incredible ways, schools functioning exponentially better, and all kinds of nature healing and being restored to greater Glory. You could dream with God for a very long time about all the changes that will happen when the creation realizes the liberation! God can show you this even now in Christ. It has already been liberated in Christ. As we realize this, it will visibly manifest in the rest of the created order!

Now, some people have misunderstood the high of God to mean that we won't be able to work, either because it won't be necessary, or because we will be too high. In one sense that may be true! However, I think that we will continue to be very industrious and active, though it surely will look differently. We won't work as if there is a curse upon us. We won't have to be stressed out, worried, struggling, or fighting with creation to succeed. Success in creative endeavors will come so much more easily. I believe occupation will exist as art and enjoyment. We were created to create!

When you are doing what you love, work is not "work." Work becomes creating with God. Serving and blessing others through industry and occupation can be as whacked as anything! I don't think that this will cease. As for being too high to work, yes, sometimes it is necessary to just lie down on the floor while enjoying God! You can get immobilized in ecstasy becoming in many ways incapacitated. On the other hand, the high of God is empowering too. If you are co-creating and working with Holy Spirit I believe that you can be all the more successful at your job. You do not need to become irresponsible in this high. No, this high is not like the high of the world causing lives to be ruined in irresponsibility. This high is empowering. It is the God high. It is an awareness that we have the nature and character of God. We are humble, loving, kind, helpful, powerful, skilled, and knowledgeable in Christ! This is the Christ high. We can succeed in our work, albeit in a more peaceful, relaxed, and stress-free way! We will build cities, and forest get-a-ways, and boats, and aircraft, and all kinds of amazing things. The future is filled with joyous endeavors, and even doing the menial tasks of every day, but with bliss, experiencing God in it all.

Now, why am I including this section on the glorious future of humanity here? It's obviously meant to be an encouraging thing! However, it is also dynamically connected to the subject of this book. For many of us, before we will allow ourselves to get all jacked up in the Glory, we need to know where it might lead! Also, it may be important for many of you to keep you from getting to a place where you begin to feel irresponsible for living your life just for being high. Yes, seeing the big picture can help in many ways. It helps to see that the high of God, while being

God's unconditional gift to you, it is also the very state of consciousness that manifests the kingdom of heaven on earth. It is releasing something powerful and surpassingly productive!

The consciousness of humanity is a powerful thing. By it we have formed worlds. We have formed the world that most people are used to, the one filled with sickness, suffering, sin, death, and decay. This stemmed from the tree of the knowledge of good and evil, which represented a consciousness of separation and independence from God. This consciousness was the root of all the non-heavenly things in this world. So, we needed to get back to the original consciousness. The original consciousness was of God, a God consciousness. Getting high on God is this original consciousness. It is an altered state whereby we co-create our world together with God. God's heavenly world flows from this God consciousness. So, getting high on God is the very thing that ushers in the new world! Jesus Christ already fully restored this new world. Realizing that makes you high, and brings that new world into manifestation or revelation. So, it's all so dynamically connected!

Do not underestimate being high on God. It is the normal state of the new world! You will effortlessly manifest heaven on earth everywhere you go while in this state. Without this state, you will effortlessly manifest some lower fallen world. The fall was in our consciousness! Jesus came to reveal and restore God's original heaven on earth reality! The restoration happens in our realm of experience as we become conscious of all that has always been true in Jesus Christ! Getting high on Jesus practically transforms the world!

Now, this doesn't have to sound super spiritual or weird. It's as simple as knowing that being aware of God brings you exceeding joy and also benefits your neighbor! This is a spiritual awareness, not just believing the right information. Our spirit is a normal part of us, and when we are rightly aware of Christ within, we can watch as the world begins to work rightly all around and among us. It's amazing! It's what we were created for! Depression doesn't exist in God's kingdom! True sobriety exists, which Biblically means "to have heaven's perspective." True sobriety means to be high on God. True sobriety, which is a Love drunk consciousness, makes earth aware as it is in heaven.

Your being high is the very catalyst by which this glorious new world is going to spring forth. I honestly see a domino effect of people getting high on God through Christ by the power of the Holy Spirit, all around the world! One by one, from the inside out, being inspired by each other, we are going to literally see the planet awaken more and more to heaven in everyday experience, until the full second coming of Jesus Christ. But, when He returns in a physical body, he may just already be fully present in all of our physical bodies as well!! This is where I see the whole thing going! Sound crazy? Well, before you relegate me to the heretic category, at least pray about it, meditate on the previously mentioned scriptures, and give it a good consideration. You don't have to agree with me! But, I think it's all going the direction of a completely high and unified humanity living in heaven on earth forever! Now that is jacked up, in the absolute best way!!!

CHAPTER 9
MORE HIGH STORIES

People love stories! We are addicted to hearing the news, watching movies, reading new novels, etc. One reason is because theoretical talk can be cheap. Seeing something actually play out in a life makes it much more real, more imaginable. So, I'm guessing that many readers will be most interested to hear more about this God high life from some stories! What has it been like? What can it be like? What have we experienced? Is it practical? Can it be dangerous? Let's tell some more stories! Some of these are mine directly and others are from friends we know in the whack.

For the sake of my blurry memory, just kidding (mostly), I'll start with stories from when I first got high, then I'll move forward from there.

HAPPY HAPPY FUN TIME

Actually, before I even felt the whack of God's weighty Presence, I had some bliss stories. I remember this particular story as a great encouragement of how the Glory unites. We saw a whole group experience genuine child-like innocence and heart felt celebration! Remember how I told you that my wife began to be intoxicated on God before I was? Yeah, well, we were at the house of some close friends of ours where we would gather to play music and pray and fellowship. I remember it was towards the end of the gathering, and some people had already gone home. We would often linger on and fellowship into the night, just shooting the breeze. That particular night though, as we were just hanging out in the kitchen of the house, something began to happen.

The Glory of God was obviously spontaneously moving in our midst. One person began laughing, and others smiling, and then another, and another just seemed overjoyed by God's Presence. I wasn't even really into it, but it seemed so genuine and sweet spirited, I went along with the group anyways. People began to get up and dance! Then they began dancing around the room, in a circle. Then we all just began to run from room to room through the house! We were running and dancing around the whole house, laughing and smiling like little kids. Even those who had previously been discouraged began to smile. Then, even the quietest persons there began to laugh, and dance, all around the house. It would have been so impossible to try to organize this. It was so silly that most adults would never have participated! But, that night, it just felt so right, and everyone was so genuinely overjoyed, just having innocent fun. Again, like I said, I had never done anything like this before, at least not as an adult! We just danced and laughed and ran through the house.

We ended up laughing and joking about it later, calling it, 'happy happy fun time.' "Remember when we had, 'happy happy fun time?'", we'd say for weeks later, kind of almost embarrassed, but not really. It was such a beautiful and spontaneous night, and even as a "non-Glory drinker" at the time, I joined in and enjoyed it.

The Glory obviously can work on us at such a level and feel so natural that sometimes people get high and do things they normally wouldn't. Usually these are things that they've always wanted to do but couldn't until that self-consciousness disappears. It was a beautiful time! Anyone who has ever tried to lead people in a spontaneous group dance, or a time of celebration, without the use of drugs and alcohol, could tell you it can be quite the challenge! Getting past self-consciousness and into a child-like innocent state of mind is very difficult for most adults! All that to say…I loved 'happy happy fun time!' I loved it so much that it got a hold of me! A few months later, both, my wife, Katie, and I had become supremely intoxicated on God as a regular part of our daily lives.

Katie and I have also had a fellowship community that we've been a part of since 2005. You heard about our personal transformation away from striving and struggling to get God to invade our own lives, and into heaven on earth experience. Well, it definitely affected our church community as well! When we got hammered, at first we kind of hid it away from even our closest friends in the community. We would gather only occasionally with a few and secretly to get drunk on God with those who were ready. (It can be really hard to explain to folks at first.) Still, after a while the whack began to take over our whole group. It was a really special and delicate time. We did lose a few community members, but the majority remained through the transition! It wasn't long until love piles and group child-like euphoria became a normal occurrence in our precious fellowship community.

Now we quite often find our whole gathering caught up in the euphoria of the "happy happy fun time." It can be pretty unusual for new folks, but many people aren't as freaked out as you might expect. I believe everyone wants child-like freedom and expression. It may be shocking at first, but people can warm up to it fast when it's presented by someone they trust. This isn't to say that we haven't had some people be super critical of our style of gathering, and they have their reasons, I guess. But, overall, I have just sensed that a beautiful, innocent intimacy has been expressed in these times. The depth of community seems so strengthened, despite the number of folks that have been freaked out in one way or another.

Some of us have felt so close together that we have moved in together, sharing lives on a daily basis, and sometimes even getting Glory drunk together daily! I know that this can sound totally foreign to the ears of someone who hasn't experienced it. We are not a hippy sex cult, or a group of new age communists. We're not talking about that at all! (You might be surprised at the accusations we've had!) The genuine community that has formed has honestly been such a way to get past formalities, a way to live with vibrant emotions, a way of letting walls down. It's definitely been healing and consciousness expanding for me! Now it just seems like normal for a heavenly life! It also makes for parties that are way crazier than you might experience almost anywhere! We've gotten so high that you really don't give a rip what people are thinking anymore. You just dive on the floor and start rolling and shaking with all your closest friends! Hahahahhaahhahahah! I can understand why it seems crazy to so many people at first.

I know I said I was going to try to share the stories in order, but that last story just got me so whacked up, I just have to go with the flow, if you know what I mean, LOL! I'm sure I'm breaking the rules of writing all over the place in this book, oh Jesus help me!

SUPERNATURAL WHACK HAPPENINGS

Anywho, so the good ol' drunken Glory is also like the doorway to the supernatural, aka the mystic realm. Jesus is actual doorway to all of God, to be clear, and when you first experience Jesus, the real person, you get supremely high on the Glory. That's how Jesus enabled us to move in the holy supernatural!

So, here's a story or two of some of our supernatural whack happenings. One time we were so whacked up in northern Georgia, with a few friends of mine who had just come from a Glory conference. We had been staying in a hotel, but were packing up to leave. It had been an amazing few days, and we were all pretty high on Jesus Christ. My good friend, Brad had pulled into the gas station next to the hotel to fill up before we were about to head out. The rest of our group was still packing up and grabbing some breakfast from the front lobby. While Brad was pumping his gas a gentlemen approached and asked him for some money. He mentioned that he was homeless and strapped for cash. He also seemed a little beat up, with several cuts on his face. Little did he know who he was approaching and what was about to happen!

Brad told the man that we would give him money and asked if we could pray for him back at the hotel. The man agreed and they walked over to the hotel, which was right next door. Brad gathered our group in one room and we began to pray for the man. The Presence of God was so strong that it literally knocked the man over, and he went out like a light. When he came to, like a minute later, he stood up and began to speak in tongues, a new heavenly prayer language. He was filled with joy, and said he felt high. We told him it was the Glory of God, a free gift of Jesus Christ. His face lit up, and he began to tell us that he had planned to commit suicide that day. Just then, we also noticed that the cuts on his face had healed. They were nearly gone altogether, a very noticeable difference. The man told us that he had gotten into a fight in a drug deal the day before but now his damaged face felt so much better! He said he felt refreshed and ready to live again. He literally looked like a new man! We gave him some clothes and money, and dropped him off at a local recovery center on our way back north to Indiana. Literally, the man was glowing, a life transformed by the whack!

Later that day, as we were still driving towards Indiana I got struck completely mute. I honestly was so overcome by the Glory of God that I couldn't speak, literally for like 6 hours. We even made a stop at a friend's house, a friend of one of the people in our group, a person I had never met. I remember feeling kind of awkward because I couldn't introduce myself to these new friends. Thankfully, they were spiritual people who were gracious enough to not be offended. I just sat there through the whole interaction at their house, mute as a board. I was as silent as a kid in the principal's office, just kidding, but, well, actually I was totally and absolutely unable to speak. I was in such an ecstasy feeling the Glory of God rocking my body with pleasure and revelation of the goodness of life. It is something I will never forget.

WILD CASES OF WHACK

There have been a number of wild cases of friends I have known who were so whacked in the Glory that they have literally needed to be carried from place to place, completely immobilized. Some friends have needed wheelchairs in order to get around. One guy had a doctor verify that he was experiencing "ligature," and gave him a doctor's note in case the inebriation came on too strong while in airports, or in public places. This way medical staff would know what was going on, and he could receive help if needed. No, literally, it has gotten that intense! I have one friend who regularly splits his pants from vibrating on the floor from the Glory. There is another friend who has a handicap helmet he wears on occasion when he knows he's going to get so drunk that he may fall at any time.

I just have to include the story of our good friend who was taken away in an ambulance from one of the Glory conferences. What!??! Yeah, well apparently this friend of ours was so inebriated during a Gospel preaching session, that he excused himself from the meeting, so as to not become a major distraction. The meeting was being held in a larger conference type facility. As our friend went into the hallway the Presence of God only increased. He wandered down the hallway, and ended up in another room, which also happened to be a Jesus related gathering. Our friend was known to no one there, and he became even louder and more boisterous than in the previous meeting room where he had started. He then somehow ended up at the front of the room hugging the person who was speaking at the meeting. This was an obvious disruption, and our friend was removed from the room and the conference center altogether. Someone had even called the police, who approached our friend, and became convinced that he was on drugs. They had him placed in an ambulance where he began to sing songs to all of the medical staff and police involved. He began to sings songs of God's love, and if I remember the story correctly, he was singing old hymns too. The staff actually seemed to like it, and had some fun driving him all the way to the hospital. He was given medicine that is supposed to sober up a drugged out person, but it didn't work on him! Surprise, surprise! Eventually he was told that he was not being held in the hospital, and he checked himself out, end of story.

Now, my point there is not to say that this is the goal, or even what should or shouldn't have happened in this situation. I've gotten to a place where I'd much rather promote not disturbing the peace most of the time, and respecting the environments where we are guests. Still, I do want people to know how high you can get on God. You can literally get so high on the Glory that people want to haul you off in a paddy wagon! My point is that this is no mere, "Oh, I'm sure feeling high on Jesus, brother" high. It's not the little goosebumps you feel when you hear an inspirational song. There's nothing wrong with that. But, this is not that. To quote the words of another dear friend, "Being high on God makes LSD look like decaf coffee!"

TELEPORTATIONS, STIGGIES, AND LEVITATIONS

We've had crazy stuff happen in the whack. I was once driving with a friend to minister at a Glory meeting in Indianapolis, and our car literally moved from one place to another supernaturally. We were over an hour late to the meeting, traveling from Fort Wayne to Indianapolis.

We had lost track of time, and were really quite hammered on God. We figured that we might as well try to get to the meeting anyway. We'd just be late. We put on some Rodney Howard Browne music in the van as we traveled. The Glory was quite tangible. All of a sudden I noticed that we were near Anderson, Indiana, but we had never passed the exits for Muncie. Also, all of a sudden our GPS time was set to arrive right on time! We didn't see anything like a Star Trek special effect or anything, we were just all of a sudden aware that we were way farther down the road than we'd expected, and on time. Needless to say we had a powerful meeting that night, and saw some lives genuinely touched by God. We've had a number of friends move from city to city supernaturally in the whack. Phillip did it in the book of Acts, by the way, but that's another story.

One time after another drunken Glory meeting one of our friends approached me showing me her hands. She was asking me about two bleeding spots that had appeared. Now, this one freaks a lot of people out, but it's true. Again, I only share it to make people aware of how wild this whack is! My friend was experiencing the stigmata. No, she wasn't experiencing the 1999 film by Rupert Wainwright. She had literal wounds appearing on her hands. This has happened several times throughout history, usually by Catholics. You can look it up on Google. It's called the stigmata. The stigmata are the wounds of Christ appearing on various parts of a person's body as a visible reminder of the crucifixion of Jesus of Nazareth. It was reported as having happened to St. Francis of Assisi as well.

I also know of at least three friends who have even began to physically float up off of the ground in ecstasy. Usually while they were worshiping Jesus in a passionate way, the joy of the Lord would hit them so strong, and they would lift off. I have never seen this one with my own eyes, but

I trust the testimony of these credible friends. Talk about being on cloud nine! Such overwhelming bliss can occur! Our friends have floated!

NOT JUST A FREAK SHOW

Now, in case you think that this ecstatic joy is being portrayed as just a freak show, let me tell you some of the deeper relational stories. There is so much more I have experienced beyond just supernatural travel or stiggies (a fun little nickname for the stigmata).
My wife, Katie and I experience such an amazing freedom in our marriage because of the whack! Yes, it actually is a blessing to family life! Any real spirituality must be a blessing to the family! It truly has encouraged us so much in openness and forgiveness. We literally almost never fight, ever. And, if we do, it is so easy to forgive. This may sound basic, but try talking to a few marriage counselors! Forgiveness and getting past fighting is usually no easy thing! Hahhahaha!

Because we have felt so satisfied and blissed out, it's just been so easy to let things go. The things that used to bother me so much, as a former perfectionist and legalist, I am now able to get past. I'm not looking for her to 'make me happy." I'm already happy. So, now that overflows to her! She feels positive energy coming from me, and I from her. We weren't big fighters before. Still, now, it's pretty hard to get us frustrated over anything at all. And, if there is something that is worth getting upset over (because circumstances in life definitely can still be challenging or down right bad), we don't blame each other or feel the need to punish one another. The bliss enables us to see one another with the love-drunk eyes of God! God feels so much genuine pride and love for each of His kids. Its super healing! We have literally been able to consistently feel this for each other. That can make for a pretty decent marriage. Hammered drunk on seeing each other as God sees us!

That reminds me of a more recent story of miracle love and forgiveness. The bliss can just make you so forgiving. You can stop being insecure, and dramatic about protecting yourself or your image! You are just too happy with life to care about petty stuff! One of our friends recently called me out on a public broadcast as if I was supporting demons and teaching demonic doctrine! Hahaahha! In some spiritual circles that would be enough to never talk with that person again. It's amazing how much division could be caused by something like that. No credit to my abilities, I was so jacked up on the love of God that I just laughed when I heard the broadcast. When I saw my friend next, we had the privilege of lovingly talking through the whole thing. We easily came to peace. I had a hard time not seeing him as he is in Christ, and being in love with him. I honestly, didn't care that he had publicly rebuked me without having talked to me about the issue in person before. I was too in love! This joy is a deep satisfaction that comes only from communion with the Presence of the One who created us to be ravished by Love. The whack works!

Hopefully, by now you aren't quite as concerned about the drunkenness of God being merely some kind of shallow freak show. I promise you, it's all about love and real relationship. It bears good fruit. That being said, maybe you'll allow me to tell some more stories that are kind of wild and wonderful.

DRUNKEN EXPERIMENTS

Some other amazing testimonies come from times when we've just been so drunk that we start playing around with the supernatural. One time when we were traveling in California we began to supernaturally stick objects to walls. These objects would just stay on the wall with no explanation. We stuck pennies, then quarters, and even got spoons and bigger items to stick to the wall without glue or any natural substance, LOL! We kept doing that for years afterward! Our house once had about 50 coins just randomly all over the walls. Our friend even stuck a spoon to a window once! Weird, stuff, I know, and not that important, maybe. But, it sure is fun!

That same night in California when we were sticking coins to the wall, we also grew my friend. Yeah, we actually just got drunk and commanded his legs to grow. He got taller. He was tall already, he didn't even need the miracle, but he grew! God is so fun that He'll let us just play with the supernatural in His Glory!

BUZZ EVANGELISM

Being drunk in the Spirit has also revitalized my street evangelism life. Evangelism was always such work before! I could do it, but I was always either intimidated or exhausted by it. I rarely saw miracles. Now, I really only do drunken evangelism. I mean, the drunk guy usually gets the phone number at the bar, right? Hahahaha, well, sometimes. Anyway, I do have a video or two online somewhere of some of these buzz evangelism encounters. It's just fun now. And, I usually only do it when I feel joy and whack on it. I mean, why share good news with someone, if they aren't going to see you feeling good about it??!!?

Several times during whacked up evangelism I've seen legs get healed. I've even seen deaf ears pop open! Miracles on the street that I never had the boldness to pray for before, I now have confidence to just go for it. It's amazing what can happen when you're buzzing with God's Glory. You feel empowered with the blind faith of a drunken stupor, too inebriated to overthink it! This is actually a big deal for most humans!

We've also on several occasions walked up to folks and asked them if they wanted a free buzz. In Nepal our team shocked a man so powerfully with the power of God that he jumped back, and was honestly a bit terrified. Yet, he got to hear the Gospel and was smiling and receptive in the end.

This happened in a local bar one night as well. I was just hanging out with some friends, listening to a great band. A lonely looking guy walked up to our table and began talking with us. He shared that he had deep anxiety and it was giving him a lot of trouble sleeping. I told him that we were healers and that this was perfect timing. He was open to us but must not have thought anything would actually happen. We prayed for him, and he said he felt the anxiety leave. Then, I asked him if he wanted to get high on God. He kind of seemed weirded out. Then, I asked him to stick his hands out. He did for just a second, and felt something go through his body. He jumped back, kind of stunned. He was like, "What kind of healers are you people?" We talked to him about Jesus and got to share the good news! Honestly, I've seen that kind of thing more times than I can remember.

One of my favorite stories of whack evangelism I just heard recently from a friend in Texas. He and his friends put together a God rave. It wasn't meant to be a religious event, they were just going to play electronic music with a few decent DJs. They were going to get people high on God if people wanted it. The flier they were handing out made it clear that, "No drugs will be necessary." I love that! So my friend was there, dressed as a giant banana. He was having the time of his life. Then some young people came up to him and said, "Hey, man, do you have any party favors?" He told them, "Yeah, I've got lots of party favors! Come over to the side room and I'll give you some." They were looking for drugs, but instead he put his juicy hands on them and they were instantly high. They weren't interested in Jesus at that time, but they will never think of Jesus the same way! Those young people experienced a high that they will never forget!

That reminds me of another story! My wife, Katie, and I love jam bands and electronic music as well. So, we try to go at least once or twice a year to a music festival. Well, last year we were at a festival, seeing one of our favorite bands, a band that has very spiritual music in general. The experience was really amazing, and we felt the Glory of God exploding all over our blanket at this outdoor venue. At the edge of our blanket a girl we'd never met just began to cry tears of joy. My wife went over to her and they just laughed and cried and stared into each other's eyes for like an hour or so! It was wild. The girl was experiencing the Glory of God and didn't even know what it was. My wife got to share with her the Gospel. Then she gave Katie a little context to what was happening to them both. The girl explained to Katie how she had just the day before almost gotten arrested for possession of the street drug ecstasy, but the police officer had let her go for no reason. That day the girl realized she never needed to use drugs again, because she knew how to get high on God! Her life was changed forever!

Honestly, evangelism and all kinds of ministry become absolutely effortless in the Glory of God. Honestly, all of life can become that easy! We were made to be possessed and carried by the Presence of God, even greater than the Garden of Eden! I have seen so much more happen in the last few years since being whacked, way more than I ever could have planned. God loves to keep us as dependent passive instruments, taking us along for the ride of Glory, letting us do stuff just for fun!

One time in California, we were spending a week in a hotel in Redding, on a Glory pilgrimage. My buddies and I were pretty wasted on Jesus Christ every day that we were there. One night a man knocked on our hotel door, and asked if we were the ones partying so loud the previous night. He also asked if we had knocked on his door the night before. Apparently, someone had knocked on his door and told him if he wanted some good drugs to go to our room. The thing was, no one we knew of had knocked on any doors! Plus, we had not been in our room the night before until very late, and went right to bed when we arrived. There was no way that he could have heard anything from us! Still, there he was knocking on our door asking for drugs.

We invited him in and chatted it up for a little while. We talked about life and made some casual conversation. Every now and then he would hint that he was ready for some good marijuana or really probably almost any other kind of drug. Eventually we were like, dude, "We are high on Jesus Christ!" Then, my friend just began to pray for him, and he got really high! He was so excited that after another hour or so of drinking Glory with us, he ran out of the room thanking us and saying, "You guys make me want to wake up in the morning and live!" Again, in that story, we did nothing at all, literally. The man somehow came right into our room, as if sent by God Himself! The realm of Glory is effortless. This realm is everywhere. You never have to work for God again!

More recently our team was ministering in Austin, Texas and we saw another effortless drunken evangelistic exploit! There are so many stories, I am sure I'm forgetting some of them. Glory to God! But, yeah, the team was just going to get some food at a local restaurant, when they stepped out of the van. The first guy near the van when they got out was asking for some money. He seemed to be pretty down and out. They told him that they had some good news for him! They told him that God had caused their paths to cross that day. And, after sharing the Gospel with him, they prayed for him. He got hammered drunk, fell to the ground, and got up speaking in tongues! The dude's entire countenance changed. Similar to the guy we met in Georgia, this man also told them that he was contemplating suicide that day. His wife had left him, and he was asking God for a sign if he was supposed to live. Needless to say, he got his sign! The dude's life was impacted forever, and all our team was doing was going for some food! Reminded me of the Bible in Acts chapter two, where it said that God was adding to the number daily of those who were being saved!

I've had some real drunken fun in the nation of Nepal as well over the years. Nepal is the highest nation on earth, geographically. Seven of the world's ten highest mountains are in Nepal. I've done mission trips to Nepal since way before I realized heaven's intoxication of earth. In that nation, though, the last few years, I've had some glorious times taking intoxicated teams to love on orphans and pray for the sick. We've also done large healing meetings, preaching the good news of Jesus Christ to thousands of people. In the first joy crusade we did, there were several thousand folks present. The effortless ministry sure was flowing that day! We saw a blind man begin to fully see, a couple of paralyzed people begin to walk, and so many other miraculous healings happened that we couldn't even keep track of them all! The amazing thing was, we only preached for like thirty minutes, and prayed for the sick for about five minutes! Then all those testimonies came flying in! At that meeting the whack was so strong there was even a man brought to us in an ambulance, but before we could pray the ambulance drove away. The man had gotten healed as we did our thirty minute preach. We never even cracked the ambulance doors to see the man or his condition. The local people told us later that the hospital had turned him away saying he was beyond medical help. They brought him to the meeting as a last resort, in need of a miracle. Apparently God did it! They drove away before we could even pray. That was easy! Thank you Jesus for your love!!

KAMIKAZE GIVING

Now, since we're talking about Nepal, let's tell a few stories about generosity in the whack! We've seen so many generous people help us to minister in Nepal, it's been amazing. But, did you know that I even sold my family car to give the money to help the poor of Nepal. Now, do I share that to impress you with me? No, I couldn't care less, honestly. I do want you to know how drunk you can be to not even care if you have a car, you'd rather give your money to help others. Now, believe me, I have no problem with keeping money for myself and my family as well. However, in this intoxication there is just a generosity that comes over you. It's what a friend of ours calls 'kamikaze giving'! Hahahhahah! You just get an awareness of your royal heavenly wealth, and you give! We sold our only family van to go to Nepal last time, who cares!? It was totally worth it! It's so drunk to give! Our small ministry has managed to come up with tens of thousands of dollars for the people of Nepal!

Now I've been empowered to give all the more so because I've been on the receiving end of what I like to call 'drunk money' myself. Once I was just riding in the car to go to the bank with a friend, and we were talking about drunk money. We were talking about how much we loved the concept. We were laughing all the way to the bank. It didn't even cross my mind that I was about to walk into a literal bank. Sure enough, as I made my deposit that day, there was $800 that had mysteriously appeared in my account out of nowhere. I literally to this day do not know where that money came from. As I got back into the car I told my friend what had happened, and as a Glory drinker himself, he was not surprised! We'd both seen God create wealth that way many times before. I've had people give me cars, multiple times. These cars weren't junkers either! I had an almost brand new Kia Rondo given to me one time. I picked it up at the dealership, totally free! Thanks be to God, and the person who was so generous to our lives and ministry.

Now my absolute favorite drunken money story came to me while I was in the state of Wisconsin. We were at a Glory conference, and a lot happened, oh my Jesus! I'll start with the drunk money story! Well, the Glory had been so thick and juicy at these gatherings, we were absolutely enamored at the beauty of Jesus Christ. A group of my four friends were in the front row, hammered drunk, and the Spirit was manifesting in many various ways, which I'll talk about later.

As the Spirit was manifesting, I had fallen face down at the front of the meeting room. I was whacked out, in a deep trance, just enjoying the Presence so much. All of a sudden a lady was tapping me on the shoulder, though I didn't even look up to see her. I was too whacked. She asked if she could pray for me. I told her to go ahead, whatever she wanted. I was too jacked up to pay much attention. As she finished praying for me, she told us that she was supposed to give into my ministry. We had never met before.

So she then asked me what my ministry was. I began to tell her the things in my heart, one of which was a coffee shop. She stopped and looked very interested. Her and her husband then said they were going to pray and come back to the next meeting to let us know something. By the time the next meeting had rolled around this couple had come to a conclusion. They approached me and explained that they had just closed a coffee shop. They felt led to give me all their old equipment. Now, I thought that this would be maybe a couple of old coffee makers, or a fridge or something. I had no idea what they meant by 'old equipment'. As it ended up, they had, stored in a warehouse, over $100,000 worth of equipment! They had the best espresso machine I had ever seen! They had fridges, an ice machine, a bakery case, a big freezer, and literally everything you would need to run an upscale coffee shop. The equipment was only two years old! Drunk money cometh! I've seen money supernaturally appear out of nowhere, dollar bills literally appearing in people's pockets. However, that last story is more than just a few dollar bills!

GOLDEN GLORY

So, back to wild drunken manifestations, at that same conference while I was drunk on the floor, doing absolutely nothing, more stuff happened! A woman was preaching from the front about signs, wonders, and miracles. It was a great meeting. Many people were being touched, healed, and transformed! Now, before the previous lady came up to pray for me and give me the coffee shop equipment, about an hour before that, a wave of Glory hit me. The woman from the front who was preaching said that she was releasing some angels. And, she truly did!

The angels smacked me with something! In fact, all four of us who had come together began to get gold dust appearing all over our hands. I had heard of this before, and wasn't quite as shocked, but two of our friends were really quite surprised by this. One of them began to cry because the gold dust was so real and undeniable, and she had never seen a miracle like this. My other friend ran to the bathroom and kept washing his hands off, but the gold would just re-appear! From that day and for the next several months I had gold dust on my hands every day. Sometimes it was very small, but it would always come. Also, for a period of like three months, anyone I prayed for would get it. I mean everyone!

We gave it to almost everyone we knew. Anyone with whom we were drunk enough to overcome the weirdness of it all, we went ahead and showed them! We even gave it to random people on the street! It was crazy, a really wild time! We were hammered drunk. It was during this time that I had the boldness to really introduce the whack to our home neighborhood fellowship community. The physical demonstrations were supremely emboldening!

We began getting people together anytime, anywhere to introduce them to this wonder-working, pleasure giving, supremely satisfying Jesus! From this point on we had jewels show up around us supernaturally, diamond rings, feathers coming out of nowhere, I even had tiny emeralds and diamonds appear out of my hands once. It still happens at the most unpredictable times. Sometime in the middle of the night at our community house, which we called 'the monastery,' we've had pillars of golden cloud appear. If you touched the pillar you just felt more whole! Waves of gold dust, usually very light and small will pass over people as they are around us sometimes. These gold and jewels speak to our hearts of the extravagance of God and how we are his special treasure, a royal people.

BLURRY ANGELS

I mentioned some angels earlier. In the drunken state, we are truly aware and receptive to the invisible world. This is the world where angels normally interact. So, when I'm drunk on God, which is pretty much a permanent state, I see angels. It's not usually with the physical eye. However, sometimes the state is as such where the invisible becomes visible. Four faced angels have appeared, orbs, tracers, small fairy looking lights, flashes of light, and other angelic phenomenon have appeared.

These angels have been sent to minister to us, the children of God. They basically work for God by serving us. Many times they encourage us just by letting us know that they are there. Other times the angels are carrying a revelation, or an anointing for wealth, or some other sort of empowering or encouraging gift. The Bible calls God, "the Lord of hosts." Hosts here means "groups of angels." In the drunken state we are way more aware of angels! I normally see an orb or two every day around somewhere doing something. I've often tested to see if they are just a reflection or coming from somewhere, but I can usually tell when they remain stationary as my head moves, or they move when my head is not moving. They aren't usually perfectly easy to see, but I see them enough, and notice that things happen when they are around.

A WONDERFULLY FRUITFUL WINE

Just a couple more stories here and we'll wind down our story portion of the book (for the most part). Let's talk about how being drunk has opened me up to hearing clearer in the Spirit. There's such an openness that has come at times, when I'm whacked. Sometimes I've even received people's names before they've told me. One time I was at the mall, and I heard this young man's name from the Holy Spirit. I had never met him before, and he was moving by me pretty fast. He actually was almost running past me. I had to chase him halfway through the mall before I caught up to him. I told him what his name was and that God had sent me that day to encourage him that God knows his name. He was absolutely stunned. While I had no proof to him that I hadn't just stalked him a bit, it sure looked like God had ministered to his heart. He seemed to really be touched by God. I've gotten people's names like that on a few other occasions. Just being whacked, I would hear them inside me somewhere. I'd go up to the person and talk to them, and it would be their name. It's been wild.

Honestly, the weird and wild stuff that has happened in the intoxicating Presence of God has been so absolutely amazing. One time a friend of ours had milk and honey start appearing in his beard out of thin air. Literally it was white milk, and fragrant honey. It could have been nothing else. The beard was totally clean just seconds before. Another girl had honey fragrance coming out of her hands. I've smelled supernatural honey, and other wonderful smells in the Glory on many occasions! It's encouraging! Still, like I mentioned earlier, there's been nothing like the love and genuine fruit of the Spirit that it has produced! I honestly feel like so much more of a patient and compassionate person when I'm wasted on Jesus. It's amazing! All I can say is that this intoxication has been wonderful. It has been supremely fruitful. I'm sure I've even forgotten as many stories as I've recounted. I love being high on God's Glory! It is wonderful! It is wonderful! IT IS WONDERFUL!

CHAPTER 10
HOW TO STAY HIGH

It's one thing to get high, right?! It's another thing to stay that way! The unawakened world has what I like to call "an inferior high." Many things could be classified in this category of inferior highs. Obviously, drugs, fame, money, sex and power can be abused to cause an inferior high, among many other things. The problem is that these inferior highs always fade. They are temporary at best, not to mention shallow. I've got great news for you, though! The high of God never fades! It's the stash that's never cashed, the supply that never runs dry, the trip that doesn't quit! This Glory smoke never goes broke! You can live continuously high, for all eternity! In the groups of Glory guzzlers that I hang with, we called this "the permawhack."

It's not just about getting high, it's about living high. It wouldn't be right not to include a chapter here for those of you who have begun to taste God but have yet to live high on the daily. I've met many folks who have gotten high a few times on Jesus, but then it seems to wear off. Maybe this has been your experience. I know it can seem extremely frustrating. It can seem inconsistent. I've seen it happen. You may be wondering what's missing. Why do some people stay high and others don't? Let's explore deeper! We can help! There are keys to STAYING hammered on the Holy Ghost! And, guess what? It's not as difficult as it may seem.

IT'S STILL ALL DEPENDENT ON JESUS CHRIST

Let me start by once again bringing it all back to Jesus Christ. If you simply get a true deep revelation of Jesus and His finished work, resonating through your entire being, this chapter and the chapter on "how to get high" will be entirely unnecessary! The love and the reality of God that Jesus Christ communicates is enough to keep anyone stoned forever! From His view point, you experience the whole world high. In Him, you only know a heaven on earth that's jacked up forever! Whenever you are truly aware of the good, glorious, intoxicated nature of heaven on earth, you cannot but stay high automatically! That's the whole of the message. God giving us all the good life, for free, preserved forever and revealed in Jesus.

Like I said in the chapter on "how to get high," only Holy Spirit can reveal Jesus and thereby make us high! So, it's all dependent on God, it's all dependent on Christ. He makes us lie down in green pastures. He makes us leap like the deer! It's all God! As much as the Bible is true, and Jesus Christ is "yes" and "amen" to all the promises of God (2 Cor. 1:20), with this much assurance I can tell you that God is going to keep you high. You are always high in the true reality, in Jesus Christ! Holy Spirit is always committed to awakening you to that perma-high that you have in Him! In other words, the future of humanity is a whole world permanently high. This includes you! Jesus wins! God is gonna keep you high forever! You can take that to the bank!

STAYING HIGH IS NATURALLY YOU

Also, like I said previously, you are always already high, and Holy Spirit is the guarantee that you will awaken to this truth! So, why do some people appear to sober up? Why do some people only feel high sometimes? Is there anything we can do to help? Great questions! These questions deserve a thorough answer, and I've been contemplating them for some years now. How can we all stay high? What can we do?

Firstly, please, forgive me. Some of this will be a bit of repeat. It just seems so difficult for us formerly religious folks to understand! We need to hear it several times over! What do we need to hear? Hear this.

We cannot help God out! Hahahhahah! It is already done! Right now the right circumstances are already going on within you to keep you high. You need not add anything to it. However, like I also wrote previously, continuing to make healthy choices is also still valuable. Having our consciousness filled with this truth still matters too. There is a seemingly mysterious connection between staying high and walking wisely. Giving natural attention to being and doing the things that are as close to your true self as you are currently aware of; this can seem to enhance, or quicken, the perma-high!

Staying high is all about His reality, aka what is actually real. It's being aware of the Glory that is always here, being aware of the finished work of Christ! When we consistently see Christ as all and in all, we will always stay high. When we continuously feel the vibrations of the Holy Spirit literally and physically coursing through our being, this is when we remain blissed out. Even talking about this can seem to quicken the bliss to our awareness. Woohoo!!

Let me share with you a picture that illustrates this even better. It's like being at a feast. The finished work guarantees you are at the feast, you can't get out! And, the Holy Ghost is the one that causes you to taste and see the feast! You experience the feast through the Holy Ghost. Now, Jesus has locked you into the feast, a.k.a. heaven on earth, and Holy Spirit is going to guarantee that you taste the feast. God does however give you some freedom on how fast you dive into that food to devour it. You can sit back at the table and refuse to eat for a while, or you can dive right in and eat and drink! Eventually the feast is going to look so tasty that you just begin to devour it all. You can start eating now, or you can start eating later. You can celebrate now, or you will celebrate later.

In that little picture, the staying high part is the feasting and drinking. The Holy Ghost is the one that opens our eyes to the feast. The Holy Ghost is also the very taste buds on our tongue that enable us to taste the feast! Jesus Christ is also the feast itself, both the room that the feast is in, and the true food and drink! The Father is feasting right along with us, as the Host who created it all and made it all possible! It's only a matter of time before we all realize that we have always been at the feast. Yet, until we realize that fully, we might stay high or sober up depending on how quickly we actually begin devouring that feast. It's all his work. Only God can give this rich intoxication. It does seem however that we have been given a limited ability to learn for ourselves of the value of enjoying the feast.

God will direct us to ways that will help us to awaken, and stay awake. We can engage these activities, like I mentioned before, in a way that is as simple as just being ourselves. Remember, everyone loves to feast! So, staying high will not be something that feels foreign to us. Everyone loves pleasure! So, these ways will feel very natural to us. These ways will resonate naturally with all of humanity. These ways will feel very natural because it is normal for a child of God to love to eat and drink the Glory. So, there are some regular ways that God will inspire you to participate in, ways that feel natural, ways that feel pleasurable, ways of feasting and staying drunk on God's intoxicating Life!

What we'll encourage in this chapter is to engage in regular rhythms of these pleasurable ways! Let's make a steady lifestyle of feasting and drinking of Jesus! These will simply be you being the real you. They should not feel like duty. They will not usually feel like disciplines. At the very first they might feel a bit strange to you, since you may not have been practicing them previously in your life. Once you have already gotten high, however, they will be super easy to maintain. All of God will be backing you. Plus, it all fits with the way that you were made! The rhythms of heaven are your mother tongue, not a foreign language.

STAYING HIGH

Let's dive into these ways of continually feasting and staying drunk! Firstly, you can stay high by just continuing to practice the tips I listed in chapter seven. Again, maintain a healthy distrust for them as formulas. Think of them simply as expressions of who you naturally are and what you love! Don't think that once you have been high for a while, that you should just leave these ways behind. I have seen folks get high on God, stay high on God for a while, but then they start to think that they have "gotten too big" to stay engaged with these. It's like someone thinking they have grown too mature to need to breathe or eat! It's like saying, "Oh well, I don't need to love anyone anymore, I'm bigger than that!" That's just silly! This is confusion, or a relapse into a false identity of pride.

Staying true to the feast analogy, let's think of it like a diet. Now, it is true that as you grow, your diet may change. However, you will still eat! It is still good to eat. You don't grow past eating! Even once you realize that you are perfectly one with God, you will still want to do these activities simply for the pleasure and joy of them, because they are expressions of who you are. Your heavenly self will always want to continue in these with the intention of staying high in God and enhancing the high of everyone around you!

Now, because I already described in detail in chapter seven my favorite ways of getting high. And, these still apply to staying high. I will simply list them here, and you can go back a couple chapters to re-read them if needed. After this I will write a bit more on some particulars that especially apply to staying high.

That list of high activities is as follows: *Art, Communion, Faith Activators, Fellowship and Community, Going on Mission or Evangelism, Laying on of Hands, Loving and/ Being Loved, Mentorship, Music, praise, and worship, Nature, Prayer, Meditation, Praying in Tongues, Preaching/ Teaching, Recreation & Hobbies, Serving and Giving, and Study.* Of course, this is not a comprehensive list, but great foundation points! Staying engaged with these types of activities is a natural outflow of who you are! Again, they will just happen spontaneously through your life when you know who you are. However, we are also given a limited freewill to continue to do these activities, with a reliance on God, and an expectation of continued refreshment in them! Do not rely on these activities! While you are enjoying or desiring to enjoy the Glory of God, fill your life with these things. Really no matter where you are in life, fill your life with these things! Not looking to them as your Savior, but still engaging in them regularly.

Filling your life with many other kinds of behavior just doesn't suit who you are! It also won't suit who you are to engage these kinds of activities with a sense of desperation or lack mentality! It's all gonna be ok! However, starting to form an unforced rhythm in these kinds of activities will surely mysteriously help you to stay high more consistently and more frequently. This rhythm will begin to feel more and more blissful, until, as you tweak and adjust it all by inspiration, it will just become the perma-whack. It may not take long at all. Don't be discouraged if it does seem to take you longer than others. Just stay with it, have fun along the way, and it will "work". The Love of God guarantees to train us up in His ways!!

SPECIFIC WAYS THAT SEEM TO MAINTAIN THE HIGH

Now that we've reviewed all that, I want to discuss some long term lifestyle attitudes and practices that perma-high people all seem to have! I mean, otherwise, why are there some people, groups, churches, etc. that just seem so dry? There are some practices that those who are mature in the whack have adopted as a part of their free flowing selves. Again, none of the lists in this book are comprehensive, nor do they cause the bliss in themselves. Still, here's a stab at what I've noticed specifically to be congruent with flowing in the perma-whack! Hahhahaha!

DESIRE FOR AND LOVE OF GOD HIMSELF AND HIS GLORY

Permawhacked people have adopted a continual desire for Glory. They stay focused on Jesus, and enjoying real intimate relationship with God in Him! They are always passionate for Glory to move, even when it's already moving. They have their attention, not merely on the visible things, but the invisible. Permawhacked people are ravenous to always feel God, to always be seeing the natural and supernatural present to one another. They are always ready to pray, worship, and talk about God, even if that is in non-traditional ways, such as just sitting around on the back porch, or laughing in their car, or many, many kinds of encounters. You can always tell that they have a focus for great love, great power, and great God type of things to happen at any moment, not in an insecure way that needs to prove anything, but just out of passion and love. They will always be filled with desire, even when feeling full and flooded with God! Their minds are set on things above (Col. 3:2)!

Once you become experienced with being drunk, you get used to moving in heaven on earth. You get used to drinking, or better yet, being the Drink. You can become so familiar with moving in the Glory that you learn how to turn it up or turn it down together with the Holy Ghost. You have this ability no matter what is going on in your life. Your normal state is as a fully functional God-man or Goddess-woman. Just like

Jesus, you have all authority on heaven and on earth to function as fully God and fully human.

Once you know this experience, just stay there!! This is called "abiding in Him." (John 15:4) This is the awakened state. Just simply don't let yourself be talked out of it by outside voices. It sounds silly to think that any awakened person would want to go back to sleep. Yet, when outside pressures or confusing voices become intense, I have seen it happen. It's not like you need to fight to stay awake. It's the easiest state to stay in! Yet, still, Jesus wouldn't have encouraged us to "abide in Him" if it was impossible to go back. You are always truly in Him, of course, no one can pluck you from His hand. However, you can go back to sleep, if only temporarily, and this is silly! When you become familiar with how to increase the whack at any moment, don't settle for the broken cisterns of the world! Stay hammered my friends, by simply continuing to value God and His whack first!

TESTIMONIES OF THE GLORY

Another powerful tip that can really keep the perma-whack flowing is continuing to hear and share testimonies of what God is doing, of the good things happening in life. Those that recount the stories of God, and not just ones from the distant past, these people seem to be able to stay whacked more often. There is just something about testimonies that often awakens our awareness. Again, more testimonies does not necessarily mean more whack, but God sure can use them! I say a healthy amount of God testimonies is a great thing! I highly recommend it!

A COMMUNITY OF ENCOURAGEMENT

Surrounding yourself with the amount of encouraging people that you need can also be key. This may be different for different people, and at different times. However, I encourage you to find the amount of encouragement that keeps you whacked! This is not the only solution by any means, but oh my, how it can help! I've seen so many people sober up because they surrounded themselves with people who were not speaking the truth. Their daily life and environment was mostly sober, mostly unaware of heaven, and therefore after a while they just forgot reality. Now, when you are super rooted in reality, like Jesus was, you can stay in any environment. However, God won't force you into an environment that you aren't ready to handle. Many times, though, you have the opportunity to create the environment that you live in on a daily basis. Most of us have tons of options just because we have the modern conveniences of telephones and internet! Whatever it may be, it is good to place within your environment a healthy amount of people who encourage you in your heavenly awareness. Staying in touch with other whacked people can help so much! It reinforces reality just by seeing, hearing, and feeling what is coming from their lives. This is a big deal! If you think that you can order your life around your job, your school, your hobbies, your "obligations" and not around a culture of heavenly relationships and encouragement, you will likely find yourself sobering up pretty quick.

MEDITATION OF THE GLORY AND BEING AROUND GLORY POINTERS

This is kind of related to the previous one, yet still important! I want to encourage you to find easy, relaxed rhythms of including meditation of truth into your life. Permawhacked people just always seem to either be meditating on truth or listening to Glory teachers, or somehow using pointers that personally trigger them in the Glory throughout their day. Now, as you really grow in the whack, this might become times of just pondering truths as you go about your day. Again, this is so personal. You must find your own rhythm! Some people like to listen to a Glory teaching on recording every day. (Just make sure it's speaking from a place of heaven and earth inseparably united once for all in Jesus Christ!) Some people like to meditate in a quiet room for hours per day. Some people just do the dishes mindful of God. I want to encourage you plainly. Find a rhythm of meditation and reminders, ways that encourage your high over and over! Don't think that you are so solid that you can fill your life with lying voices continually. Keep hearing the Gospel! Keep hearing the Truth of Jesus!

TRUSTING YOURSELF

A huge way of God in staying perma-whacked in God is to learn to continually trust your true self. You have a holy nature! Your fallen self died with Christ! This means you can trust your desires, you can trust Yourself! You have been fused together with Christ! This is a huge scandal to most religious people. So much of the world has been taught that we are sinful, or bad, or lacking, or stuck in ignorance. However, so much of staying high is beginning to go with what just feels right from deep within. This is truly following the Holy Spirit. Holy Spirit is the One who is one with your deepest you, your spirit. As 1 Cor. 6:17 says, "He who is joined to the Lord becomes one spirit with him." So, you have one spirit with God. The spirit is the deepest part of you, from whence your desires, thoughts, and everything spring. Out of your belly flows rivers of living water!

This is one of the biggest deals in this whole book! True freedom is being able to do whatever you truly want, knowing that living out of your heart will really bless the world. You, just being you is what the world needs! Not only that, it's what will help keep you perma-high!!! Nothing makes you feel better than union with God manifesting in you doing what you love! Trust this true God self that you already are, and you will stay hammered. You will be blissed out just doing the things that you want!

RESTING

This will almost be a repeat of the last one, but it's so worth repeating! Doing what you truly love every day, this is true rest. The book of Hebrews chapter four speaks of the Sabbath Rest that remains for God's people. We are living in a continual Sabbath. Union with Christ is our Sabbath rest. Sitting still, or sleeping, or napping are natural types of rest. The true rest of the Spirit is just doing what you were created to do. It is flowing with what feels the most natural, or easiest for you, in every moment. Sometimes the easiest thing to do in the world is a full day's work. You were made to be creative and to live and move! Your work can be rest when it's what you love from the heart. It is a part of your original design!

Countless people are not staying high because they are still forcing themselves to do things that just aren't them! This is the only actual "work" in the cosmos. Dead works is when you force yourself to do things that you don't love. That could be anything. It's all about allowing yourself to do what you feel springing up from deep within! This is rest! It's not about napping versus doing a lot of activity! It's about flowing from the heart.

Now, your heavenly self was not made to run around like a chicken with its' head cut off! The culture of heaven is happy, playful, with lots of recreation, and not in a hurry. Don't let yourself bow to the fallen worried, harried culture of the world. Ultimately, perma-whacked people are those that have radically rearranged their life to only do what feels restful to them. This could mean little activity, or lots. The point is to go on a journey with God, over time, finding a rhythm of life that does not feel stressful, that feels like your "yoke is easy, and burden is light (Matt. 11:30)." This helps the perma-whack greatly! Do not fear work, but also do not fear inactivity. In different times and seasons you may go from running like a sprinter to living like a snail. The point of the rest is to radically allow yourself to only do what's deep inside your heart! In this, other people may give a helpful perspective, but ultimately only you can discover what your rest looks like from within.

DOING WHAT YOUR HEAVENLY SELF ENJOYS!

Once again, this will be very similar to what I just wrote. Still, it almost cannot be over emphasized. I am convinced that God created each one of us as a perfectly functional healthy masterpiece. It would be a crime not to simply allow a masterpiece to be just as it is. A masterpiece can be trusted to do exactly what it needs to do. I believe that the main reason that the church worldwide has so often been sober and behaving in ways that are not very heavenly is dynamically related to this very issue. When we forget that we are whole, powerful, and true masterpieces in Christ, then we are left merely "trying to do the right thing." This results in a form of godliness, maybe outwardly, but not truly manifesting our unique expression of God. You see, we were not created to follow Jesus' example. We were created to literally express Jesus through our own life. To put it another way, we weren't created to act like Jesus, we were created to be Jesus. We are the body of Christ, with many different members. Doing what we truly feel created and passionate to do, doing what just feels the most like us, yes, this is how the God life is manifest. Only this will keep us high, because it agrees with the Glory within.

Practically, it's ok to start small and simple. For most of us it takes some getting used to. Most people are used to attempting to live by some sort of goal or standard that isn't felt from deep within. You may need to take some time to feel deeply what your deepest self feels like. Take some time. Take a vacation. Spend some intentional time re-evaluating your life. Start making changes over months and years, discovering what feels the healthiest from within. You probably won't want to quit your job over night, drop out of school in a week, or leave your family. Most of the time God has us make small changes that will benefit those around us in our transition as well! Remember who all you may be affecting, even while standing up for the changes you know you need to make. Take it slowly, prayerfully, with some counsel, yet boldly re-order your life around the Glory.

For me, taking some good time speaking in tongues is like letting my deepest self bubble up. It flows from my deepest place, not just in the realm of thoughts and opinions that have been flying by, but what is deep within. Can you feel your heart or hearts? Can you feel your spirit, one with God's Spirit deep within? We all can! Just take some time to do this, and after a while you will be able to continually live from that place. This gearing of your whole life around who you truly are is extremely key to staying hammered on His Life!

I remember distinctly the first few weeks when I started waking up every day and instead of seeking God outside of me somewhere for

His will for the day, instead I began to just do what felt right from deep within. Sometimes I honestly felt to just go back to bed and get some extra sleep, trusting that everything would be ok. My life began to work so much better. I was happier, and found it so easy to be whacked! Even when I felt deep within to engage in a big project or to wake up early, or do challenging things, they didn't feel like work. Now, I only do what I love, and, oh God, life is good! Sometimes what I love is having a challenging conversation with a friend or family member. Sometimes what I love means walking miles and miles. Sometimes what I love is letting myself be persecuted! It's all so whacked!

This might start with God having you eat ice cream and pizza every day because He's scandalizing you with His goodness! It might mean just relaxing when you thought you should work. God is not going to have you become some selfish irresponsible person. Don't worry! However, He may scandalize you and a few others by having you do really fun stuff all day. He might find ways to get you to stop trying so hard all the time!! Selah! See what God has deep within you, and go with it.

People may agree or disagree with your new life choices. (I'm not saying to become unteachable.) Still, hey, sometimes your holy heart may tell you to do some radical things. Go for it! Even if you make a mistake sometimes, you will get more used to hearing God through every experience while looking to follow your holy desires and insides. It works! Spontaneous following of your desires will work. You are perfectly designed to live and love well!! Remember, this is what you were made for! The God life is meant to feel GOOD! God feels good!

EXPECTING TO SEE AND EXPERIENCE GOD IN EVERY THING

I have one final point to touch on in "Staying High.". I want to mention the importance of what some have called "Panentheism." Panentheism is defined as seeing God in every person, place, thing, and activity. This is a lot like what Brother Lawrence would experience in his daily dish washing. We already discussed how Brother Lawrence experienced the love of God tangibly in everything he did. Well, as you can imagine, that kind of view could really intoxicate you! Looking for and expecting a mystical and tangible Glory Presence to be moving in, with, and through everything keeps you supremely high! And, it is simply the Truth! The Truth makes you free!

Panentheism sets us free to not be waiting for God to manifest in some other place or time. From this understanding we can encounter God everywhere! The two big lies of religion are distance and delay. Panentheism removes them both. God is both here and now. Where? Everywhere! We aren't saying that the people, places, and things are all there is, but we are saying that the mystic Presence of Christ is living in and as them all. The whole universe is held together by Him (Col. 1:17)!! With this kind of outlook, you may just find yourself begin to trip out as you hear a bird's whistle, or see a friend's face, or even in the menial tasks you used to hate. This does not mean that every circumstance that happens is God, but that you can see God present somewhere in it all. There is so much to expound upon here. Meditate and go deeper in this glorious revelation of panentheism. It's quite a rabbit hole of Glory. But, surely it is a key that those perma-whacked in God understand in their lives.

CHAPTER 11
COMMON QUESTIONS & MISCONCEPTIONS

Being high on God is such a wild, new, and strange concept to so many people! Besides this, the folks on the planet that are experiencing this bliss presently are still few and relatively inexperienced. I know of only a handful of people alive at the writing of this book that have more than twenty years of experience in being high on God. So, naturally, there have been many misconceptions, questions, and things that must be explored deeper regarding the subject! I want to help as much as I can with this! I truly want this book to give as full and deep of a presentation of the perma-whack as possible. I want to create an accessible resource for the growing number of people worldwide who are embracing the God high as a long term sustainable lifestyle!

In that hope, let's cover some common questions and misconceptions related to the bliss of heaven. I'll try to lay them out as simple as possible, exactly as many of them have been asked to me. Some of these are the literal questions that I have received over the years. Others will be general topics that cover a wide range of questions. Still others are addressing issues that I have witnessed with my own eyes among those new or inexperienced with the whack. Let's dive right in! Hopefully we will cover some of the questions or concerns that you may have had specifically as well!

I'm dividing this chapter into three sections: "Drunkenness for All," "Work Related Questions," and "Deep or Shallow." Feel free to skip to the section that may seem most relevant to your current experience.

DRUNKENNESS FOR ALL

IT JUST DOESN'T SEEM TO WORK FOR ME. WHAT DO I DO?

Firstly, let me just say that this is a common question! Don't give up hope! You are not alone! At first many folks just don't seem able to get high on God. Others initially only experience the high sporadically, every now and then. This does not mean that it won't work for you. This does not mean that something is wrong with you! No one is too hard of a case! Let me give a short response that may help...

Let's remember that this is about a change in consciousness. It is about a change of awareness, from the lies and non-realities that you had become so accustomed to, into an awareness of the truth of heaven on earth. Now, consciousness can be a funny thing! For whatever reason, certain people's consciousness changes at different rates. Some people get it super quick, for others it can take time. There are many reasons for this actually, often related to our attachments to hurts or disappointments of the past. Often a sense of jadedness, disappointment, or general distrust can be rooted in our subconscious. Trying to address these hindrances can occasionally be of some help. However, what I've found to be most effective, rather than exploring the problem in depth, focus on the powerful solution! Bask in the love of Christ. Keep hearing the truth of Christ's love, and what He's done for us! Keep hearing the Gospel of our inclusion in Him, in heaven on earth. We were all created, as a species, the same way. We may be very different people, but we all have a similar consciousness, and no one's consciousness is too far gone! It will work for you. The love of God works. The Gospel works!

It may seem to take you so much longer than others, but the stuff I wrote in chapters seven and eleven are the same for everyone! Again, don't begin to do these in some formulaic way! In essence those two chapters are about continuing to hear the Truth and being around people who live it with you. This will work for you, I guarantee it. God has put all His chips in on you! Jesus was tortured so that you could live the high life! He's going to get what He came for! Stay with it, in a relaxed way, enjoying whatever graces you can along the journey. You will get perma-high. God is committed to you! And, honestly, is there any other viable option that works better? I've tried a lot of them! God's intoxicating love far exceeds them all!

WHAT ABOUT DESERT SEASONS, OR GOD WITHDRAWING HIS PRESENCE TO MAKE US MORE PASSIONATE?

In this book, we have often discussed the whole earth having been filled with the Glory, as well as the reality of humanity's union with Christ. This is the Gospel! It does not change! To believe in desert seasons, or God withdrawing His presence would be anti-Gospel! This does not mean that we cannot go through challenges or hard times. What it does mean is that God is always with us, always one with us? Jesus died so that you can be in tangible experience of God at all times! It would be totally double minded for God to then turn around and disable our experience of the Presence! Jesus said, "Surely, I will be with you always." (Matt. 28:20)

In this current point of history there are many who are teaching that there is a difference between the "omni-Presence of God" and the "manifest Presence of God". This teaching can be extremely harmful! The only difference between these two is in our consciousness. In reality and truth there is no difference between the two. God is not 'with us, but not letting us feel Him.' That is not the nature and character of God! We may not be experiencing the manifest Presence of God at some point, but that is not God's will. If that is our experience, it is only because our consciousness is not aware at that moment. A simple hearing of the Gospel can change that! The good news is that you are inseparably united with the manifest Presence of God in Christ! No more desert seasons! It is finished! You are One with the Glory!

HOW IMPORTANT IS IT TO BE HIGH ON GOD? ISN'T IT JUST ONE OF MANY TYPES OF "ANOINTINGS" OUT THERE?

Firstly, being high on God is a gift, not a demand. This isn't another rule or law you must keep in order to be "right with God" or "on the right track." Anyone who makes you feel like the drunkenness is something to achieve, as if you are lacking, does not have a mature understanding of God's heart in this. Having ecstatic joy is a result of experiencing the unconditional love and acceptance of God over your life! It's not a 'should.' It's a 'get to!'

The whack is what happens to the human consciousness as it is made aware of the Glory of God. It may look different in different people. This is one of the beautiful things about it. However, each person in the Glory is going to feel the profound joy and ecstasy of His Presence. Psalm 16:11 says, "in your Presence is the fullness of joy." This is not just any old gift! It's not some additional side dish to salvation! The whack is just what happens! It the nature of reality! Anyone experiencing the tangible Glory of God will be intoxicated with the fullness of joy!

Sometimes I like to give people a clearer picture though the following analogy. If twenty people walked into a room that was just absolutely filled with marijuana smoke, how many of them would feel an inebriation? All of them! All twenty people would get high. It's just the way things are. Marijuana smoke is an earthly intoxicant. In the same way, if twenty people were made aware of the Glory of God in a room, they would all become inebriated. The Glory is a heavenly intoxicant, with much healthier influence than marijuana intoxication, and much more inebriating!

If being intoxicated on God is just what happens whenever someone is aware of the Glory, then it is not just important, it is vital. It's not just vital; it is the way things work. No need to even compare it to other areas of the kingdom. It just IS the way things are. God is amazing. God is perfect love. God is inebriating. It is not just an anointing out there that helps things work a little better. It is the result of communing with the Glory! You can't be around God without getting drunk! Now that doesn't mean you will always be rolling around and laughing. However, it does mean that communing with God always puts us in a fully joyful altered state.

ISN'T BEING DRUNK MORE OF A PERSONALITY TYPE?

This is pretty much covered in the previous answer. How it is expressed is a personality type. However, being intoxicated is just what happens to everyone who is walking in an awareness of God. It is not limited to certain personalities or types of people.

DO I HAVE TO BE LAUGHING OUT LOUD AND ROLLING AROUND ON THE GROUND TO BE DRUNK?

This is a common question. Good news, the answer is no! It is not about everyone looking and acting the same way! It is not about any one certain behavior or action! That would put us back under rules and image management, yuck! While it is really quite likely that you will have times of joyful shouting, laughing, falling, and shaking under the Presence, this is not some kind of required performance. This high is also not some kind of limiting or one dimensional reality. You are going to be able to do work, take care of your business, raise your kids, create art, go on adventures, write books, climb mountains, and every other kind of beautiful activity imaginable, all while high! The high can just as much express itself through a silent, still, meditative state, or a focused creative skill manifesting state. There are so many expressions of the high to explore! No one has experienced them all! Maybe you will taste one that has never been tasted! The point is that you are in an altered state, aware of the tangible Glory, feeling overwhelmingly loved! It's not about achieving any particular behavior. We need to be careful not to criticize or judge another person's expression. God has so many wide and varied expressions! Let's not limit one another or discourage one another from exploring them all!

OF WHAT VALUE IS IT TO JUST BE LAUGHING AND ROLLING AROUND?

I have often received this question, as well. My first response is often to respond with another question. Of what value is it to laugh, play, and roll around with your kids?

It's all about intimacy and close fellowship! It's all about enjoyment! It builds such a deep trust to be able to be this close with God! We have so often had a wrong understanding of God. We thought He mostly wanted to be a Judge, a Boss, or a Political Leader. He can be those things. However, Jesus revealed that God's deepest heart is to be a Father, a Sibling, a Lover, a Spouse, and a Friend! Fathers that don't laugh and play with their kids wouldn't be good fathers would they? Laughing and rolling around makes perfect sense in this context! It may be a culture shock, but God is an extremely playful, intimate God!

I DON'T LIKE THE LANGUAGE OF BEING "HIGH ON GOD".

This statement often comes up when I share in a place. And, it's totally ok! Again, this is not some legalistic rule or doctrine that must be enforced! You are totally free not to use this kind of language!

You may want to ask yourself, though, 'why don't I like this language?' Is it simply because it is new or foreign to you? Many times humanity has rejected beautiful things simply because they didn't understand them. Maybe your view of God has been of an overly serious God, or a distant father? I do not mean to be assuming or accusing of you. However, be sure to truly ask yourself these questions! I have seen many people not like the language at first, for these reasons. Later they told me how glad they were that I continued to declare the high of God, because they love it now!

Now, there are many folks who have been deeply hurt by the results of the counterfeit intoxications of the world. This can make it difficult to hear the God-high language. That is totally understandable too! So many lives have been ruined by the counterfeit highs! If this means you don't feel comfortable using this specific language, then that's totally alright. If that's the case for any other reason as well, no problem! Do what you have grace for!

All in all though, if you don't like this specific language, please don't dismiss the reality behind it. God is not concerned about the language and semantics. God is concerned about our hearts. Living in a tangible awareness of the Glory that produces an altered state of consciousness is what matters here! THIS is close to God's heart! Maybe God will give you different language for communicating this! That's amazing! I won't judge or criticize you for it! And, if you would, please don't criticize me for my language either! Whatever bears fruit, right? Whatever allows people to effortlessly enjoy a life of heaven on earth, that's what matters! Language is secondary. Being high on God is just a way that I believe God has shown me to communicate the substance of a more important reality! I haven't seen a better way to communicate it yet. If you do, let me know! I desire to live beyond semantics.

DO I NEED TO STOP BEING AN INTELLECTUAL IN ORDER TO RECEIVE THIS HIGH?

No! The mind is a beautiful thing! We could all use to have a few more geniuses manifesting in the Glory! However, this is still an important area to discuss. The Bible talks about a carnal mind which is hostile to God (Rom. 8:7). It also says that we are not to lean on our own understanding and that knowledge puffs up, but love builds up (Prov. 3:5, 1 Cor. 8:1)! These scriptures point to an important reality.

Most of us grew up relying on our own abilities, living in a consciousness based on spiritual independence and the five-sense realm only. This has created many intellectuals whose entire way of thinking is not in reliance upon the Spirit. To them, I might actually want to say that the mind is a wonderful thing to waste! What I mean is that this old way of thinking must get wasted in the Glory of God, in order to receive the renewed mind, our inheritance in Christ!

Our own self-reliant thoughts led to a humanity that was lost and confused. This was because of a profoundly wrong way of thinking. This thinking must be transformed by the genuine gift of revelation from the Spirit. Once there is a shift unto thinking under the influence of the Spirit from within, then the mind is an amazing thing! From this place it can be healthy to be an amazing intellectual! However, without this mindset, the more intellect you think you have, the more of a barrier you will put up to experiencing the Glory of God. The true wisdom is in becoming like Paul, who resolved to know nothing but Jesus Christ and him crucified (1 Cor. 2:2)! Paul did later speak of a wisdom he had. Yet, this wisdom was from the mind of Christ, not the carnal mind. There is a distinct difference!

It is because of this difference that you may hear certain phrases in the Glory community such as, "Less thinking, more drinking," "Turn your brain off for a while," or "Brain bypass." Phrases such as these, and the like, can seem offensive. It may make some wonder, "Well, why did God give us a brain, if we just have to turn it off?" Good question! The answer is not to turn off the original mind that God intended for you! It's the carnal mind that needs to be bypassed and turned off!

Most people around the world grew up only knowing the carnal mind! So, phrases like, "less thinking, more drinking" can be so helpful to many, until they learn to operate in the mind of Christ! Now, some people have misunderstood this as well to mean that we never need to think again. No! We were created to think! But, it's a new way of thinking, from the Spirit first, and then through the mind! It's a way of thinking that acknowledges God's activity and source in all things, and therefore reflects the humble, joyful, loving, powerful, supernatural, and natural nature of God's thoughts. Hopefully this helps in navigating this often challenging subject. Meditate on what I wrote here for a minute. I honestly believe it can help in understanding why the intellect can seem so wonderful and yet such a stumbling block at the same time!

BEING DRUNK DOES NOT MAKE YOU BETTER THAN SOMEONE ELSE.

I'm sure that it's obvious by now that we are absolutely encouraging the high of God as the healthiest way to live. However, it is not meant to create a pride or an elite mentality in anyone's life! This isn't about comparison or being "holier-than-thou." In fact, the true drunkenness doesn't allow for any of that. Genuine intoxication on God makes you kind, tolerant, understanding, and humble! No one should feel any guilt being projected upon them by a God-drunk person! That's not the Gospel!

Being high in the Spirit is the normal healthy way to live. However, just like when someone discovers a healthy diet in the realm of food and natural nutrition, it is a big turn off when they pressure it on you. Just like with an earthly diet, it doesn't make you better than someone else, even though it may cause you to experience greater health. Let's not over complicate things by bringing guilt, pressure, or criticism in on one another over the whack. It's about love and acceptance! You all are so beautiful! We're all awakening in our own time and way. The whack is so healthy and wonderful! I don't think anyone would truly want to miss it. But, it does not make you more valuable or holier to be whacked! We are all glorious unique expressions of the divine!

ARE YOU INCLUDING EVERYONE IN THIS HIGH? DOES EVERYONE GO TO HEAVEN? WHAT ABOUT HELL? ARE YOU A UNIVERSALIST?

These are some massive questions for many people, worthy of their own entire books in and of themselves! I'll attempt to give a few short answers here, and if anything I can provoke you to explore further…

Firstly, Jesus Christ is the Savior of the whole world! He's not just a potential Savior, He's an actual Savior. 1 Timothy 4:10 says that He's the Savior of all, especially those who believe! This is why throughout this book I've attempted to make it clear that ALL ARE INCLUDED! Yet, at the same time, when we are not believing the Truth, we don't experience all the full benefits of that Truth. Yet, the Truth is still true. Does that make sense? Ponder it for a bit…

In this book, I'm not trying to make any conclusive statements about hell. The book is more about heaven, Jesus, and the Gospel! However, I do believe that Jesus saved everyone, once and for all. Does that mean everyone will awaken to this salvation? I certainly hope so!

I can understand why the question of whether this Jesus would on one hand gives us bliss, but on the other hand torture and burn humans for all eternity would be quite disturbing. I will say this, I don't see eternal conscious torment for anyone! That's not the inebriating God of Love that I know! There may be some consequences for those who insist on remaining in the false worlds of lies and illusions, and it may even feel like hell, just as it does now many times for those who remain unawakened. But, the days of hellfire and brimstone preaching are over! That was never the heart of God, and it's time we stop associating it with the Gospel!

Throughout history there have been many well respected Christian leaders who have either leaned toward or full on believed in a Christ centered universalism. If that shocks you, just go do a real search on the subject. Look into Gregory of Nyssa, Origen, Athanasius, George MacDonald, Robert Capon and many others. The Love of Jesus is truly inebriating, and has no hidden dark side waiting to hurt you if you don't measure up! Any view we have of the after-life, and the scope of salvation must align with this. This Good News is truly better, more inclusive, and more Love-drunk than we could ever imagine!

SOMEONE WHO WAS HIGH ON GOD HURT ME, SO I DON'T LIKE IT ANYMORE.

In the course of time for any group that gathers, especially new or young groups, people are going to get hurt. This is not ok, though hopefully you can understand that it's bound to happen. I personally want to apologize to anyone reading this who has been hurt by someone in the name of the "God-high." You are amazing! You never deserved to be devalued or hurt! I only hope that this next wave of God drunks will do better. I also hope that you can understand that even the most beautiful moves of God may have immaturity in the midst of it.

People all over the world are growing in their experience of the drunkenness of God. In the meanwhile, they may make mistakes. Please don't let it ruin the Glory for you. God was not causing them to hurt you. It was their own immaturity. You may not be ready, because of your terrible experience, to embrace the God high. That is ok! Still, please allow for the chance that God will bring this tangible experience to you in a way and time that you can receive.

It is not meant to be like the high of the world where people are rude and hurtful! Honestly, most Glory drunks I've seen are not this way.

Still, I do know that it has happened. Please, allow God to minister to you directly, or through someone else, and get the joy and altered state for yourself. It will not produce negative fruit! Unfortunately, that was just another hurt person's immaturity or insensitivity! This whack is all about love, joy, and grace! You may have been extremely frustrated that a God intoxicated person would be so rude. I am with you. I'm ready to manifest the real deal, a Love-drunkenness that honors and empowers the world!

WORK RELATED QUESTIONS

HOW CAN I HOLD A JOB WHILE I'M THIS HAMMERED?

Many people when they first encounter the whack imagine that they wouldn't be able to do a good job at work if they were high. Others get super jacked up, are completely immobilized in the Glory, and they imagine that this state is all there is. They imagine that they will always be shaking and rolling around, too drunk to see! That's just not how it is!! Don't worry, this is not a buzz-kill! It's good news! There are many different types of high!

God has created you to be able to be creative, successful, and industrious! It's true, He doesn't need your help, but He's given you the joy of doing stuff on the earth! You may experience a high that puts you in a wheelchair for days, even weeks! If that is happening, go with it! Have an amazing time in these kinds of ecstasies, my God, they are wonderful! However, God won't do that to you if it's going to ruin the job, calling, or ministry He has for you. Now, hear me out, because this is a touchy subject.

God may immobilize you and ruin what you thought was your "job" or "ministry!" What He won't do is keep you from your true expression of life in occupation. Let me put it this way. Some people need to go through a shocking and extreme immobilization in order to re-establish their life in their true identity. In fact, most people probably do! Still, if you were called to be a brain surgeon, God is not going to intoxicate you so much in your operating room that you hurt someone or can't do your job!

There is a thing I like to call "garden works". These are jobs that are not under a curse of stress. They are similar to Adam's job of caring for the earth in the book of Genesis. Like I wrote earlier in the book, I believe that we will be doing jobs forever. These are jobs that we were created to do! The intoxication will not hinder these. These are enjoyable, heavenly garden works!

Now, even if you don't think that your current job or responsibility is a "garden work," please don't just be irresponsible with it! I have seen too many people blame irresponsibility on the whack! That's not right, and that will ruin it for the rest of the drunks!

If you find yourself stuck in a responsibility or job that you do not feel called to, simply ask the Lord to come up with an exit strategy. This exit strategy will be kind and honoring to all parties involved! Of course, you can't always make everybody happy! Still, as much as it depends on you, try to be at peace with all people (Rom. 12:18)! Be a blessing with your God intoxication. There will be some times where you are just too whacked for work. However, that won't be a lifestyle for most people. When that time does come, where you do have to take a shift off, a day off, a week off, or even a longer time off because of the whack, find a considerate way to do it! You can find ways to get away, to go enjoy God away from work, and still bless everyone involved!!

I do want to say one last thing about work. This whack radically changes your life. Oftentimes it does cause a person to re-arrange their entire world around them. Listen to Holy Spirit about what to do about your job. Some people will stay in their occupation, others will move on to something that better fits their new perspective on life. Either way, I want to let you know that it's ok. Also, the greatest truth here is to know that you will always be provided for. Don't let your thoughts be filled with occupation first. Let the Glory fill your whole world. Re-arrange around that. That may mean radically changing everything. Whatever it means, I encourage you to organize your whole life around what keeps you jacked up. Do that honorably and respectfully whenever possible, but be radical. You will be provided for, even if you do need to take some risks to follow the life of bliss. Be free.

THE GOD HIGH MAKES YOU RESTFUL, NOT LAZY.

One misconception that I have personally seen is when people confuse rest for inactivity. Closely related to that is confusing laziness with rest. However, the apostle Paul, probably the biggest writer concerning the restful life in all of the scriptures, labored to the ends of the earth! Paul ministered so much that by the end of his life he probably thought he had preached in all the world! He was a very active dude, and he definitely understood the whack!

Don't get me wrong. The culture of heaven IS much more relaxed and easy-going than what most people know on earth. Our being high does often cause us to be misunderstood because we are so relaxed and stress free. But, it should not make us lazy. You may go through times of being able to do very little! However, you may also go through times of doing more than the average person could possibly do! There are different types of whack! The slow, immobilizing whack has historically been called an 'absorption ecstasy." The higher energy whack has often been called a "concentration ecstasy." They are both amazing. They are both drunk!

"The rest" is about only doing what you were created to do. It's about being moved by the Holy Ghost. If the Holy Spirit is moving through you to desire to just be still, then be still. This is rest. If the Holy Spirit is moving through you to go to work in the morning to do your job, then do that. That is also rest. The real unrest is to resist doing what you are inspired to do from God within! Flowing in the Glory is the true rest, whatever that looks like! Don't miss out on the many plans and adventures purposed for your life, in the name of "rest!" The Glory may have you be the best worker at your job! The Glory may also immobilize you for years! The point is that the most restful thing you can ever experience is just going with the flow of the Glory! It's just naturally being who you were created to be! This is the highest way to live! This is the true rest!

DEEP OR SHALLOW

TOO DRUNK TO CARE?

Let me clear up another common misconception among God high newbies! I promise you, none of these will steal your joy. My heart is to see a real long term, ever-increasing whack! With that in mind, I must discuss the folks that say that they are "too drunk to care!!" Sound ridiculous right? I mean, we are high on God, and God is love. Still, let's navigate this one!

I believe that those who think they are supposed to be too drunk to care have simply gotten confused in the process of unplugging from a life where they always felt pressured, demanded of, manipulated, etc.! Jesus said, "Come to me all you who are weary and heavy laden, and I will give you rest." (Matt. 11:30)

There is a healthy not caring, and an unhealthy not caring. There is a healthy not caring that comes in the immobilizing rest. The healthy not caring is a place where you simply will not be concerned with that which you are not called to have a concern. So many of us have spent our lives caring about things that were not our concern! For example, it has never been our job to provide for ourselves! God is our provider! Having a mentality of "God helps those who help themselves" is not godly! It is extremely healthy to not have a care about providing for yourself! Now, as we just previously discussed, this is not meant to make us irresponsible or unconcerned about the jobs that we ARE called to! Still, there is such a sigh of relief when we get high in the Glory and feel the freedom to stop caring about providing for ourselves! There are some other places in life where it is healthy to have a "too drunk to care" attitude as well. 1 Peter 5:7 says, "Cast all of your cares upon Him, for He cares for you."

The unhealthy type of not caring is when someone misunderstands the high of God as something that causes us to stop loving others. It's when we stop caring about our God-given family, friends, and responsibilities. Discerning between that which was religious guilt driven responsibilities and true God given responsibilities can be challenging at first.

However, it's not that complicated. God given callings are ones where there is empowerment and grace present. God given ones won't burn you out. They will have a "lifting" on them. You will feel the favor and blessing of God on them. Caring for your family, and paying your bills are things that we obviously should care about. You don't become too drunk to do this stuff. That's not God! This may take discernment at times, because "not caring" and "caring" both have an important place in the whack! Don't be quick to judge your neighbor on these. Start with your own life. Are you stressed and worried? Then you probably need to grow in "being too drunk to care"! Are your bills not getting paid, and is your family starting to experience some genuine neglect (God forbid that it would ever actually get that far)? Well, you might just need to grow in "caring!" Holy Spirit will always guide you through this kind of stuff. Listen and abide in grace!

ISN'T ENCOURAGING FOLKS TO GET "HIGH ON GOD" KIND OF SHALLOW? DOESN'T THE ENCOURAGEMENT OF A DRUNKEN SPIRITUALITY PRODUCE A SHALLOW SPIRITUALITY?

Well, it shouldn't! When understood rightly, being high on God is the very foundation for a rich expression of spiritual life. Though we are using vernacular that is common among twisted or uneducated portions of society, there is way more to it than just the drug language. All mystics throughout the ages were familiar with the altered state. Being inebriated in the wine cellar of God's love is all though the writings of the saints of all the ages!

The state of being high on God is how all revelation comes! You may not like the drug language. It may feel shallow or even degrading to some folks. However, in looking deeper into the actual substance of what it communicates, you will find something layered and quite profound. We're not just looking for a way to "be relevant to the kids." We are talking about being in a deep joyful awareness of heaven as a healthy part of sustainable life. We are talking about a state of consciousness that encounters the original state of humanity, receives revelation, and becomes a practical blessing to humanity and all the cosmos. If that is shallow, then, yes, it is shallow! The language can seem shallow at first, but I don't see it that way at all.

ISN'T AN ALTERED STATE JUST 'AN ESCAPE'? WON'T THESE MYSTICAL EXPERIENCES MAKE SOMEONE LESS PRESENT TO THE STATE OF REALITY?

Being high on God is not about escaping to a fake reality, but waking up to the true one! It is meant to be a true awareness of God, overwhelmed by his love, joy, and bliss in everyday life. Our God is intimately involved in people's lives on this planet. So, being intoxicated on the divine should also go hand in hand with being a good listener, a present person, a very involved person in this world. It is not only possible; it is quite natural for a true ecstatic mystic to be loving and caring of their fellow man! We may be high, but the high is intertwined with all that exists. If the high results in a fantasy world, or always being "spaced out," then that is a false high. The counterfeit highs of the world are like that. The true high is not. The true high is on Jesus, who though He was anointed with the oil of gladness above all his companions (Heb. 1:9), He was able to hold a normal job, hang out with all kinds of people, and be very present to His world. The virtues of Jesus truly do flow in this altered state of consciousness.

AREN'T HIGH PEOPLE OBNOXIOUS AND RUDE?

Again, the God high is not the same as the world's high! The world's high makes people do things that they may later regret. The world's high is often unkind and lacking compassion toward others. However, like we said before, the virtues of Jesus flow in this state of consciousness! It is blissful, just as God is blissful! It ALSO carries the same humility that God carries! If someone is regularly rude, that is not the high of God.

Now, sometimes people are not accustomed to being around joy and laughter! Someone innocently being happy can often be misinterpreted rudeness. It is sad, but this can be the case, simply because of culture shock. The first time I heard people who were high on God I thought they were being rude. They were in a public place just laughing and falling down. However, in looking back, they weren't really disrupting anyone. They weren't being rude to anyone. I just wasn't used to their culture! I didn't understand why a group of people would just be laughing for no reason and falling over. I may have even been a little jealous. Still, they weren't being rude. They were just laughing and enjoying God. To be honest, if they hadn't had been there doing what I thought was rude, I may not have realized the Glory the way that I did!

If someone seems to be rude while being high, you may be perceiving it rightly, or you may need to take a step back. Try to see their hearts. Maybe they need to grow a bit in expressing the high of God. Maybe also you need to let them be and get over your culture shock. Either way, rest assured, the true high of God carries the love, sweetness, and innocence of heaven on it! This isn't about creating a world of jerks!!

ISN'T IT IRREVERENT TO BE HIGH ON GOD? DOESN'T IT DISRESPECT THE NAME OF GOD?

I have often heard people claim that to be high on God is irreverent. However, irreverence is an issue of the heart! Reverence can be defined as: a feeling or attitude of deep respect tinged with awe; veneration. This is a heart matter! If you are going to judge someone's heart then you'd better have all the information! If someone doesn't have a deep respect for God, then that is not the God high! Most Glory drinkers are absolutely in love with God, though! Most God-junkies are reverencing God deeply by displaying to the world how enjoyable He is!

Again, this is probably more of an issue of culture shock. The true God high is respecting and reverencing God so much that your entire consciousness is filled with Him!

AREN'T YOU PROMOTING AN UNRIGHTEOUS LIFE-STYLE IN THIS HIGH ON GOD?

This one should be obvious by this point in the book. We are encouraging people to be high on God so that all the virtues of Jesus will flow easily through their life. The high of the world encourages unhealthy choices. The high of God is the consciousness of heaven, producing heavenly values and lifestyles!

WHAT ABOUT BALANCE? CAN'T YOU TAKE JOY TOO FAR?

I have literally heard both of these questions. They only make sense if you also believe that love should be balanced out with hate, or that truth should be balanced out with lies. Heavens, no! There are some things that just do not need to be balanced! Joy and bliss are two such things! The God high is one of these things! I am not a big fan of the idea of "balance" anyway. The idea of balance suggests that it is up to us to figure out life and maintain our own way, like walking in just the right amount of good and evil! No! We simply are to be led by the Spirit within! If the Spirit is ridiculously happy, then go with it! If the Spirit says to sell all your possessions and give them to the poor, then go with it! Obviously, there is such a thing as wisdom in life! Balance though? Hmm, I'm not sure. I don't see that much in the Bible. Is there any Biblical warning against too much joy? I don't remember any. I've never seen anyone in danger of that!

WHAT ABOUT SOBRIETY? DOESN'T IT SAY ALL OVER THE BIBLE TO "BE SOBER"?

This is a great point! There are dozens of scriptures that tell us to be sober! Some of those scriptures are talking about not drinking alcohol excessively. That is a great exhortation. Drinking too much alcohol ruins lives! It's not healthy! Of course, that's not what this book is talking about. We're talking about drinking God here, not liquor.

The other scriptures that encourage sobriety are talking about something that may not be apparent at first glance. The sobriety that these passages speak of is more about having a clear view of reality. You could define Biblical sobriety as, "staying aware of what is real and important." With that definition, then, these very passages are actually encouraging the God high! They are not warning against it at all! What they are discouraging is that distracted, self-conscious, worldly, non-heavenly minded way of thinking. There is a drunkenness on alcohol and earthly substances, there is a drunkenness on the fallen mindsets of the world, and there is a drunkenness that is the high of God. Two of those ways are harmful, and the Bible speaks out against them. One of those is healthy, and is quite Biblical. Understanding the difference may be subtle at first, but once you understand the meaning of true drunkenness those Biblical passages become quite obvious. None of the Biblical passages encouraging sobriety, when read in context, are talking about folks who are getting too excited about God. None of them are discouraging the God high. They are all discouraging either drunkenness on alcohol or drunkenness on the fallen way of thinking.

HOW CAN I STAY HIGH IF I'VE HAD A LOT OF BAD THINGS HAPPEN IN MY LIFE?

Firstly, as I begin to answer both this and the next question listed here, let me say how important this subject is to me. If this high doesn't work in the midst of problems, challenges, and pain, then it truly is a shallow thing. The world has gone through a lot of horrific stuff. You may have experienced unimaginable things. Because of these, being high on God may seem like a frivolous, distant idea. It may seem irrelevant, impossible, or too good to be true. I want to ask of you, dear heart, to stay open. Consider taking another look at this with me, when you are ready.
The apostle Paul once said, "Not that I am speaking of being in need, for I have learned in whatever situation I am to be content. I know how to be brought low, and I know how to abound. In any and every circumstance, I have learned the secret of facing plenty and hunger, abundance and need." (Phil. 4:11-12 ESV)

Paul had faced so much pain, sorrow, and torment! He was beaten, imprisoned, shipwrecked, and left for dead! Still, Paul found a joy that caused his heart to sing, even while locked away in chains. Paul's joy was not because He was going through easy circumstances. His high was coming from deep within. He had a bliss that could not be taken away. This is the God high! It's a secret of contentment, far beyond what this world can do to us.

What is the secret of contentment? It is the tangible sense of Christ within at every moment. It is the knowing that we always have God. Not just knowing it intellectually. I may know I have a million dollars, but until I am able to experience that money, it does me no good. No, you must be able to experience God at all times to truly be able to be content. Only the Glory can satisfy our soul deep enough to keep us continually encouraged. And, that's the kicker here! His Glory will never leave you! You may have been left by family, friends, or lovers. Jesus Christ will never leave you. God is inseparably united with you! This union with God IS the secret of contentment. You will always have God. When you become truly aware of this Glory within, you can always have bliss. Your rich bliss will genuinely be able to sustain you, no matter what may happen.

We will go through trials and challenges in this life. Still, God's Glory will never leave us. Do I believe that the Glory will bless us and cause our circumstances to improve? Yes! Still, even in times where circumstances don't improve, or turn out differently than we would have liked, we still have the best circumstance ever! We still have God! Knowing God as our permanent high means that we can always feel overjoyed in any circumstance!

You still may want to grieve when a loved one dies. That is totally appropriate! Still, the Glory will be there, intoxicating in the midst of it! He will never leave us! We may hate it when someone steals or damages something precious to us, but they can't take away the Glory! I even believe that the Glory is enough to give us inward ecstasy, while being tortured or burned at the stake! Countless stories of the martyrs can attest to this. Think of Stephen in the book of Acts! Read Foxe's Book of Martyrs. Many saints attest to experiencing great ecstasy even while having their heads cut off! The Glory is so potent! God is more than enough for us. This high is the ecstasy of always being with Him, regardless of circumstances. This doesn't mean you are expected to laugh or smile at all times. No way! Please don't get trapped in a cycle of pretending! God forbid that we would become fake little happy folks! What we are saying is that deep within, you can always be ravished by His thick honey love. This is authentic good news!!!

WHAT ABOUT SUFFERING?

This question, similar to the last one, is especially dear to my heart. If you have been through, or are currently going through deep suffering, I want to say how much my heart is genuinely there with you! You are amazing. You are loved. Your life matters to God, and to me. Take heart, dear soul, you are embraced right now by Love. If you can't even bear to imagine being high on God at this point, that is totally ok. God will meet you right where you are at. Just go with the flow of what you have grace for today. Take your time. Let God walk you through it personally and individually, whether that has anything to do with being high to you right now or not! Jesus has always been right there with you. He is loving you in the midst...

That being said, I have encountered many people who want to have their questions answered about suffering in regards to the God high. I'd like to respond to those questions in a general way, to help bring some clarity!

In this world, almost everyone has been violated deeply, some to unimaginable degrees of pain. For them, how could being perma-high be realistic? How could it be the plan of God? If it is God's plan, hasn't God missed it? Without writing a whole book just on the subject of suffering, let me attempt to answer what I can.

Here's my short overview of a suffering theology. Bear with me, and please read this whole section because what I say may shock you!

First of all, I don't believe that suffering was ever meant to be here! I know that some disagree with me, but that's how I see it. Suffering is not necessary, nor is it God's will for any of us. God's purpose for us is always health and life. That's how good our God is! Now, an element of freewill was also necessary, and this made room for humanity to cause pain, and of course God knew this would happen. Still, pain has never been God's plan for anyone. It never came from God. I believe that sin, sickness, pain, suffering, and death are all simply the results of the collective fallen consciousness of mankind. It's no one person's fault, no one group of people's fault, but it is the natural result of humanity as a whole adopting an independent and self-reliant consciousness. And, until the whole planet awakens to a dependent, union with God in Christrealization, suffering will continue. That is the only reason it exists. Suffering is not caused by God, nor is it necessary.

This can seem confusing because even if you are God-conscious, that does not mean that you won't suffer. You may still suffer deeply at times, until all of humanity wakes up. Someone may persecute you for your beliefs. A friend or loved one may leave you or pass away. This does not mean that God wants it this way. It just means that God has loved us so much that He dignified humanity with true freedom, even the freedom to hurt our world. We abused that freedom, as a people, and therefore we have hurt ourselves in the process. Still, God will always be present with us in the midst of it all! God is always present emanating His deep joy to us no matter what! In this rich intoxicating joy we can find the strength to carry on and co-create a better world for the future, together with God!

I also do not believe that our suffering is redemptive. Of course, God can USE even the worst situation to teach us things, but He doesn't CAUSE those situations to teach or help us! These situations are not necessary for any growth or for any other reason. To believe those types of things about God would be to say that He abuses his kids in order to teach them. I could not get high off of that type of God! Does God discipline? Yes! But, does He cause suffering? No.

As we said before, God's high is something that can be experienced in the midst of any circumstance. Suffering does not need to negate the continual high. You may have a difficult time sorting through your thoughts and emotions at a time of suffering. This is understandable. God is never standing over us demanding that we stay high! Still, the high will always be there for you in Christ within, whenever you are ready, whenever you look to it. I just want everyone to know that it is possible to stay high even in the deepest pain. However, God always understands exactly where you are at. God will not be disappointed in you in any way if you aren't always ecstatic. The ecstasy is a gift, not a demand! And, God knows just how to minister to your heart!

In closing this little section on suffering let me just say one last thing. I know that those of us who are "perma-high" may have not been as kind or understanding as we could have been to some folks who were suffering. This is not ok. It is never cool to rub your high in the face of someone who is hurting. It is never cool to make someone feel like a "less than" because they aren't always rejoicing. All I can say is that I hope this book will help us all to understand each other better. I do hope that in the days to come we can so tenderly communicate the bliss in ways that never leave anyone feeling discouraged or left out. All of our lives are unique and filled with beauty. I, myself, plan to be as kind and compassionate as I am able in Christ, to all people, simply offering the high to those who desire it. If what someone needs is for us to be with them and cry, then there is great bliss in doing that. Jesus wept. God is the Most High, and He's also the most compassionate and empathetic to the pain of the whole world. Life can be filled with some incredibly trying circumstances and challenges, but I just know that we can all love one another through it, allowing each other to be right where we are at, and finding the deep joy of heaven permeating even the toughest times!

All this being said, don't let anyone tell you that life is meant to be tough, or that we are destined for a journey through pain. Jesus sits with us in our hell, for as long as we need, but He also lifts us out of there! Jesus came that we may have life, and life to the full (John 10:10)! God is so empathizes with us in Christ! He is with us in our pain. But, He's also already suffered, died, and resurrected to lift us out of that pain, to the heights of heaven, once and for all!

WHAT ABOUT THE BIBLE? SOME PARTS OF IT DON'T SEEM VERY INEBRIATING OR LOVE DRUNK?

This is another massive and important question that could take many books to fully answer. However, it doesn't have to be extremely complicated. The central answer to this revolves around the reality of God's progressive revelation to humanity, which culminates in Jesus Christ. The Bible, and especially the Old Testament has some extremely harsh passages which should cause us alarm, and would definitely sober us up, if they were taken by themselves! However we must see them as how God interacts with a humanity that is insisting on its' own independent, rule based reality.

God spoke in many ways to people throughout the ages, some of which were ridiculously harsh. But, this was never God's full heart. We demanded a God who would interact with us according to the world we tried to create on our own. He has interacted in that world, sometimes even harshly and terribly, but it was all ultimately to reveal to us that this false world is never what He wanted. Ultimately God came to us in Christ to reveal His full heart, and wake us up to heaven on earth. The harsh parts of the Bible are still beautiful, when we can see that they were leading us to wake up out of that false reality. A world based on independence, rules, and eye for an eye leaves the whole world blind. When interpreted rightly, leading us to a Jesus Christ based world, the whole Bible is drunk!

CHAPTER 12
HIGH CHURCH & COMMUNITIES OF THE WHACK

We have touched on the topic of 'church,' 'community,' and 'spiritual family' briefly so far in this book. This is such a powerful and important reality in my heart and life! In fact, I see it as one of the primary joys of existence, to dwell together with brothers and sisters in unity! Community is the very nature of God. God is a Trinity, a community!

Community is such an ecstasy in itself, when the Glory Presence of God is being experienced there! It literally might even be the highest ecstasy of them all. Remember that Bible passage that says, "Where two or three are gathered together in my name, there I am with them."(Matt. 18:20)? Obviously, we can still experience God when we are alone, but something special, maybe even greater, happens when we experience God together! I've often found that at first, those who are new to the whack really only get high when they are in a group setting of like-minded Glory drinkers. People have asked me why that is. I believe it's because we were created to be together! It's not a bad thing! It just shows that the Glory comes from all of us, and when we are together a greater manifestation of Christ is present. The Drink is stronger together, you might say! Hahhaha!

So, in this light, let's explore! What can it look like to keep this beautiful community flow going? How does the high of God support and bless community? How important is it to be involved with a group of like-minded folks in the whack? Once we've started experiencing the ecstatic joy of the Lord in our church, how can we keep this from being just a 'mountain top' experience? These are powerful questions worth deeper exploration. It's a big deal! Living this out together is massive. It will also be a tell-tale sign of the depth of this altered state. Let's discuss!

IT'S ALL ABOUT ONENESS AND UNCONDITIONAL LOVE

In this day where Christianity has spread throughout the world in various forms and formulas for hundreds of years, there are a growing number of people who have had a bad experience of church. So many have been hurt, burdened, worn out, or just put to sleep by 'Christian community.' Let me start by saying, "I totally understand!" The number of churches, that I know of, that are really encouraging and promoting the high life are few and far between.

This chapter has absolutely nothing to do with encouraging you to plug in or stay connected to an irrelevant system of religion. In fact, I truly don't care if you consider yourself a "Christian" at all! Christianity has so often come to mean something entirely different than what it meant to the early church of Jesus. I don't give a rip about labels or systems or religion! All that stuff has become way more of a hindrance than it ever was a help. That being said, I do care about you getting jacked up on God in Christ! I also care deeply about you connecting with friends and intentional community in a dynamic way, as the body of Christ. There are new expressions forming, new life giving, non-manipulative, non-ritualistic communities of Life are emerging! And, I'm not really referring to what has been called "the emergent church," although I don't have a problem with any particular group as a whole.

The heaven on earth reality is all about oneness and unconditional love! So, even though so many people have been discouraged and disillusioned with churches and intentional spiritual communities, isolation can't be the solution either! I also can't believe in the sort of "community anarchy" that so many spiritual people in the western world have intentionally or unintentionally adopted! No, there is great hope for real, practical, day-in-day-out communities to form! It is the destiny of this planet, a beautiful natural result of being high on God, to begin to gather in unconditional love tribes and spiritual families! These won't be ritualistic controlling cultish families that exclude or live with an elite spirit. They look more like immediate families that realize their oneness with the entire world-wide extended family of all humanity! Such a beautiful dream!

Some clarification has been needed, though. The body of Christ has experienced so much scattering, and loneliness, and confusion. Many have given up on any hope of a healthy church life at all. Being the Body of Christ has been extremely challenging and difficult to say the least at times. I think we've all just needed to get really high together! My God, it makes us too blissed out and satisfied to remain divided or offended with one another! Long term love is completely natural in the Glory. I've found that the intoxicating bliss of God can actually make community life work! Why wouldn't it?

Through the rest of this chapter I want to summarize and expound upon some of the glorious truths I've experienced while living out this high life in community. It absolutely does work. I've tasted and seen! I've spent the last several years surrounded by blissed out friends, living heaven on earth together. I'm convinced that with just a few key understandings we can lay a bare bones framework that will act as a new wineskin for all this wine! Communities of bliss and genuine spiritual fruit are possible!

Starting out, it's important to at least have one foundational realization. We must begin with a value on community itself. We must start from the conclusion that without commitment to a real flesh and blood community of specific individuals, unconditional love just cannot be lived out. Until you are a part of community, you are not able to express unconditional love to the body of Christ. There is no canvas for agape love to be expressed without people to express it to long term! Until you have a team of real people to play with, then all you have is an 'idea' of love! The world is meant to know the 'God people' by their love! It's not by our preaching. It's not by our internet presence. It's not by our books. It is by watching us in daily life in real situations with actual people! We can talk all day about 'oneness,'t but people want to see if this love really works!!

The good news is that your new nature is absolutely powerful and able to handle this kind of day in day out love! You are one with Love! You need not be afraid of real people and the mess of real life! The God high flows so naturally with juicy unconditional love! Those of you who are whacked on the Spirit know! Don't you just want to keep hanging out with your amazing friends and family? Can't you just imagine all of the great times you are going to have together!?!? Oh, there is so much life and fun we will have together! Oh, the places we'll go! This is the substance of what flows through the veins of a God-high person, to live in real life, love, and adventure with a community! To demonstrate little non-exclusive camps of lovers all over the world, with real people, having real adventures! This is your nature, oh bliss-drunk ones! The Trinity is a community! The Trinity has not given up on true church. Oh, it's got to look a whole lot different than it has in most churches! But, it's the highest way to fly! High community is the great expression of the Glory of God!

HOW DOES THE HIGH OF GOD SUPPORT COMMUNITY?

One of the main reasons that communities and churches fail is because of insecure and hurting people both leading and participating in the group! Now, the high of God is not some magic wand that you wave over a person and 'poof' they never make mistakes. Yet, I do believe that the bliss one experiences when in the Glory of God truly produces wholeness! God's tangible Glory and love experienced to the point of intoxication gives a profound sense of security to one's identity. In His Presence we feel complete, seeing ourselves as we truly are, as God's masterpiece.

The biggest factor in producing healthy human behavior is that sense of feeling whole, complete, and satisfied in being loved. When someone feels loved and satisfied in who they are, they stop manipulating and using others. So many manners of psychological conditions go away when one has a sense that they are loved just for being as they are!

Communities are so often destroyed by this one root issue, insecurities and attempting to get from other people what can only be given by the Divine. The whack is an experiential knowing of the love of God. The whack is so satisfying to the soul, for it is the ecstasy that comes as the 'God-shaped hole' in our hearts is filled. The Presence of God always speaks of our completeness in Him. Imagine whole people living in community!! The true God high is communion with the Prince of Peace, the Whole One. Naturally this produces more stable and life-giving people. Start experiencing the bliss of heaven, and all of a sudden a hundred other inter-personal problems begin to go away!

Besides the fact that this bliss produces healthier community participants, we also have the amazing reality of its encouragement towards a community atmosphere of celebration. So many communities become burdensome due to the constant serious and business-like tone of gatherings and activities. Getting high in the Holy Ghost just makes people more fun! It lends itself to more celebratory gatherings! Now, this doesn't mean that there is no place for structure or business discussions. It means that overall the God high maintains a celebratory atmosphere in the midst of it all. This makes church life much more sustainable for the average person. Ask a hundred people in your neighborhood whether they'd like to go to a business meeting or a party, and see what they prefer!

People were created to celebrate! This life of enjoyment makes community much more sustainable. Church becomes something that people look forward to. Children and young people especially feel more at home in a celebration. The atmosphere of joy just makes the wheels turn so much more easily in all facets and dimensions! This is a big deal. Take a look around you at the churches and communities that are experiencing some sense of growth and acceleration. There is almost always a healthy dynamic of celebratory life present there.

There are so many other areas that the high of God empowers in a community life. It would be worth an entire additional book! I will however just mention one last major benefit here of the God high to community. The God high facilitates an acceleration of discipleship within a community.

As we stated throughout the book, the virtues of heaven flow effortlessly in the bliss. So, a high community is one where supernatural/natural fruit will flow without numerous programs or intense scheduled discipleship. Just keep them drinking of the Glory and growth will manifest! The fruit and gifts of the Spirit will flow freely in a Glory-wine drinking church! It's such a beautiful way to live life together. There is naturally so much patience on a whacked person, so much love, so much joy, so much faithfulness, it goes on and on! In the place of ecstatic satisfaction, people are inspired to listen to their Lover within for direction, no matter what it may be. The God high quickens discipleship. Remember, we are encouraging folks to be overwhelmed and overcome by God Himself! This puts people in deep experiential touch with the ultimate Teacher, Discipler, and Father!

WHAT COULD A HIGH COMMUNITY LOOK LIKE?

Let's address the creation of the new wineskin (a reference to Mark 2:22 when Jesus says that new wine must be placed in new wineskins, e.g. a new way of life). Many folks get high on God, and then experience a rejection by their local community. Either that or the sober community that they were once a part of no longer feels healthy or relevant. For this reason, new examples of life together must be created. We can't just do things the way that sober church has been done. A new consciousness requires a new expression and lifestyle!

This is not to say that everyone should just give up on the communities they were a part of. No! Unconditional love is committed and gives all opportunity for people to grow along with you. Your community can be loved even if they continue to disagree with you. Obviously, though, this can be a challenging place to navigate. What happens when you realize the heaven on earth whack before your church does? What can we do if we awaken to genuine Glory but our community does not? Well, there is not one pat answer for this. It takes time, listening to the Spirit, and a real sense of practical wisdom. No one person's decision here will be the same as another's. Be a listener and feel it out with compassion and care, hearing the hearts of those you've been committed to. It could be very possible that there is an openness to you there. Maybe you didn't even notice it at first. Maybe you can grow together with them! The big issue is this one specific area, openness.

If I could give one word of counsel here, it would be this: pay attention to the openness. If the group and especially those who are seen as leaders are open, then that makes a big difference. You also must be open to learning from them too. It goes both ways. It is so ideal to value long term love and commitment; to not just give up on people quickly! However, if the group is not open to your growth and whack, especially after giving them an honest chance through conversation, it can be healthy for you, and even them, for you to move on. Don't write them off as hopeless or "less-than!" However, you need to connect with those who share at least some foundational values. The Good News of heaven on earth and the manifest Glory of God are pretty big starting points. You need to connect with those who will at least allow you to be you without stifling the Gospel's revelation in your life. Maybe they will be open to that, give them a good long chance! If they are not open, however, do not feel bad about connecting with another group as your immediate spiritual family. Honor all people as part of your extended family in Christ! But, don't be squelched by spending long years in a specific place where you are not encouraged to be yourself.

Once you determine where your community is meant to be, through listening to the call of God and your holy heart, then dive in! Begin to move forward in new expressions of Glory community aka 'whack community' aka church! I, myself, have been a part of a home fellowship called Hillside Covenant Community since 2005. It has been amazing. I will share a little bit about this group here, to maybe give a picture of one healthy example. And, then we can also discuss some other cool ideas you may consider for real whack community formation as well! I'm excited!! I love to see this real life stuff come into fruition!

When you get high on Jesus your priorities change. One of the things that happen is that you just begin to fall in love with people. You begin to see people the way that God sees them. You begin to feel the way God feels about them. You actually like people! The easily annoyed and quickly frustrated attitude you once had towards people fades away. You begin to enjoy just hanging around God's kids! You aren't looking at them for what you can get out of them. You aren't looking at them with suspicion, either. You just enjoy and appreciate who God has made them to be. You see them as the most precious thing in all of heaven on earth! It no longer becomes necessary to discipline yourself into going to church. You love worshiping, praying, and fellowshipping with people, but not in a religious way. A natural desire to commune with God and your fellow friends and neighbors in everyday life begins to emerge.

Because of this new addiction, not only to the high of God, but to the high of God in fellowshipping with your fellow humans, new structures must emerge for church. It's difficult to even call them structures, because they will be just bare bones enough to support the natural flow of the body life. Still, it will be essential to your love of Life to find new long term ways of doing community.

NEW WINESKINS FOR THE NEW WINE

The example I'm most familiar with has been my home community, Hillside Covenant Community. What we have done is to get together in homes, at least one evening a week, for the last ten years. But, more than just a once a week home gathering, many of us have moved into the same neighborhood! We just love each other! It would be too hard to only see each other once a week! We see our co-workers and school mates way more than that! To enable our community to really have time together living, partying, and growing, we have moved into the same geographic location. It became a goal of ours to be able to walk to one another's houses!

As well as moving close to one another, we also adopted a more open format for our gatherings than most churches have had. Our gatherings are often just open format, where anyone can speak or share what God is doing with them or just ideas, prayer requests, and the like. We have a family table that we often sit at to just chew the fat and talk about life. It's not about one man preaching, and a bunch of other people tithing. We have adopted more of an intentional communal focus, where all the parts of Christ's body are allowed to function, and the format can look different each week.

The big deal when we get together though, too, is to keep the Gospel and the Glory central! This is the source of our bliss! So, we will usually have someone at every gathering sharing the simple message of heaven on earth in Jesus, with demonstrations and manifestations. Whether in song, or in outright teaching, the message of Jesus comes forth. It's just too much bliss not to remind each other weekly of the source of it all. That weekly reminder is one of the highlights of my week every time. Everything else just works better when we hear the Gospel and get all jacked up off of the substance of its Reality! Our meetings get crazy often times, and we have learned to not criticize people's manifestations in our gatherings. We let the God inebriation flow. Sometimes people are howling, laughing for extended periods of time, or all kinds of joyous expressions. As long as it's not hurting anyone, we have given much room for ecstatic expressions in the community. So many times, people have been healed in these atmospheres! The party bears fruit of all kinds! And, even if sometimes people are not always fully manifesting directly from the Spirit of God, we avoid being critical or controlling, letting people learn for themselves for the most part.

More than just meetings and sitting at the table, we also have begun to embrace getting into the community to demonstrate real societal change. We opened a coffee shop for four years, just to get to know our neighbors and share our joy with them over coffee or tea. We had a room in the back where we would pray for folks, and we saw some crazy outbreaks of miracles and joy in that prayer room! We love to host gatherings for people to come and experience the Presence that is in our midst. We are even currently looking at buying land together to demonstrate more of an organic farming type of life, communing with nature, and to possibly run a retreat center for holistic refreshment! In the midst of all of this, we are just living normal life, being in the world, but not of it. Many times our community will see outbreaks of love in normal places like malls, bars, or street corners. Just being together manifests crazy life wherever we go!

Now, that's how my community is doing it. But, you may have other expressions! The important part is that you are really enabling the true party of heaven to explode! Do you really know the people you are committed to? Oh yeah, that reminds me! My home community has expressed our commitment to one another by an exchanging of rings together! Each one of us, when we are ready to tell the group, "Hey, I'm in this for the long haul," we get them a ring. It's been a cool way to let one another know that we are not just here when it's convenient, but we are down for partying long-term, through thick and thin! Hahahah! But, like I said, you may have a different expression! The point is that you gather, get to really know one another, commit to them as people, and get hammered drunk together living out the Gospel! Your goal of hanging out together is not to fix each other, but to celebrate God! Your goal is not to fix the world, but to demonstrate unconditional love with the joy of the Lord as your strength! And, in this heavy intoxicating joy, your community will be strong!

Even if you only know one or two people at first that are open to you getting whacked. Gather together with them! Ask God if this can be your community! It doesn't have to start as this big glamorous thing. Just meet once a week in a cafe and encourage one another with stories, scriptures, and whacky fun. Fellowship somewhere with someone regularly in the Holy Ghost! Have a drunken Friday night party in your basement! There are very few regions where something small like this couldn't start. Don't be discouraged, you may feel like the only one for a while! Yet, God always has someone that will come into your life at just the right time, maybe a group of someones! You can get together regularly, be committed to one another, and drink the Gospel! God is passionate about placing the lonely in families! It's as simple as that! There is obviously more we could explore, in growing a community, the nature of leadership, buildings, money, ministry, and whatever else, but I am confident if you engage the simple things, all the rest will follow. Even if you are reforming a pre-existing group, the truth is still the same! Drink together, and He will build it, and they will come! LOL!

Lastly, let me say something about the community anarchy mindset. Why is it important to have a wineskin at all? Like, I mentioned earlier, many western believers have adopted an idea, whether they know it or not, that all true fellowship must happen spontaneously. While I am a big advocate of swinging the pendulum closer to pure spontaneity than to its' alternative, rigid control, I still believe in some intentionality and structure. It doesn't have to take much. Some kind of mutually agreed upon regular gatherings or get-togethers are so vital, even if it's just once a month, or through the internet, though I would recommend more than that. The solution to the problem of religion and sobriety in church life is not to throw out all wineskins altogether. I believe that a loose, freedom based, flexible intentionality and structure can emerge in any context. Not much more is needed to be said on that. However, for the record, I do believe that after all the boxes are broken, our regular gathering together will still remain as an awesome life giving way to party! Having some kind of organized group that is mutually committed in Christ is healthy, even if when you get together you just roll around and laugh all night!

HOW AN INTENTIONAL WHACK COMMUNITY HELPS YOU

More than telling you how to do community specifically, I am further motivated simply to encourage you to engage it in the first place. I want you to see its' value deeply in your heart, so you will naturally have the passion to overcome obstacles in figuring out the 'how' that works for your unique group. If you understand the value then you will stay with it to tweak your wineskin with the Holy Ghost. You will embrace the challenging fun times of trial and error! Remember, there is no formula. There is no one right way to do Glory community! Mega-church can work! House church can work! Even internet church can work sometimes in this era of history! There is no set way to do it! You and your community get the privilege of co-creating with God together, a beautiful individual community!

So, what other reasons are there to connect with this value of Glory community? Well, for one thing, it helps to encourage your own personal bliss! Hahah!! Honestly, I have seen too many Holy Ghost drunks start to feel all sobered up because they didn't value staying connected with other like-minded friends in an intentional way. Don't be foolish! The body of Christ is your body! You won't be happy without them!

As many hard times as you may have experienced with your body, you still need it! Don't commit spiritual suicide by disconnecting from your body! Now, sometimes there may be an unusual season, especially when recovering from church drama, or needing a sabbatical alone with your spouse and kids. During these short seasons, you might go into a time of not fellowshipping with many people around the Gospel. Yet, don't let this become a life-style! I'm a big believer in the old song that says, "The more we get together the happier we'll be!" Isaiah 65:8 also says, "The new wine is found in the cluster." It's just amazing how encouraged you can get, not by attending religious services and rituals but by remaining in real intimate fellowship with those who love and believe in you! It's worth it for the encouraging high alone!!

Not only does whack community encourage your heart, it also allows you to experience and partner with parts of God that you wouldn't taste by yourself! This is a big key! There are a lot of folks in spiritual circles today who are emphasizing how complete we are in Christ! This is an amazing thing! I am all about that too, believe me! Still, this does not mean that we will experience all of God without our brothers and sisters! 1 Corinthians 12:21 says, "The eye cannot say to the hand, I don't need you." We actually need our brothers and sisters regularly in our lives in order to manifest all of Christ! I see several different ways that we actually need our brothers and sisters. We need them for the love and relational fulfillment. We need them for their perspective. We need them for their spiritual gifts. We need them to complete the masterpiece of wholeness that humanity can display. This does not mean that we are in lacking in any situation, for we will always have access to the people that we truly need at any given moment. This also doesn't mean that we should become "needy" trying to use our neighbor in some unhealthy way. It simply means to go with the flow, and be intentional about staying in touch with your community. And, as you do begin to love on your neighborhoods, cities, regions, and the world, you will function so much more powerfully having all these gifts in operation. When you want to minister and do "stuff" together, you'll see exponential fruit being intimately involved with a well-oiled love machine! Did you ever see the old cartoon, "Captain Planet?" Hahahhahaa, yeah, well anyways…

Another personal benefit for staying connected to an intentional Glory community is that it keeps you sharp! It keeps your consciousness rooted in reality when you have so many differing worldviews interacting with each other. When there is no one around it can be easy to get lost in pie in the sky ideas that don't encourage life. Being around others, keeps you honest, humble, and down to earth. Sometimes this will be the most challenging thing! Your community won't always agree with you! During those times it can often be tempting to withdraw and back away from your friends. It is at that very time that remaining close can be so beneficial! They may not even be right when they disagree with you, but they can still be of help. It's in that moment that you have opportunity to reject the illusion of ego, embrace patience, and display the pure beauty of unconditional love! Without commitment to them in community, they may never truly be able to experience the love of another who will never give up on them. You get to be Christ to them, and continue to empower their heart, listening to their voice, even when they're wrong. And, heaven forbid that you are ever wrong, if you have a respect and humble attitude toward your community, they may just help you get back on track too.

We don't need to adopt complicated or hierarchical accountability structures. That has made so many people feel afraid, manipulated, or hindered by community. If you just truly spend time together, being vulnerable in life, you will have a natural accountability that comes in just being involved in each other's lives. Just because you are high in the Glory doesn't mean you won't ever make mistakes! Having others who are communing with heaven all around you, gives you a sweet help and encouragement net that can be truly be protective and empowering in any season of life.

SUSTAINING THE LONG TERM HIGH OF GLORY COMMUNITY

One of the biggest concerns of my heart is to see these beautiful whacked out communities last! I want to see them thriving in greater and greater ways, on into eternity. I'm convinced that these communities will do just that, being the fulfillment of the restoration of all things! In the tangible Presence of Jesus, this is quite natural and effortless. Still, this means the using of Glory wisdom. In my few years of flowing in this ecstatic state, I've already seen multiple communities flourish and then disappear. Sometimes afterwards these drunken Jesus lovers don't even want to be friends anymore. Sometimes they don't even want to drink the Glory anymore. This is not cool! That is not the Glory! So, my heart is inspired, not as much by those negative stories, but simply by the love of God and humanity to share what I've learned. I think a few simple keys can keep us drinking together, from Glory to Glory, continuing in momentum for many, many years to come!

One key to sustaining long term community is to have a high value on not giving up on people. Keeping a focus on the fact that these people are always going to be family is very important! If you have not discussed and communicated this high value of unconditional love and commitment to one another, then it's easy to just move on to something else. I feel that this is too valuable to just push off to the side. The community must discuss and remind one another regularly of the value of their relationships and not giving up on one another. This must always be done in a way where people know that they are always free to go where they feel led. It's not a controlling thing! However, communicating that long term value on remaining close is valuable and important. In the midst of the commitment and long term love, though, keep it fun! Heaven is a fun place! Earth is a fun place! If the atmosphere of the group gets too heavy people won't be able to hack it week after week. Stay intentional, but keep it light. Remember, sustaining the kingdom and saving the world doesn't depend on your efforts! Jesus came that we might have life, and life to the full (John 10:10)! So, don't just worship and do ministry together! Have fun and enjoy life together!

Dynamically connected with the fun and lightness of the community is the whack itself! I have seen communities sober up! What a tragedy! Heaven is always whacked! The Glory is only more and more intoxicating each day. Somehow though, through false teaching and the distractions of life, some people seem to just 'move on.' I have literally heard people say that their church had matured past the whack. This is not the nature of heaven! That's like saying God has matured past virtue. It's not even an option! Value the whack. Value the wisdom of chapter ten of this book. I think we've pretty well established the importance of the whack in this book already! Stay high, my friends! It's a not so obvious open secret of maintaining community. Hahahahaha!

Another big deal in community is to let everyone's voice be heard. This can sound like another obvious thing, and yet for some reason the old wineskins often lend themselves to the creation of an elite class within community! Whacked community is one where everyone can express

Christ, for we are all One with Him! Understanding Christ in every person can awaken a respect and ability to listen to each person within the group. Even when a person seems very confused or immature, God will still remain present in them. This doesn't mean that we need to make every person a primary teaching voice in the group, but find ways to include all people. Do what you can to create an atmosphere where, for the long term, people can feel heard and freely express their heart. The party depends on this. It's just more fun to party all together!

Sustaining the party will also depend deeply on the way you treat doctrine or teachings. Love, expressed through the Gospel of Jesus Christ, is a necessity. All other teachings are secondary. If someone is against love, or the source of love awakening, aka the Good News, then you have a pretty important thing to discuss. This might cause a community to discuss if they are all able to continue in close spiritual fellowship together without part of the group believing the Gospel. However, if someone disagrees with you about almost any other doctrine, it's important to give them room within the group, (unless it's obviously harming people). Even when some folks don't believe the Gospel, if they are willing to love and remain humble, you may easily still be able to fellowship with them.

The point is, having a solid foundation of the good news that releases love is primary. All else is secondary. Community is not based on doctrine, it is based on love. It is based on relationships. The whack is a love whack! To stay in whacked community, you need the love first! Now, the Gospel awakens this kind of God love. But, to make any other doctrine a non-negotiable is a trap. Stay with your team! Keep partying with your friends even through the craziest of doctrinal disagreements. Even, when their behavior is not love, or they seem deceived in some way, draw close. There is way more continual whack on staying involved and intimate with one another through the disagreements and trials of life. Remember, we are family!

Lastly, you do want to stay engaged with loving on people and ministering to your region. You don't want to just gather around projects primarily. Have fun and just go to birthday parties and sporting events! Still, also, it is so key to stay focused on loving your region, loving your neighbors! A river that stops flowing outward will become merely a stagnant pool. You were created to have rivers of living water flowing from your heart. It feels good for you, refreshing and flowing, when you are spilling that river onto others! The body of Christ is the steward of a region. Care for the poor! Love the hurting! Minister among the suicidal, the drug addicts, the prostitutes, the needy! You and your community will love the way it feels when you do this in a relaxed yet steady way. There is just so much whack on loving your neighbors! It is a great way to keep things fresh. Look especially for ministries that flow naturally from the hearts of the community. Try to find service and ministry opportunities that several community members are passionate about. This won't be a problem in the whack, because heavenly drunks love to love! Spontaneous love and ministry are important, and so are intentional ongoing outreaches. This will so often help to keep the party cranking!

HOW TO AVOID BEING A CULT

Lastly, in our chapter on Glory intoxicated communities, we should address the issue of cults. There are many people across the world at this point in history that will likely label you as a cult simply because you get high on God. I wouldn't try to defend myself too much. Let the fruit of your life speak to them. It is very hard to argue with someone about it, unless they are asking with an open heart. This doesn't mean you can't have a healthy conversation with folks. Still, many people will label any spiritual group that doesn't make sense to them as a 'cult'. You may also get cult accusations just because you are a part of a smaller group, or a house church group, or a group that meets more than once a week. These are all frivolous accusations as well. The size, frequency, or location of the meetings makes no difference.

What does make a group "a cult?" If you are already concerned about whack communities being a cult, it may be hard for you to read this section at all (or any part of this book for that matter). You might be having a very hard time trusting my words. I understand that. This stuff is drastically different than what most churches are like currently! So, I encourage you to please do your own research to discover a more objective perspective. I am not asking for unquestioning devotion in this book whatsoever! Examine everything. Talk to God about it! However, in my understanding there are two things that make a group a cult. I believe that you can identify a cult by either manipulation or foundationally unorthodox beliefs.

MANIPULATION

You and your community can avoid becoming cultish by avoiding all forms of manipulation. Manipulation is also tied very closely with control. The very essence of this Gospel is that God has made Himself one with us and awakens our hearts to this glorious reality through radical trust! You do not need to control anyone! You do not need to use pressure to motivate someone into doing anything for you or your group! Also, if they do find themselves joining with your community, please do not use any tactics to attempt to manipulate them to stay.

Everyone who is in a community usually feels deeply about their involvement there, or else they wouldn't have joined. Do not let this passion for the group or its' mission turn into something that violates others by pressuring them to do what your group wants. This can manifest through the "us and them" mentality where by people are treated as "less-than" if they aren't in your group. This can also turn strange when "leaders," or devotees to the "leaders," begin to pressure others to do things for the leaders' sake. If someone wants to give money, attention, or blessings freely to someone they respect or have benefitted from, then that's one thing. However, when there is manipulation to benefit a leader in some way, it's cultish. Using guilt, condemnation, or any sort of pressure to cause people to do anything that the group may be promoting is manipulation, and is the tell-tale sign of a cult. Avoid manipulation, and you pretty much avoid half of all cultish-ness. Walk in love grace and freedom, and you will avoid being a cult.

UNORTHODOX BELIEFS

I believe that there is so much room in the body of Christ for differing perspectives on so many issues. In fact, the subject matter of this book will be considered by many to be unorthodox and heretical already, though I obviously believe that it is not. It may be unusual, pushing the envelope for many, but we are still promoting the historical central teachings of Jesus Christ and his church. It is for this reason that I want to make something even more clear. Your community does need a healthy foundation in the historic essentials of the church!

The church hasn't got it all wrong through the ages. There have been some major truths that have emerged as healthy beliefs. These will bring great benefit when understood and applied passionately throughout your community! Do not despise what your forefathers and mothers have stood upon throughout the ages! These foundational orthodox beliefs can be found in historic creeds such as the Apostle's Creed or the Nicene Creed.

These healthy foundations are essentially about keeping a focus on Jesus Christ and Him crucified, including a few key elements dynamically related to that. Things like knowing the Trinity, believing in Jesus Christ as a literal person, as Lord and Savior, revealing the Father, by the power of the Holy Spirit. Sticking to the centrality of what Jesus Christ reveals is so healthy and life giving! God as Love, Jesus giving humanity the free effortless gift of union with God, these things are truly orthodox. Stick to these basics, not just in head knowledge but in vibrant living experience. These foundations will keep you from becoming a cult.

Just because someone is high on God does not mean that they get to introduce doctrines that take away from the focus on Jesus and the pure love of God. Also, great manifestations of power or Glory do not necessarily mean that someone's teaching is healthy or true. It's still ok for drunks to use discernment, and stick to the historic foundations of the faith! These historic foundations may not be the same as modern day evangelicals or mainstream Christians currently believe, however. That brings us to the next chapter of our intoxicating adventure. Have another big ol' Glory drink, and let's read on…

CHAPTER 13
BEYOND "CHRISTIAN" BOXES

The last chapter ended by reminding us of the historic foundations of the church of Jesus Christ. These foundations of faith in Christ are the foundations of staying jacked up on God! There is no other way that communicates the love of God so clearly, so intimately, so freely for all. There is no other way that gives real, free salvation to humanity. Jesus Christ reveals the clearest, purest, highest, and only sustainable lasting ecstasy for all the cosmos! I truly believe this. I am convinced of no other way but Jesus, in reality and authenticity!

However, Jesus has been widely misunderstood in the Christian church for generations. So many of these misunderstandings regarding what Jesus is about continue on to this day. We also understand that God has surely been present and active, speaking to people in all times and in all places. There are many groups of people that have experienced Christ outside the box of so-called Christianity! On top of all of this there are also many revelations, manifestations, phenomena, and scientific discoveries which are also outside the box of traditional Christianity even though they don't necessarily disagree with the foundational elements of Christocentric doctrine.

I realize that by writing a chapter like this, I risk losing what little support I still have from Christian sources. However, I am compelled to continue.

I don't think that Jesus ever had any other agenda other than loving people and wanting them to be truly high on Life! For this reason, I have adopted the same mindset. Jesus was friends with tax-collectors and drunkards. Jesus' scope of life seemed to be able to find resonance wherever He went, regardless of whether or not the people he was with seemed to fit any specific type of spiritual box or orthodox background. I think this was one of the most powerful and important parts of Jesus' life. It is worth asking why and how Jesus lived this way. The answer could result in the blessing of so many more people!

Through this kind of authentic relevance and ability to connect with the various places of consciousness in humanity, I believe that we can release a greater awareness of the full scope of salvation, as Jesus did. These may be outside of what is commonly being thought of as 'Christian', while still remaining faithful to the true historic essentials of the faith.

The Christian church has added too many restrictions and non-essentials to the message of Christ. Don't get me wrong, I believe that salvation is found in Christ alone. However, I think that the Christ experience can be dynamically widened and expanded. We may be able to live such richer and fuller lives by exploring some new concepts without fear. We may be able to re-define and/or expand the common understanding of Christ life in a powerful way, without losing its' essence. In fact, we hopefully can simply reveal its' most potent, original essence!

I mean, something needs to change in the church world, right? I am not at all excited about bringing new folks into most of the churches I know of today. There are various reasons for this. My point is not to list problems that I see with the Christian church today. Nor is my point to be discouraging to believers in Jesus. It is my desire to communicate, to both those who think of themselves as 'Christians' and to those who don't, that this God high is not about some religious set of doctrines that you must agree to. It's about life! It's about living for all that we were created for! It's about joy! It is for freedom that Christ has set us free (Gal. 5:1)!

I want to point out that there is much to explore in this glorious full scope of existence! Jesus Christ is not the end of exploration. Jesus is the foundation of all true exploration! I also want to say that although this book has been profoundly Jesus centered, it is also just as much focused on a real expansive happy and high way to live. I love the God high because it relates to so much more than the western Christian worldview! Being high on Jesus has very little to do with the Christian culture of the day. That culture is full of beautiful people, many of whom are so genuine, and well-meaning! Yet, I often do not even label myself as a Christian because of the various popular Christian teachings and practices that I abhor.

I love the foundational teachings of Jesus Christ and the basics of His historic church! However, I have found many concepts that are not commonly thought of as in agreement with the Christ life that in fact only reveal it all the more clearly! Some of these have come from interacting with those of various backgrounds, religions, and worldviews. I want us to recognize that there are many ways that God has been moving in and among those who don't claim to be Christians. God has been active everywhere at all times! No one has been left alone. His grace among all of us is truly so beautiful.

In this chapter I'd like to discuss some of these concepts I just mentioned, as they relate to life and the God high! These may come as either a shock or a relief for you to read! But, please just don't just toss them out! Consider how they could be more Christ centered than you maybe thought! Whether you are a 'Christian' or not…take a big breath of Glory!!! Let's explore!

GOD IS EVERYWHERE

The revelation of Jesus is that of "Emmanuel", which means, "God with us." This was one of the names that they called Jesus himself. This revelation was to come as a comfort, not just because God was appearing at one point in human history, as Jesus Christ, but that God had always been with humanity, and always will be. The 139th Psalm makes it truly clear that there is nowhere we could go where God is not. God was with you when you felt abandoned and alone. God was with you in your greatest moments of success and joy as well. We have been seen, and we are known. God has never been far away. And, Romans chapter 8 says that nothing can separate us from the love of Christ! So, not only has

God always been near, but God has always been loving humanity!

This kind of commitment and intimacy in ever presence can enable a continual God high! Not only that, but it also means that anyone can get high on God at any time! They don't even have to be a 'Christian.' I mean, if the Glory is filling the whole earth, as it says in Isaiah chapter six, then who is separate from the Glory? No, the message of Christ is not communicating an exclusion of certain people, but an inclusion of all! Anyone who does not understand this is not communicating a full message of Jesus Christ. This has always been about God's love for all, in all times, and in all places. The God high is for everyone, no matter what their background, no matter their past, present, or even future. This is such a powerful and profound reality! To see the Presence of God present in, with, and among all people, in all its' Glory, will change so much about the way we live. Consider that this was so much of what Christ came to communicate!

THE GOD HIGH IS NOT ABOUT CONVERTING PEOPLE

There is another reality that I find profoundly connected to God's omni-presence. God does not have an agenda of converting people! If God has always been with us, then we don't need to invite Him into our lives. God just wants us to be loved and happy. God has always been in our lives, and will always continue to bless us no matter what. God is a good creator, father, and friend. He's way too healthy of a Person to have formed us for a shallow existence of conditional love. He doesn't have an agenda to enforce upon us. Christ did not show up on planet earth to form a new religion or gather converts. This book is not about that either!

There will be way more whack when we are simply able to enjoy and spend time with one another, regardless of beliefs, without agendas. We can discuss spiritual things, absolutely. But, this is not about spreading the fear of hell, or fear of anything for that matter. Jesus Christ came to offer a high life with no threats or hidden agendas. Jesus was so fully aware that God had already been moving in people's lives. In Acts chapter 10, Peter finds out that God shows no partiality to interacting with people no matter where they come from, even spiritually (Acts 10:34). So, Jesus also didn't come to talk down to people, or force his conversations either. Christ has beautiful truth to offer, but in a humble, happy, helpful way! Let's stick to the same pattern with one another! Holy Spirit is moving day and night around every person, you need not worry that your agenda is necessary to show them the Light. In fact, non-Christians may often times have many amazing whacked things that they understand and experience, sometimes even more so than some parts of the church. Why? God has been active in their lives from before they were born! And, they too have a unique destiny that God has been shaping in specific and unique ways for quite some time!

This is not to say that Abba, Jesus, and Holy Spirit don't want people to wake up to the Truth! And, as we spend time with people, we will feel genuine inspiration to share the Gospel, and minister powerfully. However, ministry to others is meant to be a much more respectful partnership with the beauty of who they already are and what God has already put inside of them, rather than the "pressure to convert" mentality that has so often been normal in modern church!

NON-CHRISTIAN ECSTATICS

In light of God's Presence everywhere, it would be remiss not to mention some 'non- Christian' ecstatics in this book! I didn't include them in the ecstatic history part of the book mostly because my Christian readership would be less likely to receive from that section if I had. I do also believe that a clear focus on Jesus Christ makes for the highest and most beneficial high. This book does not at all hide the fact that I believe salvation to be found in no one else. So, I do want to mention a few here, but I may not give them as much focus as I did to the Christian ecstatics of history. This does not mean that there is not much benefit to looking them up for yourself. I highly recommend reading their biographies and looking for the Glory gems found there! These guys had some really high on God experiences. Does that mean that all of their experiences were 100% pure or right on? Not at all! But, neither are all the experiences of the Christian ecstatics! Have fun and dig deeper! Explore outside the box. Be free! Holy Spirit will lead you into all Truth, Truth that will not disagree with Jesus.

Here are a few interesting ecstatics that are outside of Christian boxes:

JALAL AL-DIN RUMI (1207-1273) – Persian Sufi Muslim poet whose writings reflect experiences being high on God, and was known to spin into ecstatic experiences.

BA'AL SHEM TOV (1698-1760) – Founder of Hasidic Judaism who had ecstatic mystical experiences and encouraged dancing and joy in God.

SRI RAMAKRISHNA OF BENGAL (1836-1886) – Hindu mystic priest who had more ecstatic experiences than many of even the most prominent mystics.

MEHER BABA (1894-1969) – Indian 'Avatar' who encouraged God intoxication, discouraged drug use, and taught throughout the world, despite maintaining silence for the last 44 years of his life.

BILL WILSON(1895-1971) – Co-founder of Alcoholics Anonymous, who may or may not have been a Christian. He had an experience of being high on God after which he was set free from addictive alcoholic behavior.

ALAN WATTS (1915-1973) – Philosopher and Episcopal priest, combined Zen Buddhist, Hindu, mystical Christian, and Western ideas. Experienced spiritual ecstasies and was an influential speaker.

TIMOTHY LEARY (1920-1996) – American psychologist who promoted experimentation with drugs and getting high as a means of therapy and consciousness expansion, more of an atheist.

TERRENCE MCKENNA (1946-2000) – Author and lecturer who deeply studied psychedelic drugs looking for the various benefits to the human race that altered states have to offer

MOOJI (1954-PRESENT) – An Advaita spiritual teacher/guru, often referred to as the "laughing Buddha" for the ecstatic experiences he has had and seems to effect on others.

JASON SILVA (1982-PRESENT) – Film maker and ecstatic futurist who promotes hedonism and various forms of consciousness expansion unto creating a better world, also an atheist.

Now, in the lives of all of these ecstatics, we can find something that God was revealing to them, yes, even to the atheists! I list them to provoke you. Go on your own journey. Listen to the Holy Spirit! Do I believe that the ultimate revelation is found in Jesus Christ? Yes! But, God is active all around you. If you truly want to learn about a subject, you need to explore all the sources related to that subject. Eat the meat, and spit out the bones. There is so much more high to be had when we are open to God everywhere! Ultimately it is all about what proves to be real, and has the most real love, joy, peace, kindness, goodness, etc. on it. Don't just believe anything! Trust Holy Spirit within. If it produces good fruit, listen, for you will find God's Truth there!

THE GOD HIGH TRANSCENDS LANGUAGE

Speaking of good fruit, isn't the most desirable fruit the juicy fruit that we call 'love'? Everyone loves love. Everyone wants to be love drunk! This is another reason that I love the God high. It absolutely blows away the boundaries of any religion or set of beliefs. The drunkenness of God relates to all people. I've never met a person who, deep down, didn't want to be high on God. It's a universal language! Now, I'm not saying that we all desire it in the same way. Some people are more subtle or refined about their desire. Most people's pursuit of the ecstasy of love or God gets mis-directed toward some temporal pleasure. However, the desire is always present and active in some way. My point is that we are all about happiness. We are all about passion. We are all looking for love's ecstasy. It's the fulfillment of our whole person.

Getting in touch with the universal language that exists within all mankind is so important. When we can communicate with people at the deepest level, beyond demographic boundaries and cultural barriers, there is so much more freedom that can be experienced! For Christians, it can help to get rid of the 'Christianese,' the limited cultural Christian language that is only really understood in certain circles. All groups can get stuck in lingo and catch phrases that carry little meaning to outsiders. Getting at the essence of the God high can transcend all of that. That's much of what this book is about. God isn't recruiting for a new country club or exclusive gang. God just wants each one of us to be incredibly happy. God has a life for us that is authentically ecstatic in love. This can be a hard pill for many to swallow at first, to allow ourselves to associate God with experiential ecstatic love! Yet, when truly understood, it resonates within every heart. The high of a full life is what we were born for! I just had to include something about this transcendence in this book. We don't need another exclusive little stream of people with a new language or full doctrinal agreement. This is about the universal desire of humanity, to experience the richest love, the fullest life, and the most exhilarated state of consciousness possible. Let's go for whatever encourages that! Let's get beyond language and cultural approval! No agendas. It's a humble offer to one another to encourage each other's bliss, no matter what, beyond semantics and exterior appearances. We can speak to the heart of every person's desire for bliss!

EXPLORING SCIENCE AND THE GOD HIGH

Another area of massive importance that has often been considered outside the box of modern Christian emphasis is the field of science and technology. The God high is not at all at odds with technology and science! In fact, when seen rightly they both are confirming and supporting one another. Previously in the book, we mentioned studies in physics and psychology that support and display the power of altered states of consciousness. Vibrations, energy, chemicals, matter, and machines are all profoundly spiritual as much as they are scientific. Our exploration of them can absolutely encourage the God high. Spirit and science go together! It's all one reality. This is all about fully experiencing that reality! We need not ever be afraid of what may encourage awareness of reality, be it scientific, spiritual, or otherwise. Let's briefly look deeper.

Scientists have been studying the power of altered states of consciousness to assist and empower the human race for generations. Notably in the last 75 years was the work of Dr. Timothy Leary, Terrence McKenna, and Dr. Rick Strassman. Now, much of their field of research was in connection with psychedelic drugs, which we are in no way advocating in this book. Yet, their studies made some profound scientific breakthroughs. I realize that this is controversial ground. However, there may be much we could learn from any scientific observations of an altered state. I pray that we would have scientists and people of all walks of life who would engage the God high with as much passion as these men did in their pursuits. How amazing would it be to be able to set up labs and spend years studying and observing people getting high on God? I dream of that someday!

Dr. Timothy Leary experimented with altered states especially using the drug LSD. In one set of experiments he saw dozens of professors, graduate students, and others respond by saying the altered states were some of the most educational and revealing experiences of their lives. Leary also experimented with altered states in the rehabilitation of alcoholics and criminals, with a significant measure of success.

Dr. Rick Strassman's research was most interesting in that he made mention that the extremely powerful psychedelic drug DMT is already existent in the human body. His studies with DMT, though inconclusive, may point to the practicals of how the God high works within us physically. Through looking at Strassman's research one may theorize that just as God can work in and through the electrical impulses in our brain to produce holy thoughts, so also, God may be using the DMT that is resident in our bodies to produce ecstatic spiritual experiences. The connections here have only begun to be explored. The point is that science is our friend. The God high, while spiritual, can only be assisted by the deeper study of science into its what's how's and why's!

Terrence McKenna said, "(The human race has) a crisis of two things: of consciousness and conditioning. These are the two things that the psychedelics attack. We have the technological power, the engineering skills to save our planet, to cure disease, to feed the hungry, to end war; But we lack the intellectual vision, the ability to change our minds. We must decondition ourselves from 10,000 years of bad behavior. And, it's not easy." (McKenna, Terence (September 11, 1993). This World... and Its Double. Mill Valley, California: Sound Photosynthesis)

I believe that in his discoveries, McKenna had encountered some powerful truth. Instead of using psychedelic drugs, I believe that the revelation of Jesus Christ manifesting through the God high can so much more quickly, easily, and fully bring that deconditioning! That's the message of Christ's cross! The false self died with Jesus. We can now associate ourselves with a whole new awakened consciousness in Him!

There have been many other scientists who have studied fields that could be related to the science of the God high as well. Most of these scientists are much more accepted than Leary, McKenna, and Strassman. One field of related research is in the field of other naturally occurring pleasure chemicals of the brain. Chemicals such as endorphins, dopamine, adrenalin, serotonin, melatonin, etc. have been discovered to greatly affect the state of consciousness within a human being. Studying these chemicals should not negate a belief in the God high, rather merely give a 'how' to the way it is being carried out. I have had a few folks talk to me about the God high as if it can easy be explained as "merely chemicals." Yet, just because we know what chemicals are being released in a person when they feel love, does not mean that love does not exist. It merely means that we know what is carrying out the feeling of love. If God created the universe to run a certain way, including how our bodies function, and we discover that 'how,' it does not nullify God's activity and presence there. It merely gives us greater understanding of the process. God is working in and among everything. God is in the body. God is in the chemical. Let's not negate something just because we can see it at its' smallest level. Let's simply celebrate that we see more clearly how it is happening, and that it is happening!

Science is also making breakthroughs in understanding light sound and vibrations. This is fascinating and important too! Through the study of vibrations, we are beginning to understand why some music is more pleasing than other music. Through scientific understanding of vibrations we are now able to use light and sound therapy in operating rooms and therapy sessions. It is interesting to note that God created the cosmos by speaking a sound. Jesus Christ Himself is called, "The Word." Despite the many strange and unverified statements that have been made in many spiritual circles about vibrations, what real truth can be discovered or confirmed by studying the field of vibration? Have you ever noticed that you can have a spiritual experience while watching video or listening to audio of someone else's spiritual experience? What if angels, or even God's very Presence was able to be recorded due to its' vibrational frequency? So many things to explore through science!

Some other areas of scientific interest, related to the God high, are multiple dimensional study, the power of perception, and string theory, etc. Just as we mentioned at the beginning of the book, the Gospel of Jesus Christ declares that heaven is already here on earth. As we begin to perceive this heaven on earth, reality shifts around us. This is the very source of the God high, a conscious perception of heaven on earth!

Scientists like physicist Dr. Michio Kaku are exploring scientifically some truths very similar to this Gospel understanding. They are looking into how the perception of a person does actually change reality. Also, the possibility of additional dimensions existing at once has not been ignored. Dr. Kaku's work on string theory only seems to be opening up more understanding regarding how heaven could be on earth in more ways than we have ever imagined. If in any way we can look deeper objectively into the nature of how our reality works, I am all for it. The God high is not threatened by this! In fact, based on what is already being discovered, I'm encouraged that our ecstatic experiences will only be verified all the more! If this interests you, I encourage a deeper study of Dr. Kaku's work, as well as string theory, and various fields related to the power of perception and dimensions. Such fun!

WIDE OPEN SPACES

In closing this chapter, please hear my heart. I want it to be known that the God high is not for some close-minded, socially and religiously conditioned culture. We are set free in God's Glory to explore and adventure through this beautiful existence! It is not about promoting the Christian stereotype, or recruiting in some 'relevant' new way to 'the youth.' No, living in the altered state of consciousness of the God high is deeply connected to the real down to earth state of humanity. It's about engaging deeply in the affairs of planet earth, to hear its' true rustlings and groanings. Sometimes it's about caring about the reality of humanity so much that we laugh and play and get high in the midst of it, for its sake. Sometimes we care about real life so much that we study it and find it to be not so real!

God's Glory was revealed in Jesus Christ perfectly! Yet, through the misrepresentations and misunderstandings of our day, Jesus has not seemed loving, wise, powerful, aware, or relevant. It's time that we ask more questions and are less bound by fear. It's time to dive into the ruckus of this world and get our hands dirty. The dirt is holy! The dirt is beautiful! In the dirt, we may find mysteries that we haven't even begun to explore! The dirt might just be what gets God high! Continue to explore, my friends!!!

CHAPTER 14
HIGH DEVOTIONAL MEDITATIONS & PRAYERS

In the final chapter, I've wanted to include helpful and encouraging resources for ongoing experience of the God high. I want to leave you all jacked up on Jesus!!! Many times Holy Spirit will flow powerfully though a poem, a devotional, or a meditative writing, quickening your being into greater awareness of the Glory of God! Devotionals and meditations can be so fun! However, I've found personally that there are very few pure intoxicating resources out there that really communicate and encourage meditation on the Jesus bliss. I'm probably more excited than all of you about getting my hands on some good blissed out devotional readings!

So I asked several of my closest God intoxicated friends to write or submit a short meditative writing. I've asked them to write something that could be read quietly or aloud as a prayer or meditation. I was honored to receive so many submissions! I am also deeply honored to know so many friends that are staying high on Jesus in their everyday life! They've written some amazing material here that can be read and re-read to encourage your ecstasy!

Obviously, these devotionals are yours to use as you please. I do, however, recommend them as something to chew on slowly. Savor each delicious line! You might consider reading them aloud in a group, slowly and with inflection. It's amazing how God will often begin to minister through a group meditation. Suddenly the whole room is tangibly experiencing heaven on earth! I just love that! I've already read some of these in groups and had that very experience! I am so blessed by the content that is contained in each person's written meditation. So, take them slow, experience them deeply, and begin to look with the eyes of your heart upon the beauty of Christ in you and His reality! Enjoy God's bliss! Cheers!

UNCREATED REALITIES

by: Dru D'arnell

I never want the lie of dry.
Lord, help me to never believe the lie of dry.
I choose ecstasy, I choose awareness.
The very dew of heaven is right here, right now.
I breathe the very dew of heaven right now,
Because it is already in the atmosphere of the Breath of God

Where this is something out of nothing.
Even when I see the space between the top of the table, and the bottom of the ceiling
The open space above me through the hallway, or all around me; this very space is Heaven
And it is as tangible as walking through the bottom of the ocean,
Free from a deep sea suit or free falling from 10,000 feet above earth!
Heaven's Breath, every time I breathe in, I am IN remembrance...
The ecstatic reality of uninterrupted union with Christ. I no longer exist.
I am an observer of Christ life as and in and through me.
Everywhere I go today; every situation, task, word, encounter...
I am fully aware of the tangible Bliss of Heaven...
Today, right now, I take the eyes of my spirit and look in my inner most being, my belly.
I look, I sink relax into, this blissful Christ awareness.
I note my body relating the same way - head, neck, slump,
Unseparated as my spirit eyes continue
In the calm gaze into the now engulfing substance of ecstatic peace - bliss.
I may smile, I may laugh, ...I AM... I am just being…
I'm the Christ Goo, substance of absolute love, acceptance,
Without thought, beyond thought and recognition.
There is no focused attention, just calm awareness, as my Christ being
As my Christ being unfolds and expands around me.
Ecstasy is mine…
The atoms an substance of my body have disappeared
Into the frequency of the all in all Christ awareness.
Now, being aware of simple objects, joy has overtaken and melted boundaries of created things.
I am a witness of the playhouse of my spirit.

I may have a conversation toward The Divine...or we may be silent.
All is nothing and all is everything, all in the ecstatic, timeless bliss.
It's like a dream, this life...my breathing is the rhythm and Breath of Heaven. Can it be this easy?
Thoughts, incongruent with this heavenly reality,
I swoop them, brush them off, wave them off - send them on their way.
I laugh.
The only real reality, the only true substance is the bliss
That I am more and more aware of...it surrounds me in form.
Angels - all of Heaven is with me as I walk into any situation
Peace - Heaven overtakes these circumstances - noises.
And as I see myself outside myself a bit,
And love myself in the surrounding bliss that overtakes everything
And turns it into peace, (the 'I' no longer exists - it's Christ)...
My awareness - my senses are keen - I listen through the ears of love –
I am above all situations and circumstances
Fully at rest, fully satisfied - fully engulfed in seamless unity
We are one - all is ecstasy, unconditional Love
What is laughter?
It is the very sap of the confidence, the very signature of the accomplishment of the creator.
He who is in heaven laughs. (Psalm 2:4)
The God of Love Laughs
The very spirit of innocence is the thread
The river of the known relinquishment of self
And the exaltation in friendship and fellowship with God.
Seamless unity of heart, soul, spirit, and mind with the all-knowing
All encompassing, expression of the ultimate personality of goodness,
Fathomless presence- inexpressible depth – yet lightness – in accessible love;

Is only a hint , a glimpse of the catching away into the fruity digital laughter of God.
This exalted laughter now is your own, but in tandem with and of the divine,
And the echoes and echoing come like a plethora of layers of realties
Faintly dancing and often forming and conjoining like raindrops of a spring rain
On a window pane, coming together in unexpected but surprisingly typified patterns of freshness
In your consciousness – patterns of freshness – once you see awakened freshness and clarity –
Out of what you thought was nothing, but is now a whole new universe of revelatory expression
You are in the hilarity of the new covenant conscious heavenly reality expression – Christ love.
Now, where confusion, depression, and more had been substantive weights,
Dried in permanency – just break away like launch shells of a NASA rocket perpetually
Disarming themselves and falling and disappearing from heavenly realities ,
As you are just an onlooker,
Joining in the hilarity of the momentum of the timeless moment of eternal bliss.
Expansive clarity takes over the substances of
What you understood to be 'life' and the heavenly places
Take on substantive reality as He reveals You as All in All;
The seat – the prize masterpiece of His creation.
You see that this is where you always have been,
The early morning 'crusties' are wiped from your eyes

As the sleeper awakens to what you've always known –
The multi-layered dream come true, the real you, awakened and awakened
Dream beyond what your wildest comprehensive wisher could ever conceptualize.
All of this in an instant in the laughter glory trance of Heaven –
Accomplishing what generations have longed for in the unified clarity of God, of the Trinity,
The very dream of dreams come true.
You are His wish come true – you have come home. It feels like a dream, this love.
Born from Heaven, full wonderland capacity that you are now and always have been of above.
The new wind of His (new) covenant has always been yours
In your hand, like the throttle – at your command.
You have been given the keys to the car – the Kingdom is yours.
Heaven is Here, Heaven is Yours.
You have never been outside – the New Wine is the Key, the Bliss of Heaven you bear –
For all to see. You can't help but wear it – it fits like a glove,
Your hand, the dependent passive instrument born from above.
Drink your fill, oh lovers, to full capacity – always as a fountain,
Over flowing, like you have been created to be.
I've never wanted the law, that idea was yours –
Face to face – eye to eye – nose to nose – mouth to mouth – equilibrium, never off course.
It's always fresh, always exciting - effortlessness.
It's all explaining who I AM and we say 'what's next Papa, what's next.
- - - - - Jesus's word to new wine lovers - - -
This new wine is a perpetual festival – endless days under the Son.

How can laughter be evil, it's the unveiling of 'it's done'.
Come feast, come enjoy – all free, beyond all dreams you have dreamt.
Jump higher than ecstatic trampolines, this Circus of Next.
Come get to know Me, I've always known you through and through –
The Key is your undoing – the Key is the Real You.
I am beyond books and words and experience, beyond all these.
You will KNOW beyond future and foretelling,
I'll show you what you already know and see, and in all of this you'll get it,
Beyond what you expect. Just listen to your heart, don't expect what you expect.
So, go each day afresh, and come each day with me.
Together we'll create our greatest dreams and new realities.
I value what you have to say, I want you – these things to decide.
Yes, it's true I trust what you think, because you see, I AM inside.
But, you are original and unique divine expression of all there is.
This plan is still being written, together in the wonderland of Bliss.
Eternity is right now and I so want to be with you –
We have always been together my beloved, Me and You!

A Slice of Time
Loving what is, fully accepting this moment as a gift from our creator is
Like fully accepting a perfectly prepared slice of eternal pie.
The creator of the universe has brought you to the eternal kitchen table
And made this exact moment, this slice of eternity, exactly what it is...
Accepting and embracing everything about it is
Taking off the form/limits that we understand as 'time'.
Accepting and sensing His presence right in this moment
Is like taking the walls off of this space/form that we understand as 'time'

And we fully experience the seamless unity, without distance or delay of Love Itself...
I just invite you to set, possibly with eyes closed, just hear and feel and sense
All that is around you at this moment...
You may have been labeling it as noise, fear, angst...and a lot of other 'unheavenly' things...
And not been wanting to accept and embrace 'what is', the 'now'...
But even in these early hours of a new day...3:30 am to 6:00 am...or whenever this is read...
Fully accept, which leads to being fully aware...of it
And you will feel His Presence…and the reality of Heaven on Earth...
In this slice of eternity will be accepted in the form of seamless love...
And you can get through this moment, and suddenly find yourself getting through,
With ecstatic joy the next, and next, and next moments as Heaven On Earth,
And communing with your Divine maker with perfect unity of love.
Lemon meringue time is served up...'just for you'. Enjoy what is! Enjoy the Now! Enjoy!

THE WINE OF GOD

by: Bert Thompson

They shall be inebriated with the plenty of your house;
And will give them to drink of the torrent of your delight,
Because with you is the fountain of life - Your love is better than wine!
PSALM 36:8-9

When people drink wine they become influenced by it.

There is a place before God, A place of abandoned love,
A place that seems irrelevant to a religious heart.
A place where, we drink deeply of the wine of God,
And become "intoxicated" on his love and presence!
The more we drink the more abandoned & intoxicated we become.

Therefore we need the wine of God!
Because when we become intoxicated in His love, we become abandoned to its influence!
The world looks upon our intoxicated nature and says: " I want what they're having"
Having tried every cheap imitation, they want the REAL DEAL,
They want a drink for they are thirsty.
Our cry therefore is, " Fill me with your love Jesus! Draw me away in your love Jesus!
Cause me to be intoxicated in your Love Jesus!"
Because that sort of abandoned heart is possessed by that which it abandons itself to.
Let us drink the wine of his love and be intoxicated by his grace.
What is it we are to "drink" as suggested above?
The WINE of His love.
For this love is purely INTOXICATING to those who drink of it,
In the Song of Solomon1:4 the woman who has kissed her beloved is accused
Of having visited the King's wine caller and being drunk.
To which she explains, "His kisses are like wine!"
Remember the King only kisses those who are his
And his kisses are for those He loves.

In the book of Acts 2:15-16 Peter explains, "These are not drunk as you

suppose!"
He never denied they were drunk, he says NOT like you think.
To drink the Kings wine, is to drink of His love and you WILL be intoxicated on it,
For His love is intoxicating & heady more than any earthly wines.

(Psalm 36:7-9) Strong's 8248 "Shaqah" הקָשְׁ Transliteration: shaqah
Phonetic Spelling: (shaw-kaw') in Hebrew =
DRINK = to QUAFF = to drink largely & luxuriously = to irrigate or furnish a potion to =
Cause to drown, moisten; from 7937 SHAKAR רכַשָׁ
Transliteration: shakar to become tipsy; to satiate w/stimulating drink OR influence;
To be filled w/drink ABUNDANTLY; to be drunk; be merry;
8354 SHAKAR = to imbibe...we get intoxicated on the wine of His love!
This is not a time of great ministries, great egos; not a time of fabulous power.
This is the time of LOVERS.
This is the time of INTIMACY and INTOXICATION in the WINE of His love!
The KING has taken us into His chambers to KNOW us and RAVISH us with His love!
Others who have never been in the King's chambers of love, can never understand.
They don't understand your love and devotion to your love.
You can only smile and tell them, "He has ravished me with his love.
Let him kiss me with the kisses of his mouth: for his love is sweeter than wine."
The King has taken me into the chambers of His love;
He has "ravished" me with His affections till the early morning's dawn.

I am uncovered and known by Love Himself; my passion is set afire,
I cannot contain my longing, my desire for Him anymore.
I am DRUNK with LOVE, I am become LOVE!
Having tasted the new wine of his love, all else seems like a cheap imitation of the real deal,
They are loath to try cheaper wines, for none intoxicates the soul like HIS.
The king led me into the wine-cellar, he set love in order in me.'
Take me away to your Wine cellar, and let us drink of your love till morning light!
Zechariah 9:15 - The LORD of hosts will defend them.
And they will devour and trample on the sling stones;
And they will drink and be boisterous as with wine;
And they will be filled like a sacrificial basin, Drenched like the corners of the altar. (NASB)
Psalms 36:8 - They shall be inebriated with the plenty of thy house; and thou shalt make them
Drink of the torrent of thy pleasure. (DRB)
Song of Songs 5:1 - He: I came to my garden, my sister, my bride,
I gathered my myrrh with my spice, I ate my honeycomb with my honey,
I drank my wine with my milk. Others: Eat, friends, drink, and be drunk with love! (ESV)
Isaiah 25:6 - And in this mountain shall the LORD of hosts
Make unto all people a feast of fat things, a feast of wines on the lees,
Of fat things full of marrow, of wines on the lees well refined. (KJV)
Isaiah 55:1 - "All you people who are thirsty, come! Here is water for you to drink.
Don't worry if you have no money. Come, eat and drink until you are full!
You don't need money. The milk and wine are free. (ERV)

TANGIBLE BLISS

by Luke Nystrom Pratt

You are at the center of Life. Life is at the center of you.
Life and all its fullness has become a permanent fixture in your heart.
Inside you there's an Eternal Sunny Day. External forecasts can't define you.
You are the Relationship that communes with all of your relationships.
You are already connected to the people you love and value.
This connection goes outwards to strangers and people you haven't met yet too!
There is a deep, underlying communion we all are a part of.
Being human and apart of humanity connects you with the divine life and divine attributes.
You are inherently part of this Eternal Love.
This relationship connects the dots between reception and contribution.
True love puts you at the center of giving and receiving.
The deeper you go in your "journey of self", the more you are able to pour into others.
Religion calls self-care "selfish" or "self-centered", negating the importance of meditation.
But your natural desire to love and be loved is of divine intention and divine motivation.
As a center-piece in the grand story of love, your worth is a reflection of humanity's.
Celebrate yourself, celebrate your fellow man.
Celebrate the connection of love between yourself and humanity.
Your life is a blank coloring book - fill it with the colorful stories only you can tell!

You are a direct line to the Healer and true Healing.
Any growth we go through in life is not from death to life, but life to more abundant life!
In our worst estate, we were still as valuable as ever.
When we have made our worst mistakes, we were still ourselves. We were still beautiful.
We are growing up from our pasts - the very real pain done to us or by us.
We are creating avenues for reconciliation to begin. We are exploring ideas of redemption.
We are becoming Masters of our relationships, Masters of our minds and emotions.
We receive freely the various tools and abilities we need to demonstrate present-tense Heaven.
All these abilities and more can be found at the center of You, at the center of Life.
Religion has a way of keeping us in our pasts or desperately running towards the future.
Spirituality, or True Religion, amends our pasts and futures, keeping us grounded in the present.
We are meant to have a healthy reflection on our pasts and a mindful focus on the horizon.
We are meant to join the yesterdays and tomorrows with the here and now!
You can find peace between the two at the center of you.
Love has made its home in you, so you are the very real operating center for the Divine!
As one of the many parts to the body of Love, your part is so unique, essential, and interesting.
Your perspective offers unique insight into the heart of God, the plea-

sures of God.
Your intentions and endeavors find their peace in the paths of love and understanding.
When you set your mind or heart to something, you will never return empty handed.
All of our situations in life are turned into "win wins", one way or another.
We have a tangible connection with the Divine that can never be severed.

Even when the external dissuades us from visualizing a perfect world...
Heaven rises up all the more vibrantly and powerfully within us.
It is almost as if trial and tribulation awaken deeper Heavens within us.
Even more of You.
In our darkest hour, let us be reminded of the pure inner voice, always pointing us towards hope.
A hope embedded in our spirits. A hope founded on our identity. A hope nurtured by affection.
This hope is not a desperate attempt to conjure up temporary solutions exclusively.
This hope was meant to thrive in the hearts of the living and bring life to brokenness.
This is the Living and Active Hope of our Hearts.
Your Heart navigates the rocky river of life, finding a way in stormy waters.
Your Perfection is perfect theology Personified.
Your Perfection is a relational perfection. Never isolated, your perfection includes the world.
Your Perfection is based on the human and divine finding consummation with each other.

Your Perfection is expressed purely in your artistic freedom and lightness of heart.
Your Perfection is a fully-functioning reality. It is there when you're awake or asleep.
Your Perfection is a growing experience. We're filling up with Love and Continual Renewal.
Your Perfection is a Family endeavor. We're meeting each other in times of sorrow and joy.
Relationships purely empower and reinforce the workings of our hearts.
It is in our relationships we discover ourselves. We are pointed continually to the Source.
Our alone time points us to the dance of the community...
And the dance of community releases us into our personal destiny.
One feeds the other, each taking turns to nourish the other.
Every season of the soul teaching us something new about ourselves.
And the Life working on the inside of us is always helping us along the way.
Always making our steps a little bit lighter, our landscape a little more brighter.
Like the sun shining through the trees after a rainstorm…
So our hearts glow with fervency after the storms of our lives.
There are answers to the brokenness we sometimes feel in our lives.
And all the answers take us back to our Source. That sweet light coming from inside…
Nothing quite answers the pain we experience like the cloud of light and love...
This cloud passes in and through us, covering us with the grace we need.
Thick with rest, laced with the fermented fruits of joy, and tasty with divine delight.

This irresistible wine infuses itself into our skin and throughout our atmosphere.
It is the Pure Communion of the Ages, passing into and out of us.
Our lungs inhale deeply this cloud of glory, this rich smoke of sacrifice...
Filling our mouths with appetite, our noses with memory, and our eyes with light...
Losing ourselves in its' rapturous occurrence, we go out with a lightness of step.
Filled to the brink with life, life escapes our mouths with meaningful conversation.
Maybe you are laughing. Maybe you are listening. Maybe you're lost in the moment.
This glory is personal. It finds itself at home with your preferences and personifications.
I am filled up on music. Music synchronizes itself to heaven's heartbeat within me.
Can you feel the heartbeat of Eternity, bursting full with Heaven for you?
Yes, even inside you?

We are on this journey together - you are not alone.
We are heading towards a grander Heaven than Eternity has yet to dream of.
Tomorrow's promises come true inside our very hearts.
We're realizing that we're not bound to the constraints of yesterday...
We're discovering new ways to express ourselves intimately, full of love and Love's Fullness.
Heaven can't take its eyes off of you - you are its' greatest longing. It's true direction.

Our various journeys only take us closer to each other.
Separation loses its power in the unity we have with each other.
We are compelled to encourage each other along this journey of life.
We are not lost in the accomplishments of one another.
We share in our brother's and sister's victories.
We share in the richness of Heaven.
We are grounded in the steadfast longing of Love for all the earth. For all mankind.
We are set free to discover all the passions and purposes set in our hearts.
We are set free to evolve with divine; Simply loved, yet complex in our expressions…
Founded in the bedrock of our Hearts, love's roots burrow in deeply…
Our hearts blessed to be expressed in our day to day lives
A never-ending exploration of God's heart.
We now have unrestricted access to the rich, rare intoxications of Heaven inside us.
At every stage of this bliss, we operate expressively with the needs set directly at hand.
We're personally empowered to speak with clarity into confusion's storm.
Like the Divine, we stand at the rail of the ship, calming waters with simple words.
Our Voice catches the fervent fire of Heaven's wide embracing desire.
Enclosed inside us, behind our beautiful skin and bones…
Is a wonderful Dreamer of dreams, a heart restored into a Home.
All the cries of the world find comfort in His arms.
All the pains will find their release.
No longer bound to the days gone by or the hope of days to come...
This Tangible Bliss now is our Oneness.

IN VINO VERITAS

By: Shane Runnels

We are glad and satisfied with your more than satisfactory work,
King Jesus - the life you lived, blood you spilt, and humanity you raised to life.
I once knew you as a far-away King, but You showed me, in Your perfect timing,
Just how close You were and are and will be to me.
You are no longer simply a historical figure, but an indwelling Person guiding my members
And directing my paths into Glory from Glory.
Thank you for realigning and reintroducing me to my original origin – You.
I thank you for your goodness and mercy.
Even when I hear mention of Your name, I feel Your presence.
You never fail to intoxicate me.
Even when I feel like hope is fleeting in my life, your bliss fuels me.
I know there is hope in the drink.
I'm not quite sure how to practice Your presence anymore.
I have trouble "practicing" anything in the enjoyment of Your Glory.
I feel as if you are mastering my presence. You are my Master, and you masterfully love me.
As my being effortlessly drinks in Your reality, I find myself unable to think
About anything but the bliss I'm experiencing.
My words become useless to me to convey any thoughts
Besides the high thoughts I have regarding Your presence.
Moans and groans and unintelligible tongues seem to carry me deeper

into the bliss
And I am trapped for however long the pressing lasts.
You make me lie down in green pastures.
I have no choice but to drink the still waters of Your peace.
The only plans you have for me are to orchestrate situations
To amplify my intimacy and trust in You.
Surely, goodness and mercy are stalking me like hungry beasts.
My only choice is to let them overtake me.
Their claws dig into me and with every inch they tear, new ecstasies come forth from within me.
The rivers are gushing out of my belly and there's no stopping the flow.
Your gelatinous Glory envelops me
And I'm unable to discern what is Earthly and what is of Heaven.
My vision is blurred enough that I can finally see
That there is no longer a difference in You, The Christ.
Everything has been made good and Holy and only exists to increase my happiness.
All things now reside in Union with You.
In my rapturous state, my eyes believe that they see better when they are closed
In which visions of all things good and holy and righteous come cascading into my spirit.
I once was lost, but now I'm found. Was blind, but now blurry.
Lord, we want nothing but your bliss.
Your will be done, My King. Your happiness be shown to the world.
My Father who is drunk in Heaven, Holy be Your name.
Your Kingdom come, Your drink be drunk, on Earth as it is in Heaven.
Give us today our daily wine, and forgive us of our sobriety
As we forgive those who act sober against us.
Lead us not into moderation, but deliver us from our clear minds.

My body is becoming numb and my eyes are getting heavy. The Lords will is being done.
Drinky Drinky. Shinky Dinky. I can't seem to focus. The pleasures are invading my body.
I've lost all interest in anything but the breasts of El Shaddai. Your milk is sweet like chocolate.
It's chocolate milk.
Your Wine changes and influences our actions, Oh Lord.
I can feel your peace even upon those that lift verbal swords against me.
Rocks thrown have become pillows I hold onto, lest I stumble and fall in the Glory.
Lord, I thank you for pillows. I wish all floors were made out of pillows.
I have no idea what's happening. I feel as if all of my eloquent speech has disappeared.
My brain functions are slowing.
The Glory has overtaken me and I only care about the shing ding I'm experiencing.
I feel the cloud in the room.
Everything seems possible, yet impossible at the same time.
I feel as if I can accomplish feats of valor, but I can't seem to move to do so.
I'm drunk. Thank you, Lord, for Your drink. Drink me in, Jesus. Amen.
In Vinos Veritas

THE BLISS OF GOD

By: Crystal Dawn

Oh the eternal bliss,
Of one whose been kissed,

By the most High,
And time seems to slow down or fly by..
It really gets me jacked up,
When I sup,
With the One who loves me,
Eternally loved, eternally free..
Just one breath can get me high
As I soar out into the sky
His beauty and His glory,
I can't cease to tell His Story..
The ecstasy and the bliss
Of the one who's been kissed
By the most High..
Every time He draws nigh
I go into an eternal bliss,
And it's really hard to miss..
You go into a deep ecstasy
And your heart has been freed
Once you've encountered the bliss
From the one who's been kissed
By the most High
The time is here and now,
Sometimes all I can say is shamwow..
And sometimes it's all I can do to speak,
Hijacked and gone for weeks and weeks..
Being lost in Jesus is the best way to be..
Being happy and absolutely free
And sometimes I go deep into a trance,
And it seems like we dance,
And visions and dreams will come to me,

And open portals and angels dancing around me..
Just a taste of His everlasting love,
From Heaven, which isn't above,
It's here and now for all to see,
The ecstasy and the bliss
Of the one who's been kissed
By the most High
His holy laughter overtakes me at times,
These are just a few of the signs,
Of how much He loves me,
And yearns to set hearts free.
Oh, taste and see of His ecstasy!
The beauty of what He did for me!
I couldn't do anything on my own,
My heart was sad and forlorn,
When all hope I thought I had was lost,
My heart was torn and tossed,
He came and he kissed me..
Showering me
With His absolute love
And I started soaring far above,
When Heaven came down to me,
Setting my heart absolutely free
Because of the eternal bliss,
I'm the one who's been kissed,
By the most High,
Then it begins to dawn on me,
Whose heart He has set free..
He gets high off of me..
He gets eternally blissed

Just by kissing me
Whose heart he has set free
Heaven is the party,
And it's free,
You don't need any drugs or alcohol,
He's your pure substance, all in all,
His love is more pure than any drug,
And you can't sweep it under a rug,
He wants to party through you,
It's powerful, lovely, and true.
When Jesus said It is finished,
The party got started, and hasn't diminished,
He hijacked you from the foundation of the world,
Knowing what would unfurl..
His love goes beyond all we can know,
It's time to lay down the works so
The ecstasy and the bliss
Of the one who's been kissed
By the most High
Heaven has drawn nigh
And then I felt,
Like my face begin to melt,
And I'm translated to the Heavenly Place
Where time doesn't matter, nor space,
God and I sometimes will walk together,
And we walk on and go on forever,
I get to sometimes co-create with Him,
Galaxies and stars explode to life alongside of Him.
All of Heaven and Earth cannot contain,
And they sing Hallelujah, His Praise they can't refrain,

The Priest in the temple of old,
Couldn't even stand, His presence was so bold..
How much more since Jesus said it is finished?
If anything, His presence hasn't diminished
It just keeps getting stronger,
And I can no longer,
Keep silent any more,
Jesus is the open door,
Oh the eternal bliss,
Of one whose been kissed,
By the most High,
Simply because Heaven is nigh,
Then looking into His eyes,
And in His love, I can't deny,
I see myself as Him
My head begin to swim,
He and I are one together,
Undeniably forever,
And then I realize that the Godhead is me,
When Jesus died on that tree,
The three became four,
Opening up Heaven's door,
Oh, the ecstasy and bliss,
Of one whose been kissed,
By the most High,
Simply because Heaven is nigh,
He loves to romance you and I,
And tells little secrets, no one can deny..
My favorite one is this,
And it causes me such bliss,

You are immortal,
You are heaven's gateway portal,
Signs and wonders will follow you,
Look around you and realize it's true..
You cannot die,
Even if you did try,
Being an immortal,
And being heaven's gateway portal,
God took care of Death for you,
It's all true..
Everything has been finished before time began,
And it was all taken care of in Him,
Oh the eternal bliss,
Of one whose been kissed,
By the most High,
Simply because Heaven is nigh,
I whisper a Thank you,
And again what happens is true,
He hijacks my mind back into heavenly places,
I glance around and see so many faces,
And once more I feel him singing to me,
Come away, my beloved, and be free..
I feel like I am soaring,
At the same time, it's like surfing,
I see the rainbow in the sky
And I cannot deny
Oh the eternal bliss,
Of one whose been kissed,
By the most High,
Simply because Heaven is nigh,

Oh, what matter of love God has shown for us,
And has entrusted us,
That we are His children,
And in being in Him,
We can no longer sin,
There's nothing separating us anymore,
We have an open door,
God showing His love for us,
And never putting up a fuss,
He just wanted to be together,
Forever and ever,
We felt unjust and unworthy,
And he wanted to open our eyes to see,
We asked for the law instead of going to God,
We even tried to hide from God,
Yet deep in His mercy and in His love,
The Godhead showed us His love,
He let us have the law,
And we beat ourselves until we were raw,
And hoped we pleased God,
But all he longed to do was to kiss us,
And remind us that He loved us..
Of the eternal bliss,
Of one whose been kissed,
By the most High,
Simply because Heaven is nigh,
Jesus' blood is divine,
It's better than all the fine wine,
One taste of His bliss,
The glory is infused within this,

Changes everything that you think is wrong,
Into a glorious love song..
There's nothing like being High on Him,
My heart leaps and exalts Him,
Jesus, My love, my darling,
Come and let us sing
Of your beauty in all things,
Heaven and earth rings
Out the glory of who you are,
You're more glorious than the North Star
And this, my dear ones,
Is what I call fun,
Being tripped out, and in ecstasy,
And He opened my eyes to see,
What is the eternal bliss,
Of one whose been kissed,
By the most High
When Heaven has drawn nigh..
His love will cover a multitude of sins,
And it all is taken care of in Him,
It is finished, for now and forever,
Nothing can separate you ever..
This is the beauty of the King,
And in Him I cannot help but sing,
Holy, Holy, Holy, is the Lord God Almighty!
You opened my heart to be free,
And reminding me once more,
Of the eternal bliss,
Of one whose been kissed,
By the most High

Simply because Heaven has drawn nigh,
And not only has Heaven drawn nigh,
Which would be hard to deny,
Heaven is here, right now,
All of creation bows,
And worships Him who sits on the throne of our Heart,
And in Him I will always take part,
Of the eternal bliss,
By the one who has been kissed,
By the most High,
For Heaven has drawn nigh

INTERGALACTIC WONDERLAND

By: Allen "A.J." Nichols

Seated in Christ, High and lifted up, above every principality and power.
Co-Heirs, given ultimate authority,
By the Living Word, The Son of God:
Jesus – the Lover of my soul.
I am completely accepted in the Beloved.
His precious blood, spilled out for me,
Brought me into a whole new world.
His love, perfect love, perfect – and yet so powerful!
I am a drowned man, yet fully alive!
Completely united and intertwined with the great I AM.
Constantly swooning in the midst of this ecstatic love affair,
This love, this perfect love, holds me secure, forever.
I AM… has made me fearless.
There is no escape!

I am completely helpless!
I am a victim of His superior gladness and joy!
I live out this existence elated, elevated and stimulated.
High and lifted up!
Severely intoxicated on the eternal life we share,
Heaven – here and now and forevermore!
Every need supplied, everything I ever dreamed,
My cup runs over, all over everything.
It is constantly gushing.
This love has made me a fiend!
This is the addiction of all addictions.
The perfect, intoxicating love of God,
Tangible, boldly overwhelming, and constant.
Nothing can stop it!
All of my understanding flew out the window!
I ascended into the Holy of Holies.
The Holy of Holies descended into me.
Together, bound up in an everlasting encounter beyond earthly description!
Way beyond my wildest fantasy, He is my dream come true!
Completely caught off guard by the insanity of this bliss!
Nothing the world has to offer can compare to this heavenly kiss.
It causes me to have outrageous outbursts of laughter!
This perfect plan, still unfolding – yet completely finished.
Outside of time and space,
My Father watches over everything.
I live in a state of absolute peace.
His eyes are always gazing upon me.
I rest.
Once I was so anxious,

Now, fully satisfied.
The Prince of Peace,
Rocks me in His lap.
To Him, my most intimate secrets I can confidently confide.
I am safe and secure,
I have nothing to fear.
My lover lives inside of me,
Closer than a friend or brother.
He lovingly leads and guides me.
We were smelted together,
United as One,
In a flaming vat of love!
I no longer live, my old man died,
But in Christ, I have overcome!
He raised me from the dead,
And took me, swiftly, to His lair.
The center of the universe,
Home sweet home. His chair.
Seated in the heavenlies, lost somewhere in space!
The pearl of the most expensive price,
I am His favored reward,
The victory is both of ours,
This joy is simply absurd.
Free, so completely free!
Thanks be to God!
This gift is inexpressible,
This love is like a dream come true.
It's immeasurable!
It was His plan all along!
To rescue us, and release us from the grip of death!

To give us back our confidence,
And unshackle us from captivity - into His reality.
Now we sing His song.
And we dance, in this sweet romance.
Together, forever.
That is what is meant by the Scriptures which say that no mere man has ever seen, heard, or even imagined what wonderful things God has ready for those who love the Lord. 1 Corinthians 2:9 TLB

MY LIFE IS MEDITATION

by Britney Cook

High on God, the easiest thing to do is share my life...

Sitting at a mini table outside of the salon I worked at, it was like an office for me.

I looked over my shoulder, there stood a foot or two from the front door an elderly woman who was just about to open the door. "Can I help you?" I said.

She let go of the door and sat down with me. A blue bandanna over her hair, long thick skirt for coverage, faded pink blouse, she quietly spoke "Yes I am looking for someone to do my hair...Are you a stylist?"

"Yeah! How can I help you?" I was a bit curious, but intrigued.

"Ok, but you don't have to do it. I am embarrassed. I had two stylists turn me down already." She was avoiding eye contact as she spoke.

"What do you mean?" I was thinking it can't be that bad.
She then continued, "I was stuck in the hospital for three months and no one has touched my hair since. Its ok if you don't want to do it, I understand it's really bad. If you have to shave it all off, I looked at wigs already, I am really embarrassed."

"Well let's go inside and take a look." I gathered up my belongings and walked inside.
She sat down in my stylist chair, and I stood in front of her to talk face to face. "I'm really embarrassed you don't have to do it."

"You're an amazing woman, I am doing your hair. Why don't you take off your bandanna Debra, so we can get started." She untied the knot, and took it off. Her hair was like a ponytail slick to the head, but was one big matted gray dread instead that didn't move if I tried, and no way would combing it out make any difference. "I have an idea, we don't have to shave it all off, I am going to take the clippers and cut through it because my shears will not cut through this. That way we can hopefully save an inch or two of hair and have a nice short haircut!"

"I'm so embarrassed. You don't have to do this."

"Stop saying that, you're in my chair, I am doing this. Your amazing Debra, you're in the right place." Turned on my clippers, and cut through the forest. The first dent I made, you could smell the stench. All of a sudden I see an alive bug come out, and mold in the mess. I continue slicing my way through all away around. The smell was pretty bad, and I decided to grab gloves to see if I can loosen up the dread now that two inches or so was left to brush through on the head. As I was doing that, I could start to see the scalp. In all of history, worse than the books that showed you what diseases look like, was what was endured on her head. I wish I was making this up.

I finished brushing through it, and said, "All right lets go wash your hair!" We walked over to the shampoo bowl, gloves still on, squirted some shampoo in my hands and scrubbed her hair. Rinsed and shampooed again. It was still pretty bad, but I continued putting conditioner in my hands. Rubbed it all over her hair, and did a relaxing scalp massage to bless her. Ended up praying under my breath for a miracle while that was happening. Rinsed and towel dried.

"Lets go back to my chair Debra." Walked back, grabbed the comb, gloves still on. I couldn't believe my eyes. "Debra this is a miracle, your scalp is perfect like nothing ever happened! Holy smokes! Haha" No joke. Completely spotless.

"Really? Wow I came to the right place. Wanna know something? I was praying to God what salon to go to, and there is another salon right next to you and I was about to go to that one but God told me go to the next one. Wow your an angel, I am so embarrassed."

"Stop saying that. Your beautiful, and God loves you so much!" Finished drying her hair and styling it. Walked her outside and prayed for her before she continued on through her day.

When you realize how unconditionally loved you are, fruit effortlessly manifests into reality... Its drunk. Drunken grapes snack on you..nom-nomnom. Woah what if you are heavens feast? Fruity feast.. Anyways, lets continue...

Ever since I was a young girl, I have always loved just styling hair. I would play with my aunts hair during holidays, and always be experimenting with my own. My dream was to do hair for a runway show. Doors never opened for me as I tried several times. This past year, I moved to Southern California in San Diego. After a couple months of living there, I found out a friend has been living in Los Angeles. The last time I saw her was three years ago in Texas, and while we were there, found out both of us grew up in Minnesota.
So, we get together and got to a point where I ended up sharing with her that it would be so fun to do hair for a runway show because I love the fast pace of just styling hair, and that it was a dream of mine since I was young. She told me she knew a celebrity stylist that does that, and gave me her number that instant. Told me to call her asap. I did just that.
I find out that I was invited to do hair for LA Fashion Week. Sharing with my friend, she says those are the biggest runway shows in LA! Well that was cool. Time comes around and BAM! I'm backstage. Fast pace environment, everyone is stressed, but I'm in Heaven really enjoying the whole thing. Straying off to a different area backstage, I met a few different designers.

"Are you a hair stylist?" Hangers full of clothes in both hands, frantically looking for help.

"Yawhats up?"

"I need a hair style with what she is wearing." Gave me his model and I sat her down.

Wow I loved every minute of creating styles with the designers clothing line! Next model, next model... Kept going.

A model whose hair I was doing asked me, "Have you been drinking?"

"Haha all I had was water!"

"It seems like your drunk!"

"Its Jesus!"
"I knew there was something different about you, I have never felt so peaceful with someone doing my hair before."

"Ya I just want to let you know you're so loved, pure and accepted! So, beautiful you're gonna rock that runway!" Sprayed her hair and did the finishing touches.

"OMG your gonna make me cry, I just got my makeup done!" haha left and right it was poppin backstage!

What do you love? Go do it! God is the fullfiller of those dreams. You my friend are fully blissed.

He will go above and beyond what you could ever ask, think or imagine. In doubt? Ask God to show you how good He is, we have the best Dad ever! Don't believe me just watch... hey! Hey! hey! Hey!

Watch out He might spoil you with goodness, it will never stop flowing. That oozy, gooey honey dripping off your nose, bubbling in that warm milky hot tub shabba fully satisfied. Yes your there.

Woah! Just take a breath right now. Glory is all around you and in you flowing through you! Hey did you know your intoxicado? The wine never stops, even if your mind isn't there all the time... The people around you will encounter it. I get random people coming to the door of my house thinking I'm on something when I answer it, but I feel completely normal. What is normal to you, is literally an encounter with God to them. They haven't been aware of what you have been aware of and when they knock into the realm your so used to, the reality that you live in, they will call and ask what is it? I want it! Woah! You'll be there to help them see the truth that has been there the whole time.

Some people don't know it but they sure do show it! Ever see someone smile? Wash the dishes for you? Vacuum? Write an encouraging note? Give you a manicure? Its LOVE! God is love! Love is who you are and always been! Perfect union with Mr. Love himself...Nothing can separate you! Not even sin! Woah! Did you know the sin problem was taken care of at the cross? Hahaha Papa God is happy with you! You're a good son or daughter of the God of this universe! He owns everything! The earth is His, and you are too! HahaRealizing who you are, it changes what you do. O happy day! Meditate o yes soak in the bliss of innocence.

EMBRACING YOUR HIGHNESS

by: Travis Harris

Hey man, do you want to get high?
The first step in "getting high" is realizing that you already are "high."
If the Lord is "high and lifted up," and you are in the Lord
In him all things live and move and have their being
What does that say about you?
You are also high and lifted up.
Awareness of your place in Christ, seated in heaven and seeded with

heaven,
Opens the door to constant, tangible, everlasting bliss.
Set your gaze on the face of Jesus
And become aware of his arms wrapped around you in an everlasting embrace
He is your Highness.
You are so embraced by Your Highness that heaven manifests
And leads others into bliss wherever you go.

Colossians 3:1-2
See yourselves co-raised with Christ!
Now ponder with persuasion the consequences of your co inclusion in him.
Relocate yourselves mentally!
Engage your thoughts with throne room realities where you are co-seated with Christ
In the executive authority of God's right hand.
Becoming affectionately acquainted with throne room thoughts will keep you
From being distracted again by the earthly realm. (The Mirror Bible)
This is why we preach the gospel: so that people may know what realm they're in and from.
You are from and currently exist in heaven.
We're eternal beings outside of space and time
All the while experiencing life within space and time.
We experience the presence of Jesus is in the present.
You can't fully engage with a future Jesus, or a past Jesus
Unless you yourself go backward or forward in time.
You can only fully engage with the Jesus within your present moment.
Jesus said he's coming soon, because he calls all times soon.

He comes at every single point in your timeline
Every "now" you find yourself in, there He will be also.
The kingdom of heaven is always at hand.
You may experience hell sometimes but your true reality is always heaven
Has always been heaven, and will always be heaven.

What is reality?
Is there anything more solid than our union with Christ?
Is there anything truer about us
Than our co-incarnation, co-life, co-crucifixion,
Co-death, co-burial, co-resurrection, and our co-ascension?
You are a thought, a dream, an expression of God
Enjoying this life in a human experience and perspective.
Your circumstances and perspective of those circumstances do not dictate the truth
About you or the truth about reality.
Never go back to being a slave of a false reality and of the problems you think you have.
There is only one true reality, and we partake in this true reality
By setting our affections on things above.
Christ defines you and your reality.
Meditate on the fact that Christ is all and is in all (Colossians 3:11).
We must realize that every situation of our lives is an invitation to bliss.
He has actually redeemed everything.
Once upon a time I was sitting in my favorite chair and decided to partake
In the enjoyment of a delicious candy bar.
As I bit into the beauty, I became aware for the first time in my life
Of the marvelous texture of said candy bar.

I sat there for a solid 15 seconds thinking of nothing in the world
Other than the texture of that candy bar.
For 15 straight seconds I was 100% present in what I was enjoying.
I became so aware of my present intoxication
And felt the love and presence of Jesus so strongly
And heard him say to me, "Enjoy the holiness of this moment."
And I continued to eat the candy bar as best as I could
While being entirely blitzed out of my mind in a fit of laughter and tears
All the while my body felt exponentially lighter.
It was as if my mind hit the eject button and soared high as a kite
Tethered only by the necessity to come back and keep eating the candy bar.
I was embraced by my Highness.
The "secular" has been bathed in the "sacred."
Finding bliss in the mundane is paramount
To moment-by-moment decisions of trusting Holy Spirit and following your bliss.
Choose bliss, realizing that bliss has already chosen you.
Jesus has set your emotional wavelengths to gratitude.
Trust that God trusts you and your redeemed desires.
Realize that every false or borrowed desire has been crucified with Christ.
You have unlimited amazing ideas that will lead you from glory to glory.
Trust your bliss. Trust Holy Spirit. Trust the family of bliss; the origin of bliss.
Do you want to be "led by the Spirit?"
Then follow your bliss, because the Spirit is bliss.
You're desires will not lead you astray when
You trust your Father who declares you perfect, righteous, and holy.
Be convinced of your holiness.

Holiness is wholeness, oneness, unity and acceptance of your truest self
And your union with Father, Son, and Holy Spirit.
It's displayed as wild, crazy, inexplicable love for yourself and everyone around you
And eyes that can't help but see beauty all around
As you manifest your holiness your actions may be mistaken for sacrifice
But your face tells a different story
You're entrenched in a stupefying love for Jesus and humanity
To where laying down your life is effortless.
Jesus said, "This is my commandment that you love one another that your joy may be full."
You are one with patience; no inconvenience, big or small
Could ever draw you away from your Highness.
Be ye brainwashed.
Take a minute to close your eyes and imagine
(Your imagination has been redeemed as well in case you were wondering)
Your cerebrospinal fluid and your blood-brain barrier being swapped
For the blood and water that flowed from Jesus' side.
Imagine it flushing out and cleansing every last crevice and fold
Of your beautifully wrinkly brain
And from there, down your spinal cord and out
Into your arms and legs, fingertips and toes
Washing over all your organs on its way through.
Let peace and ecstasy fill you and bring you into an awareness
Of your redeemed, resurrected, healthy, whole, body. You are loved.
Fear not!
No fear or insecurity can sneak its way into your renewed Christ-mind.
Perfect Love completely and permanently displaces fear.

There is no place in your being for fear to go because you are so full of Christ.
You have all the bravery, peace, fearlessness, and freedom of Christ
Because you are fully saturated with Love.
If you feel fear or any form of insecurity, take heart, and know that it is a false reality
Sure to crumble under the heavy weighty glory of your Highness
Which will bring clarity and an honest perspective to your present circumstances.
Take a deep breath.
Awaken to the fact that you can't even take a breath without being filled with heaven
Because you are at this very present moment in heaven.
There's nothing but good vibes in this atmosphere.
You inhale positive energy, and you exhale positive energy.
You are a perfect, beautiful, and clean conduit for heaven on earth.
There is no more darkness or imperfection in you than there is in Jesus Christ himself.
And if your mind is conditioned to thinking you have to do something
To be embraced by your highness, no worries! Breathe in; breathe out.
"Activate" the faith of God within you by breathing in
As much of this Christological, bliss-saturated, air as possible
And holding it in while imagining it permeating every cell in your body.
You are in for a beautiful, tangible, surprise
A plunge into the depths of true, honest, authentic reality of bliss—a divine embrace of your Highness.
Philippians 4:8-9
Summing it all up, friends, I'd say you'll do best by filling your minds and meditating on things true, noble, reputable, authentic, compelling, gracious—the best, not the worst; the beautiful, not the ugly; things to

praise, not things to curse. Put into practice what you learned from me, what you heard and saw and realized. Do that, and God, who makes everything work together, will work you into his most excellent harmonies. (The Message)

CAN YOU FEEL ME?

By: Nathan James Dickerson

Place Your Hand On Your Heart
You're Feeling Me Now
That Beat…Thump Thump…Thump Thump…Is Sustained By My Very Word and Power
It Is In Me You Live and Move and Have Your Existence
This Means That You Do Nothing Without Me Nothing Outside Of Me
Although Your Subjective Perspective Of Distance and Separation Feels As Though It Is So Real…
I Am Closer To You Than You Are To You
Although At Times You Try So Hard To Hide From Me…
Building Invisible Walls Around Your Heart and Then Calling Yourself Tough…
We Both Know That Deep Inside of You Is A River Of Love
Just Waiting For Your Acknowledgement Of It's Existence
To Burst Forth, Gushing Like A Mighty Fountain Out Of Your Belly
My Love, If You Could Only Feel What I Feel and Hear What I Hear
If You Could Only See What I See
Your Desire Of Walking In Love Would Effortlessly Manifest
If For One Moment You Could Experience This Eternal Fire Of Delight and Pleasure

That I Take In The Masterpiece You Are
You Would Never Again Need Someone Else's Approval
You Would Never Again Need To Rely On An External Source
To Escape The Hellish Experience Your Mind Re-Lives Day In and Out
You Would Never Again Need To Hide
In Your Designer Clothes Of Guilt And Shame,
Although Those Clothes Are Made By Your Hands And Not Mine
I Am NOT The One Who Shames You Beloved,
I Am Drunk On You
So High On What I See,
The Perfection Of Your Innocence
This Is NOT A Daydream Full Of Wishful Thinking
But Rather You Have Always Been My Dream Come True
Giving Me A Non-Stop, One Way Flight Into The Paradise Of My Choice
This Romance Of The Ages Was My Idea and You Were At The Center Of My Vacation,
My Purpose, My Paradise
If My Private Island Of Rest Had A Name, It Would Be Your Name
When I Imagined The Cosmos, I Never Imagined The Stars Without You,
But You Were The Inspiration For All Of The Creative Light That Has Ever Left My Hands
At The Forefront Of My Mind, When Carefully Sculpting The Planets and The Sun, Was You!
All I Could Think About Was You!
And Even Now, I Am Still Stuck On You!
I Stand In Awe Of Your Beauty
I Sit In Awe Of Your Existence
I Kneel At Your Feet In Service

In Your Presence I Am Humbled and Honored To Be Your Poppa
The Greatest Gift and Honor Is Having You As My Child
As Your Poppa, I Love Watching You Grow
I Love Changing Your Poopy Diapers
The Fragrance Of Your Mess Releases Such An Atmosphere Of Bliss
As I Know A Moment Of Change, A Moment Of Embrace Is Coming
And It Is One Day Closer To The Day You Are Potty Trained
And Ready For Your Big Boy Pants That Are Simply Waiting For You
Your Growing Up In Me Does Not Take Time,
Just As A Tree Does Not Grow Because Of Time, But Rather Because Of
It's Environment
Watching Your Transformation Gives Me The Greatest Delight
As It Is Only Through Intimacy With Me That Your Transfiguration
Will Explode Out Of You
Through The Awareness and Participation Of Our Blissful Union
That I Initiated,
Will You Begin To Walk In The Reality Of Who I Have Designed You To
Be
I AM Your Bliss and You Are Mine
Will You Let Me Be Your Drink?
Will You Let Me Be Your I AM?
Will You Let Go Of The Person Who You Think You Are
and Embrace Who I AM as Who You Are?
Will You Let Me Show You Your Face Hid In Mine?
I Have No Other Desire Than To Lavish My Love,
My Weighty, Unconditional, Non-Judgmental, Healing, Love On You
It Was Not A One Time Deal That I Only Did At Calvary,
But My Love Is A Continual, Un-Ceasing, Gushing White-Water River
That Drowns Those Who Are Weighty
Let ALL That I AM Influence You To Stop Fighting The River

But Let This Love Wash Over You and Exchange Your Weight
Of Anxiety and Fear With My Ever-Present, Indwelling Peace and Bliss
The Glory Within You, Christ, Is More Than Enough
In Your Weakness, I AM Made Strong
What I Have Already Placed and Invested,
What I Have Deposited On The Inside Of You,
The Spirit's Influence In Your Heart Is What Strengthens You IN Those Moments Of Weakness
My Beloved, Those Moments Do NOT Scare Me Or Concern Me,
I AM NOT Afraid Of You Weakness
I AM NOT Terrified Of The Monster That YOU See, Because That Monster Does NOT Exist
What Does Exist Is My Magnificent Obsession, YOU
The Real You, The Actual, Factual You Which I Declared Over You
Before I Created The Cosmos Is Good
Beloved, DO NOT Condemn Yourself Over What You Think I AM Disappointed In
I AM NOT Disappointed With You Rather I AM Ecstatically Beyond Satisfied and Delighted In The Essence Of You
Just One Glance Of Your Eye Jacks Me Up and Fuels This Ever Increasing Light, This Ever Expanding Cosmos
My Justice Is Not Something To Be Afraid Of
If You Are Afraid Of Me, You Do Not Know Me
When Jesus, My Beloved Son
Who Embodied The Revelation Of Me and
AT The Same Time The Revelation Of Which Rock You Were Cut From,
Wept Over Lazarus and Released The Prostitute From Her Accuser
He Was Releasing My Justice
My Justice Has Already Been Released Upon The Earth
All Is Forgiven and My Compassion Will Continue

To Be The Forefront Of Spirit's Heartbeat
I Love You My Child
I Love My Bride
Yield Your Heart To My Overwhelming Love
and See The Places You'll Go
and What You Will Accomplish As Your Passion Is Fueled By My Bliss
and Joy
YOU.

WAVES IN THE OCEAN

by: Matt Spinks

Come away and sit with me for just a minute this morning, afternoon,
or evening.
Not out of discipline, religion, or routine
But today, just out of love
Love for me, love for yourself, love for your neighbor
Out of this love, come away simply to enjoy
By learning to come away out of pure enjoyment, and love
We can find ourselves always centered, always rooted and grounded
To the place where we no longer need to come away
For our hearts will be fully aware in every circumstance
We can enjoy this love in every circumstance
Our bliss is real, in the midst of every circumstance, even transcending
every circumstance
Ultimately transforming every circumstance
Father, I thank you for this unmerited favor
Unmerited favor, unmerited favor
Your absolutely free gift of blessing and blissing

Absolutely free, favor, full blessing, pure extravagant blissing
I thank you Jesus that you are unstoppable Love
Holy Spirit I recognize your ceaseless passion for me
Delivering me completely, your work was successful
Hallelujah, thank you God, in you, now, I am completely free!
I look intently into the mirror and see the true me today
The true me, perfectly reflected there in the mirror of Jesus Christ
Absolutely embraced in the Trinity, as a full-fledged child of God
Whatever is true of Jesus, is now true of me
What great love the Father has lavished on us that we should be called the children of God
And that is what we are!
I come to complete and perfect rest
Absolute confident stillness, not adding or taking away from this moment
For I am lacking nothing, I shall not be in want
I don't need to complete a thing. I am utterly satisfied in You
In me in You
In what You have done, for me for You
We are One!
This means I have your joy! The fullness of joy
The Lord's joy is mine! A full and complete joy!
I allow this energizing joy of the Lord to overwhelm me now!
Nothing can diminish this, not in your true reality
I sink deeper and deeper into this infinitely immense reality
Specifically, your joy
Specifically, your bliss
Specifically, your intoxicating goodness in me
Wave after wave after wave after wave of God
This is my center, this is my home!

My Father which art in heaven in me, You are always in a heavenly state of bliss
My Father is in heaven, therefore I am always in heaven
Drinking with Dad
Drinking with Holy Ghost
I am seated with Jesus Christ
Jesus, you were anointed with the oil of joy above all your companions
You are the most joyful person ever to live
This is my identity now
Exceeding overwhelming joy
Ceaseless, endless, horizon after horizon a sea of bliss and endlessness in joy
This is what I possess in You, Jesus
So, I let it bubble
I let it bubble up
Bubble up, bubble up, bubble up, bubble up
Bubble, bubble, bubble, bubble, bubble, bubble, bubble, bubble up
Laughter of God!
I am in the laughter of God!
I am high on the laughter of God!
Let's party!
Your yoke is easy, and your burden is light!
Why have I never seen it like this before?!?
You never created me for boredom!
You never created me for depression!
Your joy is the serious business of heaven!
Thank you, my sweet Jesus for this overwhelming joy
You, flowing through me, twenty four hours a day
My life is a continual festival celebrating deliverance from sin
We are celebrating deliverance in to Life

Our Trinitarian life is pure delight
Sel-ahhhhhhhhhhhhhhhhhhhhhhh!
To whom else could I go?
You alone have the words of ecstatic life!
I have tried many a shallow drink
Oh, but Jesus Christ! You are no shallow drink!
To what could I compare you?
You are better than all the drugs put together!
Jesus, your heaven on earth ecstasy is better than candy to a five year old girl!
This bubbling is better than the finest wine, more potent than the strongest ale
Liquor may be quicker, but nothing is richer!
And, to be honest what's quicker than the Lamb slain from the foundation of the world
I'm already blitzed! I'm fully buzzed.
I refuse to wait for another drink.
In you, Jesus, I see me. I am already permanently high!
We're on our level, that next level, The Most High!
I breathe in the air of heaven now!
Oh, the sights, the sounds, the smells!!!
This air smells like Glory! I can taste the colors of your being!
Thank you Abba, Jesus, and Holy Spirit for creating such a wonderful world!
I refuse the lower, twisted, complaining, shell of a world that so many are convinced of!
God, as I feel your exceeding goodness, I recognize the goodness of all created things!
Reality is as high as I am!
We are not ignoring reality!

We are seeing the world in its' wonderful redeemed state!
High and mighty! We are never in lack!
Your Holy Ghost Glory is pulsing through it all
In its' true form
Just as I have been preserved in you Jesus
I see the whole world in your hands!
This high life is everywhere!
Pulsing through everything, You are!
The whole earth is full of Your Glory!
This is my reality now! I will never be alone!
I will never be discouraged!
As long as I see my God, the Most High
Bubbling through it all!
As we are now, resting away in your love
This has become my center
The endless horizon of your love, flooding the whole earth with joy
We WILL live happily ever after!

EXPLANATION OF ABBREVIATIONS

Throughout this book, we drink deep from multiple translations of the Bible! To enhance your bliss, the clearest and most inebriating versions are often referenced. There is such a great joy in reading many translations, as each one presents another facet of the diamond that is Holy Scripture. Here are the abbreviations used in the book, so you can go on your own adventure with them...

An explanation of abbreviations

The translations used in this book can be identified by the following codes:

AMP – The Amplified Bible (Grand Rapids: Zondervan Publishing House and The Lockman Foundation, 1954, 1958, 1962, 1964, 1965, 1987). Translated mostly by Frances Siewert.

Brenton – The Septuagint with Apocrypha: Greek and English (Hendrickson Publishers, 1986)Translated by Sir Lancelot Brenton

DRB – Douay-Rheims Bible 1582-1609 (Fitzwilliam, NH: Loreto Publications, 2007).

ERV – Holy Bible: Easy-to-Read Version (World Bible Translation Center, 2006)

ESV – The English Standard Version Bible: Containing the Old and New Testaments with Apocrypha (Oxford: Oxford University Press, 2009).

Fenton – The Holy Bible in Modern English (Destiny Publishers Merrimac, MA 1966) Translated by Ferrar Fenton

GNB – Good News Bible (American Bible Society 2001)

GSNT – The New Testament, An American Translation (Chicago: University of

Chicago Press, 1923). Edgar J. Goodspeed.

HCSB – The Holman Christian Standard Bible (Holman Bible Publishers, 2004)

KJV – The Holy Bible King James Version: 1611 Edition.

LITV – Green's Literal Translation (Sovereign Grace Publishers, 1985) Translated by Jay P. Green, Sr.

MIR – Mirror Translation (Visit www.mirrorword.net). Francois du Toit.

MOF – The Bible: James Moffatt Translation (San Francisco: Harper Collins, 1922/1994). James Moffatt.

MSG – The Message (Colorado Springs: NavPress Publishing Group, 2005 ed.). Eugene Peterson.

NASB – New American Standard Bible (La Habra, Ca.: The Lockman Foundation, 1977, 1995).

Rotherham – *Rotherham's Emphasized Bible* (Kregel Classics, 1959) Translated by Joseph Bryant Rotherham

The author has emphasized some scripture texts in bold lettering. Verses listed without translation references are partially quoted, inferred, paraphrased, or summarized.

TOPICAL INDEX OF BLISS

ABOUT THE AUTHOR

Matt Spinks and his wife, Katie, direct The Fire House Projects Co., a not-for-profit organization based out of Fort Wayne, Indiana, focusing on empowering people in more enjoyable community experiences through understanding their identity and experiencing the supernatural of Jesus.

Matt Spinks was born and raised in Indiana, and has been in Christian ministry from a young age. He's served with many different ministries including Youth With A Mission, the International House of Prayer, Foursquare Churches, and multiple churches both locally and abroad. Matt Spinks has a successful podcast and Youtube channel which reaches thousands of people per month on subjects similar the content of this book, High on God. He also travels multiple times per year for mission trips, and to speak at conferences, churches, and seminaries.
Matt and Katie have been married for twelve years and are the parents of two children: Samuel(age 8) and Rainbow(age 6). They live in the Fort Wayne, Indiana area where Matt serves as director of The Fire House Projects ministry, and on the community leadership team of Hillside Christian Fellowship.

www.thefirehouseprojects.com